THE POLITICAL ECONOMY OF THE CREATIVE AND CULTURAL INDUSTRIES

The creative and cultural industries (CCIs) are often seen by markets as critical drivers of economic growth and by governments as feasible ways to foster development. The link between these two perspectives lies in the CCIs' capacity to generate both economic value and social innovation simultaneously. While markets value their direct contribution to GDP and employment, governments recognise their potential to catalyse broader societal development through cultural expression, innovation and community engagement.

Divided into key sections covering theoretical foundations, economic growth and development, innovation, policy and data analysis, this book presents a multifaceted view of CCIs' role in modern economies and societies. It challenges traditional economic models, advocates for a holistic approach to socio-economic development and examines the transformative impact of digital technologies on creative work. This work makes significant contributions to the field by advancing the political economy of CCIs, synthesising current debates and clarifying critical concepts. It explores innovative approaches to measuring the economic impact of CCIs and proposes a roadmap for harnessing their full potential in driving sustainable and inclusive growth. With its flexible structure allowing for customised learning experiences, this book is an essential resource for understanding the complexities of creative industries in our rapidly changing world.

This interdisciplinary volume bridges theory and practice, providing invaluable insights relevant to students of CCIs, economics, arts and cultural management, as well as for academics, policymakers and practitioners.

Leandro Valiati Senior Lecturer in Creative and Cultural Industries at the University of Manchester, UK.

Routledge Research in the Creative and Cultural Industries

Series Editor: Ruth Rentschler

This series brings together book-length original research in creative and cultural industries from a range of perspectives. Charting developments in contemporary creative and cultural industries thinking around the world, the series aims to shape the research agenda to reflect the expanding significance of the creative sector in a globalised world.

Cultural Politics of the Creative Industries
Phil Graham

Business Model Innovation in *Creative and Cultural Industries*
Edited by Pierre Roy and Estelle Pellegrin-Boucher

Innovative Cultural Tourism in European Peripheries
Edited by Karol Jan Borowiecki, Antonella Fresa and José María Martín Civantos

Global Art Markets
History and Current Trends
Edited by Iain Robertson, Derrick Chong and Luís U. Afonso

The Political Economy of the Creative and Cultural Industries
Stitching Perspectives for Research, Policy and Practice
Leandro Valiati

For more information about this series, please visit: www.routledge.com/Routledge-Research-in-the-Creative-and-Cultural-Industries/book-series/RRCCI

THE POLITICAL ECONOMY OF THE CREATIVE AND CULTURAL INDUSTRIES

Stitching Perspectives for Research, Policy and Practice

Leandro Valiati

Routledge
Taylor & Francis Group
LONDON AND NEW YORK

Designed cover image: letty17 / E+ / Getty Images

First published 2025
by Routledge
4 Park Square, Milton Park, Abingdon, Oxon OX14 4RN

and by Routledge
605 Third Avenue, New York, NY 10158

Routledge is an imprint of the Taylor & Francis Group, an informa business

British Library Cataloguing-in-Publication Data
A catalogue record for this book is available from the British Library

ISBN: 9781032561813 (hbk)
ISBN: 9781032561783 (pbk)
ISBN: 9781003434252 (ebk)

DOI: 10.4324/9781003434252

Typeset in Sabon
by codeMantra

CONTENTS

ACKNOWLEDGEMENTS

This book culminates thoughts, conversations, brainstorms and insights from lectures, conference talks and countless professional moments in different countries. While it bears my authorship, the intellectual current that fed its creation is indebted to my students, audiences, colleagues and likeminded encounters.

I owe gratitude to each of my mentors in spread globally. Their consistent support and wisdom have been instrumental in shaping my academic and policy journey, and their generosity has been a guiding light throughout this process.

Several institutions, each with a unique contribution, have been instrumental in shaping my career path. The Federal University of Rio Grande do Sul in Brazil provided fertile ground for my international research. The University of Valencia taught me the importance of timing; Sorbonne (Paris 13, Labex) in France instilled in me the values of depth and consistency. The People's Palace Projects at Queen Mary University, focusing on the real-life exchange, broadened my perspectives. The University of Manchester's welcoming and stimulating environment of excellence has been the perfect stage for consolidating my research on the global stage and establishing myself in the UK academic ecosystem.

New urban landscapes, Murakami, Auster, Manchester United, and listening and playing to the music have all contributed to this year-around work, providing necessary respite and allowing the mind space to "crack the code" of the book.

Above all, this work is deeply dedicated to my small but unwavering team: Buza, Theo, Pipa and Leon. Their love and support are structure and foundation.

INTRODUCTION

1.1 An Infinitely Personal, Atomic-Scale Preface: Serendipity's Role in My Creative and Cultural Industries Journey

My journey into the creative and cultural industries (CCIs) began with a chance encounter, like the start of an unexpected song. Imagine a young economics student wandering through the campus of the Federal University of Rio Grande do Sul in Porto Alegre, Brazil. This southern city, known as the "Brazilian Manchester" for its lively rock scene, art, cold and erratic weather and progressive spirit, was about to shape my career.

That day, the unpredictable parallel 30 weather unleashed a heavy downpour. Looking for shelter, I ducked into a university café, its aroma of mediocre espresso starkly contrasted with the noise of typical university people. As I shook off the droplets, my eyes wandered across the bulletin board – a kaleidoscope of campus life. Amidst concert posters (The Strokes were coming to town!) and thesis defence announcements, a particular flyer caught my attention: a call for papers on Culture and Economics sponsored by the Brazilian Development Bank.

At that moment – bang! – two worlds collided. As an economics student whose heartbeat is more in time with Beatles chord progressions than with the steady rhythm of equilibrium microeconomics equations, this seemed like a harmonious blend of my passions. Music and economics tell stories anyway – one beautiful and soul-stirring, the other often cynical yet crucial to understanding our world. I have always believed that economics ultimately shapes lenses to understand well-being, happiness, human behaviour and the positive and negative impacts of our choices as a society. Arts, among several other things, are pretty much the same. Why not bridge these narratives?

DOI: 10.4324/9781003434252-1

Inspired, I wrote a paper on artistic value and public arts funding. To my absolute surprise, my work impressed the judges (or perhaps the Strokes flyers got all the attention from the prize call), winning me a prize and a chance to present it at a meeting of lusophone economists in Portugal and Angola. That was the scariest (nothing to do with the old and good A340) and one of the most beautiful flights I ever made. Was it just luck? Maybe. But it wasn't random. It felt like the start of something bigger.

More lines were added to this song sheet: a master's degree, then a PhD, each step building on the last. I found myself teaching and researching the Economics of Arts and Culture, a nice mixture appealing to different academic groups. My work took me to teach and research in universities worldwide – France, Spain, Italy and the United Kingdom – each country adding to my understanding of creative industries. I received awards, including one for outstanding academic work in Creative Industries (hey, British Academy). I've written books and papers – often juggling with deadlines after long periods of "cracking the code." I've worked with UNESCO, OEI, UNCTAD and the UN, adding more global perspectives to my research. I've spoken to various audiences in over 20 countries about creativity, culture and economics.

Now I'm based in Manchester – maybe the British version of Porto Alegre? – where new ideas flow as steadily as the rain in this revolutionary and fabulous city. From here, I invite students, artists and curious minds: I hope you find your own moment of inspiration in this book. Whether seeking shelter from a metaphorical storm or just passing the time, I hope these pages offer ideas that might help any element in your path through CCIs.

After all, isn't that what art and economics try to do? To change views, question assumptions and create new harmonies from the mix of human experiences? So, as you start this journey through the CCIs, remember that the most beautiful song sometimes begins with a single, unexpected note.

Looking back, I realise this book contains everything I wish I'd known when I first saw that flyer in Porto Alegre. It's a collection of knowledge, experiences and insights I've gathered from many sources throughout my career – from academic theories to real-world applications, from policy discussions to industry innovations. This book represents the connections I've made and the references I've collected, now combined into a comprehensive resource. I hope it serves as both a guide and motivation for those starting their adventures in the CCIs, offering a foundation and perspective for newcomers and stablished creatives in this academic, policy and practical field.

1.2 The Creative Industries Atelier: A Sewing Kit for the 21st Century

Welcome, dear reader, to a unique journey through the landscape of CCIs. This book is not just a collection of pages bound together; it's a carefully curated sewing kit filled with threads of various colours, textures and strengths.

Each chapter is a scissor, each concept a needle, and each theory a stitch technique. With these tools, you're invited to craft your creation of understanding, policy and innovation in CCIs.

1.2.1 A Patchwork of Ideas

In the ground-breaking novel Hopscotch, Julio Cortazar challenged the linear nature of storytelling; I invite you to approach this book in a similar non-linear fashion. Start wherever your curiosity leads you. Jump from chapter to chapter. Create your pattern through the array of ideas presented here. There's no wrong way to read this book – only different designs to discover and insights to uncover. Play and have a fun journey.

1.2.2 The Threads We Offer

In this sewing kit, you'll find threads of various hues and textures. Each represents a unique contribution to the field of CCI studies:

1. The Golden Thread of Bridge-building: the book combines theoretical backgrounds rarely combined in CCI studies, creating fresh insights. By intertwining economic theory with cultural studies, sociology and policy, you will find a multifaceted perspective on the value and impact of creative industries. This thread allows you to stitch together concepts from diverse fields, revealing patterns and connections previously hidden from view. Too often, these fields exist in separate silos, but the reality of creative industries demands a more integrated approach. Use this thread to weave together insights from multiple disciplines, creating a more robust, more resilient fabric of understanding.
2. The Political Economy Silk: A delicate yet strong fibre that contributes to establishing the political economy of CCIs as a vital field of study. This thread illuminates the complex interplay between creative production, market forces and policy decisions. By incorporating it into your work, you'll gain a nuanced understanding of how power structures and economic systems shape the creative landscape.
3. The National Models Cotton: A versatile thread that captures ongoing debates in academia, policy and markets regarding Creative Industries Models at the national level. From the UK's DCMS model to Brazil's Plan of Creative Economy, this thread allows you to compare different approaches, adapting and combining elements to suit your context.
4. The Conceptual Wool: A warm and fuzzy strand that helps define and differentiate creative industries, creative economy and cultural industries for academic and policy purposes. This thread offers clarity and precision in a field often plagued by terminological ambiguity. Use it to craft clear arguments and develop well-defined policy proposals.

5 The Data and Policy Polyester: A durable, easy-care thread that discusses data production context for CCIs and sources and summarises historical and contemporary policy debates. This practical thread grounds your work in empirical evidence and real-world policy contexts, ensuring that your creative piece is beautiful but also functional and relevant.

1.2.3 Crafting Your Understanding

As you flip through these pages, think of yourself as an artisan. Pick up the threads that intrigue you. Combine them in ways that spark your creativity. Use the needles of critical thinking to stitch together concepts. Apply the stitches of practical experience to protect yourself from oversimplification.

You might start by threading the golden needle of new knowledge, creating a piece that spans academic disciplines. For instance, you could explore how economic innovation theories intersect with sociological concepts of cultural capital, revealing new insights into the dynamics of creative clusters. Or you'll prefer to embroider with the political economy silk and the national models' cotton, crafting a policy proposal that's both theoretically sound and practically applicable. This could lead to a comparative analysis of how different national strategies for promoting CCIs interact with global economic forces, potentially revealing best practices for nurturing local creative economies in a globalised world. For those more inclined towards data-driven approaches, try combining the data and policy polyester with the conceptual wool. This could result in a rigorous empirical study that not only measures the economic impact of CCIs but also grapples with the thorny question of how to quantify cultural value.

1.2.4 A Living Creation

Remember, the piece you create with this book is not meant to be static. It should be dynamic, adaptable and open to constant reimagination like the CCIs. As new threads emerge in technological advancements, policy shifts or cultural trends, don't hesitate to incorporate them into your work. Consider, for example, how the rise of artificial intelligence is transforming creative processes across industries. Or reflect on how the global pandemic has accelerated digital transformation in the cultural sector. Your creation should evolve to reflect these changes, incorporating new patterns and textures as the landscape of CCIs continues to shift.

1.2.5 An Invitation to Co-Create

This book is not just a monologue but an invitation to dialogue. I encourage you to share your creations as you work with the threads and tools provided here. How have you combined different concepts? What new patterns have you discovered? What policy proposals have you crafted?

By sharing creations, we develop a rich, diverse and ever-expanding understanding of CCIs. We become co-creators of knowledge, collectively pushing the boundaries of what's possible in this dynamic field.

So, dear reader, are you ready to pick up your needle? The world of CCIs awaits your unique perspective. Let's start sewing, and together, let's craft a future where creativity, culture and commerce intertwine in beautiful and sustainable ways.

Welcome to your Creative Industries sewing kit. The first stitch awaits your inspiration!

1.3 Introduction: The Rise of CCIs: From the Dawn of Globalisation in 2000 to the Fractured World of 2024

As Big Ben chimed in with the arrival of the year 2000, most of the large crowd hadn't anticipated the massive changes that would sweep through the global creative, cultural and economic landscape in the next decade. The new millennium launched an era when creativity, technology and content would become the lifeblood of a new economy, challenging and invigorating our understanding of work, culture and innovation.

The dawn of the 21st century was a transformative era for digital communication and social media, with the years 2000–2010 witnessing the birth and explosive growth of platforms that would fundamentally alter global connectivity and information sharing. This decade saw a cascade of innovations that reshaped the digital landscape: Wikipedia emerged in 2001, revolutionising collaborative knowledge sharing; LinkedIn launched in 2003, professionalising online networking; Facebook debuted in 2004, swiftly becoming the dominant social networking site; YouTube arrived in 2005, democratising video sharing; Twitter introduced microblogging and real-time updates in 2006; and the iPhone's 2007 release heralded the smartphone era, paving the way for mobile-first services and media usage. These developments collectively laid the foundation for a hyperconnected and digital-centric world, forever changing how people interact, consume information and express themselves online.

In the same context, the world saw the aftermath of Cool Britannia, and the United Kingdom found itself at the forefront of a global movement to recognise and nurture the economic potential of creativity. The Department for Culture, Media and Sport boldly declared creative industries rooted in "individual creativity, skill and talent" were the new drivers for economic growth. This proclamation resonated far beyond our shores, inspiring policymakers worldwide to reconsider the value of sectors once dismissed as marginal.

The world was shrinking, or so it seemed. Globalisation, a force gathering momentum since the fall of the Berlin Wall, suddenly accelerated. Borders became more porous, not just to goods and capital but also to ideas and cultural expressions. In this fertile soil, the seeds of the creative industries began to sprout and flourish. Picture a fashion designer in Manchester, her creations no longer confined to local boutiques in the Northern Quarter but finding their way into New York and Tokyo wardrobes. Imagine a musician in Bristol, his melodies reaching ears in Sydney and São Paulo, all at the click of a button. The world had become a vast, interconnected stage, and creatives were eager to take their bow.

This shift wasn't limited to any one country or industry. From Silicon Valley startups to European design houses, from Asian tech hubs to African mobile payment systems, a wave of creative disruption began to reshape social and economic exchanges worldwide. Traditional business models were revolutionised, while new forms of artistic expression flourished in the digital realm. The lines between disciplines blurred as technology and art, science, and design began to interconnect in unprecedented ways.

Yet, this global stage was not a level playing field. The transformation also brought challenges, such as the concentration of power and a new, somewhat global division of labour. The international division of labour in the creative economy often mirrored existing global inequalities. Following historical paradigms in past industrial revolutions, the 21st-century revolution also depended on placing countries (and people) at different stages to generate unbalanced results and maximise profits. While some sectors thrived in this new creative economy, others needed help to adapt. The rapid pace of change left many wondering about the future of work and the skills required to succeed in this evolving landscape.

While developed nations like the United Kingdom, the United States of America and parts of Europe positioned themselves as hubs of innovation and high-value creative work, developing countries often found themselves relegated to roles of content production or digital labour. The promise of a democratised creative economy was tempered by unequal access to technology, education and global markets. This disparity led to a new form of creative colonialism, where ideas and cultural products from the Global North dominated. In contrast, creative voices from the Global South struggled for recognition and fair compensation in the international arena.

1.3.1 The Shifting Landscape: 2000 vs 2020

The world underwent a profound transformation between 2000 and 2020, marked by significant shifts in globalisation, political climate, conflict, and economic policies. The dawn of the new millennium was characterised by unbridled optimism towards globalisation, fuelled by the fall of the Berlin Wall and the end of the Cold War, which seemed to herald an era of increased international cooperation and economic integration. However, by 2020, this optimism had given way to a more nuanced and often sceptical view, as the 2008 financial crisis exposed the vulnerabilities of an interconnected global economy.

The political landscape also experienced a dramatic shift during this period. The year 2000 saw many Western democracies embracing centrist "Third Way" politics, exemplified by figures like Tony Blair in the United Kingdom and Bill Clinton in the US, which sought to blend market economics with social welfare policies. In stark contrast, by 2020, political centrism had largely given way to increased polarisation, with the rise of populist movements on both the right and left challenging established political norms. Events such as Brexit in the United Kingdom, the election of Donald Trump in the US, and the growth of far-right parties in Europe signalled a shift away from globalisation and towards nationalism.

The nature of war and conflict evolved significantly during these two decades. While regional conflicts persisted in 2000, including the ongoing tensions between Israel and Palestine, there was hope for a more peaceful world order following the end of the Cold War. By 2020, however, the landscape of conflict had dramatically shifted. The 9/11 attacks and subsequent "War on Terror" ushered in an era of asymmetric warfare and non-state actors, while the rise of cyber warfare and information warfare blurred the lines between war and peace. The Israel-Palestine conflict remained unresolved, and Russia's annexation of Crimea in 2014 and the subsequent conflict in eastern Ukraine marked a return to more traditional geopolitical tensions.

The economic policy landscape witnessed a notable transformation. The early 2000s saw a continued push towards free trade and financial liberalisation. However, by 2020, protectionist sentiments had surged in many countries. The US-China trade war, initiated under the Trump administration's "America First" policy, marked a significant shift away from free trade orthodoxy, while even traditionally free-trade advocates like the United Kingdom grappled with new trade realities post-Brexit.

The COVID-19 pandemic, which emerged in late 2019 and spread globally in 2020, was a stark punctuation mark to these two decades of change. It further exposed the vulnerabilities of global supply chains and interdependence, accelerated the adoption of digital technologies and amplified existing political and economic tensions. The pandemic challenged the foundations of globalisation, forcing countries to close borders, restrict travel and prioritise national interests in ways unseen since World War II. It also highlighted global inequalities, particularly in healthcare access and economic resilience, and intensified the debate about balancing international cooperation and national self-reliance.

This period thus encapsulates a dramatic shift from a world of optimism, globalism and economic openness to one characterised by scepticism, polarisation and protectionist tendencies, further complicated by persistent regional conflicts, emerging geopolitical challenges and a global health crisis that reshaped societies worldwide.

1.3.2 Impact on Creative Industries

These shifts have profoundly impacted the creative industries, reshaping the landscape in which artists, content creators and cultural institutions operate. The digital transformation, while not a new phenomenon, has accelerated dramatically, creating a paradoxical environment where globalisation in the traditional sense may have slowed, but digital globalisation has surged forward. This dual trend has opened unprecedented opportunities for creative industries to reach global audiences, while simultaneously intensifying competition on an international scale. Content creators compete for attention in a vast digital marketplace where geographic boundaries have become increasingly irrelevant.

In response to these changes, a trend towards cultural protectionism has emerged in various countries. Governments, recognising their creative sectors' economic and cultural significance, have implemented measures to safeguard local industries. These range from content quotas for streaming services, ensuring a certain percentage of locally produced material, to subsidies for domestic film production. Such policies aim to preserve cultural diversity and support local creative economies in the face of global competition.

Geopolitical tensions have cast a long shadow over the creative industries, affecting cultural exchanges and collaborations in ways that were less pronounced at the turn of the millennium. The complex relationship between major powers, particularly the United States and China, has led to restrictions on technology companies that have become integral to content distribution. The challenges faced by platforms like TikTok in some Western countries exemplify how geopolitical considerations can directly impact creative platforms' global reach and operations.

The COVID-19 pandemic served as a catalyst for rapid and widespread change within the creative industries. Faced with lockdowns and social distancing measures, these sectors swiftly adapted to a world of limited physical interaction. This unprecedented situation accelerated existing trends towards digital consumption and virtual experiences. Museums launched virtual tours, musicians streamed concerts from their homes, and film festivals went online. These adaptations helped the creative industries survive a challenging period and opened new avenues for audience engagement and content distribution that are likely to persist and evolve in the post-pandemic world.

These developments collectively paint a picture of creative industries influx, navigating a complex landscape shaped by technological innovation, geopolitical realities and global crises. As they move forward, these industries must continue to adapt, finding ways to harness the opportunities presented by digital globalisation while addressing the challenges of increased competition, cultural preservation and rapidly changing consumer behaviours.

1.3.3 The Path Forward for Creative Industries

As we move further into the 2020s, the creative industries face a landscape of both unprecedented challenges and exciting opportunities. The sector must navigate this complex terrain, balancing the opportunities of digital globalisation with the challenges of an increasingly fragmented and uncertain world order. Some crucial elements to be considered are:

1. **Embracing Digital Transformation:** The acceleration of digital trends presents a double-edged sword. On one hand, it offers creatives unprecedented access to global audiences and new forms of expression. For instance, virtual reality (VR) and augmented reality (AR) technologies are opening up new frontiers in immersive storytelling and experiential art. On the other hand, the digital realm brings challenges of oversaturation, shorter attention spans, and the need for constant innovation to stand out in a crowded digital marketplace.
2. **Navigating Cultural Protectionism:** As nations become more protective of their cultural heritage and domestic industries, creative professionals must respect local sensibilities while pushing for global cultural exchange. This might involve more co-productions, cultural fusion projects or leveraging digital platforms to bypass traditional gatekeepers. The challenge will be maintaining artistic integrity and freedom of expression in the face of potential censorship or market access restrictions.
3. **Adapting to Geopolitical Realities:** The creative industries will need to become more adept at navigating complex geopolitical landscapes. This might involve diversifying supply chains, building more resilient distribution networks or finding innovative ways to collaborate across borders despite political tensions. The creative sector can also play a role in fostering international understanding and dialogue through cultural diplomacy.
4. **Post-Pandemic Resilience:** The lessons learned during the COVID-19 pandemic will continue to shape the sector. This includes the acceleration of digital consumption and a renewed appreciation for live, in-person experiences. Creative industries must develop hybrid models that can seamlessly blend digital and physical elements, ensuring resilience against future disruptions while meeting evolving consumer expectations.
5. **Addressing Inequality:** As the world grapples with growing inequality, creative industries have a role in reflecting these challenges and proposing solutions. This might involve more diverse storytelling, inclusive hiring practices or using art and media to raise awareness about social issues. There's also a need to address inequality within the creative sector itself, ensuring fair compensation and opportunities for creators from all backgrounds.

6 **Sustainability and Ethics:** With increasing awareness of climate change and ethical consumption, creative industries must prioritise sustainability in their practices. This could range from eco-friendly film productions to sustainable fashion design. Creatives can also lead the way in imagining and promoting more sustainable futures through their work.
7 **Balancing AI and Human Creativity:** As artificial intelligence becomes more sophisticated, creative industries must find the right balance between leveraging AI tools and preserving the unique value of human creativity. This might involve using AI for tasks like data analysis or essential content generation while focusing human efforts on higher-level creative direction and emotional storytelling.
8 **New Business Models:** The changing landscape will necessitate innovative business models. This could include more direct-to-consumer approaches, subscription-based services or new collective ownership and profit-sharing forms in creative projects. Blockchain technology, for instance, might revolutionise how intellectual property is managed and monetised.

In navigating these challenges and opportunities, the creative industries have a chance to adapt to the new global realities and play a leading role in shaping them. By fostering cross-cultural understanding, imagining new possibilities and giving voice to diverse perspectives, the creative sector can help build bridges in an increasingly fragmented world.

As we look to the future, the resilience, adaptability and innovative spirit that have always characterised the creative industries will be more crucial than ever. By embracing change while staying true to the core values of creativity and cultural expression, these industries can continue to thrive, inspire and drive positive change in the years to come.

1.4 About This Book: Navigating the Complex Landscape of CCIs

This book offers a comprehensive and multifaceted exploration of CCIs. These dynamic and rapidly evolving industry sectors have gained significant attention from academics, policymakers and practitioners in recent years. Our approach to this complex subject is deliberately interdisciplinary and flexible, designed to accommodate our readers' diverse interests and needs. The Political Economy of Cultural and Creative Industries represents an interdisciplinary framework that examines the complex relationships amongst creative production, market forces, and policy decisions in the cultural and creative sectors. What distinguishes PECCIs is its normative approach, which goes beyond merely analysing how things are (positivist) to questioning and proposing how they should be.

1.4.1 Structure and Approach

This book begins by unpacking the fundamental concepts of cultural industries, creative industries, and the creative economy (Chapter 1). It explores how these interrelated ideas have evolved, shaping our understanding of creativity's role in economic and social development. The text then shifts gears to examine how CCIs fit into economic growth theory (Chapter 2), challenging traditional models and showcasing how these industries, with their unique characteristics, push the boundaries of how we think about economic growth.

The book broadens its scope beyond conventional economic metrics to examine CCIs' impact on socio-economic development (Chapter 3). It advocates for a more holistic view of progress, exploring how creative industries contribute to social inclusion, well-being and cultural preservation. The focus then narrows to the workforce (Chapter 4), examining how digital transformation and the gig economy reshape creative occupations (structure) and how the workers respond to that using tactics tackling the challenges and opportunities facing creative professionals in this rapidly evolving landscape. The narrative explores the symbiotic relationship between CCIs and innovation (Chapter 5), illustrating how CCIs are at the forefront of "creative destruction," constantly reshaping cultural production and consumption. The book then takes a global perspective, presenting a comparative analysis of public policies for CCIs across various countries (Chapter 6). It highlights the diverse ways governments support and shape their creative sectors and the challenges they face in doing so. Grappling with the complex task of measuring CCIs' economic impact, the text explores innovative approaches to capture the full value of creative activities. It moves beyond traditional economic indicators to more nuanced, context-sensitive frameworks (Chapter 7). The book concludes by looking ahead and exploring the future role of CCIs in economic development (Chapter 8). It outlines key areas for future research and policy focus, proposing a roadmap for harnessing the full potential of creative industries in driving sustainable and inclusive growth.

Within these sections, readers will find chapters that can be read independently or in conjunction with others, allowing for a customised learning experience.

1.4.2 Key Contributions

This volume aims to make several significant contributions to the field of CCI studies:

1 Interdisciplinary Knowledge Creation: offering fresh insights and perspectives by connecting theoretical backgrounds from diverse disciplines in dialogue with CCIs. This multidisciplinary approach combines mainstream

and heterodox economic theory, cultural studies, sociology and other relevant fields to understand CCIs comprehensively.
2 Advancing the Political Economy of CCIs: contributing to establishing the political economy of CCIs as a distinct and significant field of study within creative and cultural studies, both in the United Kingdom and globally, by exploring the complex interplay between creative production, market forces and policy decisions.
3 Synthesising Current Debates: This synthesis brings together various ongoing debates in academia, policy and markets regarding Creative Industries Models at the national level. It provides readers with a comprehensive overview of current thinking and practice in the field.
4 Conceptual Clarification: By exercising a theoretical analysis, we aim to clarify and differentiate critical concepts such as creative, creative economy and cultural industries. This conceptual work is crucial for both academic studies and policy formulation.
5 Data Sources and Policy Analysis: serving as a handbook, compiling relevant data sources for further research and summarising historical and contemporary debates in CCIs and social-economic development.

1.4.3 Intended Audience

This book is designed to serve a broad audience, including:

- Academics and researchers in the fields of CCIs, arts management, economics, cultural studies and related disciplines
- Policymakers and government officials involved in CCI policy
- Practitioners and professionals working in various sectors of the CCIs
- Students at undergraduate and postgraduate levels studying CCIs, economics, arts management, cultural policy or related subjects
- Any person interested in recent transformations in the world

In presenting this comprehensive exploration of CCIs, the readers are invited to engage critically with the ideas, debates and evidence presented. The non-linear structure of the book encourages active engagement. It allows readers to create their pathways through the material, reflecting the dynamic and interconnected nature of the creative industries. This volume will contribute to the academic discourse on CCIs and inform policy decisions and industry practices. In an era where creativity and culture play an increasingly central role in our economies and societies, understanding the complexities of these industries is more crucial than ever.

1

CREATIVE AND CULTURAL INDUSTRIES

An Overview

The intersection of creativity, culture and economics has given rise to a complex and evolving conceptual landscape. This framework explores three interconnected concepts: economy of culture, creative industries, cultural industries and the creative economy. Each concept offers a nuanced perspective on the role of creativity and culture in economic and social development, reflecting shifts in policy approaches and academic discourse over the past few decades. While there is considerable overlap between these concepts, they each emphasise different aspects of the relationship between creativity, culture and economic activity. Understanding these nuances is crucial for policymakers, researchers and practitioners. Below, you can find a theoretical exercise that will serve as a reference for this book each time these terms are used:

1.1 Economy of Creative and Cultural Industries

The economy of creative and cultural industries (CCIs) is a broad concept encompassing the application of economic science theoretical tools in cultural production, distribution and consumption. It recognises culture as a source of intrinsic value and a driver of economic activity. This concept has evolved and is approached from various perspectives, emphasising different aspects of the relationship between culture and economics. The mainstream approach to the economy of culture, often aligned with neoclassical economic thinking, focuses primarily on the measurable economic impacts of cultural activities. It emphasises culture's potential as a resource for economic growth, promoting cultural entrepreneurship and market-oriented strategies. This perspective has been influential in shaping policies that aim to maximise

DOI: 10.4324/9781003434252-2

the economic potential of cultural assets, often through commercialisation and investment in cultural infrastructure.

In contrast, the political economy of CCIs offers a critical framework that examines how economic structures, political institutions and power dynamics influence cultural production and consumption. This approach challenges the commodification of culture and the application of market logic to all cultural spheres. It highlights issues such as labour conditions in creative industries, the role of large corporations in shaping cultural content and the global flows of cultural goods and services. The political economy perspective argues that cultural production and consumption are not neutral processes but are deeply embedded in broader socioeconomic and political contexts. It calls attention to inequality, cultural diversity and the sustainability of growth-oriented cultural economy strategies. This approach emphasises the need to consider cultural policies' broader social and political implications beyond their economic impacts.

Both perspectives contribute to our understanding of the economy of CCIs, albeit with different emphases. The mainstream approach has been instrumental in elevating the status of culture in economic policy discussions. At the same time, the political economy of CCIs perspective provides a crucial counterpoint, highlighting the complexities and potential pitfalls of viewing culture primarily through a financial lens.

1.2 Creative Economy

The creative economy represents the most comprehensive and expansive of these concepts. As defined by the United Nations Conference on Trade and Development (UNCTAD), it's "an evolving concept based on creative assets potentially generating economic growth and development" (UNCTAD, 2008). This approach extends beyond specific industries, considering how creativity, knowledge and information catalyse economic growth and development in an increasingly globalised world.

The creative economy paradigm represents a fundamental shift in understanding the role of creativity and culture in economic and social development. It suggests that in the 21st century, financial success will increasingly depend on the ability to generate ideas, innovate, and leverage intellectual capital rather than relying solely on traditional factors of production.

Key features of the creative economy include:

1. Integration of economic, cultural, technological and social aspects of development
2. Emphasis on innovation across all economic sectors, not just traditionally "creative" or "cultural" ones

3 Recognition of the growing importance of intellectual capital and intangible assets in economic growth
4 Promotion of social inclusion, cultural diversity and human development
5 Incorporation of both formal and informal creative activities
6 Focus on the role of digital technologies and the internet in facilitating creative production and distribution
7 Recognition of the importance of creative clusters and ecosystems in fostering innovation

The creative economy approach has gained significant traction in policy circles, with many countries and cities developing strategies to foster their creative economies. For instance, the European Union's New European Agenda for Culture emphasises the role of culture and creativity in social cohesion and economic growth (European Commission, 2018).

Moreover, the concept of the creative economy has expanded to include ideas such as the "Orange Economy" in Latin America, which emphasises the transformative potential of creativity and culture in developing economies (Buitrago & Duque, 2013). It also aligns with broader economic trends such as the experience and knowledge economies.

Some critics argue that this concept can sometimes oversimplify complex cultural and social processes, potentially leading to policies prioritising economic outcomes over cultural and social values. Given the intangible nature of many of its outputs, there's also an ongoing debate about how to measure the creative economy effectively. Despite these challenges, the creative economy remains a robust framework for understanding the evolving role of creativity and culture in contemporary economic and social development.

1.3 Creative Industries

The concept of creative industries, first popularised by the UK's Department for Culture, Media and Sport (DCMS) in 1998, marked a significant shift in understanding the economic potential of creativity (DCMS, 1998). According to the DCMS, creative industries are "those originating in individual creativity, skill and talent and which have a potential for wealth and job creation through the generation and exploitation of intellectual property" (DCMS, 2001).

This definition encompasses various sectors, including advertising, architecture, art, crafts, design, fashion, film, music, performing arts, publishing, software, television and radio, and video games (UNESCO, 2013). The creative industries approach emphasises the economic value of creativity, viewing it as a resource that can drive innovation, economic growth and job creation.

Key characteristics of creative industries include:

1 Reliance on individual creativity and talent
2 Generation and exploitation of intellectual property
3 Utilisation of new technologies, particularly ICT
4 Creation of both economic and cultural value
5 Potential for innovation and cross-sector spillovers
6 A high degree of risk and uncertainty in product development
7 Short product lifecycles and rapid obsolescence

The creative industries concept has gained widespread adoption in policy circles and academia. It has influenced urban development strategies, with many cities worldwide seeking to foster creative clusters or districts (Landry, 2000). The approach has also been linked to ideas of the 'creative class' and its role in economic development (Florida, 2002).

However, the creative industries concept has faced criticism. Some scholars argue that it overly commodifies culture and creativity, potentially neglecting forms of creative expression that don't have immediate commercial value (Galloway & Dunlop, 2007). Others point out that the focus on individual creativity may overlook the collaborative nature of much creative work (Pratt, 2008). Besides the criticisms, this concept remains influential, evolving in response to technological changes and shifting economic paradigms. Recent developments include increased attention to the role of digital platforms in creative production and distribution and growing recognition of the importance of creative skills across the broader economy.

1.4 Cultural Industries

The concept of cultural industries, as defined by UNESCO, focuses on sectors that combine the creation, production and commercialisation of intangible and cultural content (UNESCO, 2009). This approach emphasises the dual nature of cultural goods and services, recognising their economic and cultural value.

The concept of cultural industries has its roots in critical theory, particularly the work of Adorno and Horkheimer (2002), who used the term 'culture industry' to critique the commodification of culture. Over time, the concept has evolved to encompass a more neutral, descriptive approach to understanding how cultural production intersects with economic systems.

Key aspects of cultural industries include:

1 Focus on intangible, cultural content
2 Emphasis on cultural diversity and heritage preservation
3 Recognition of both economic and cultural value

4 Promotion of democratic access to culture
5 Acknowledgement of the role of public institutions and policy in supporting cultural production
6 Consideration of non-profit and informal cultural activities
7 Attention to issues of cultural rights and identity

The cultural industries approach is closely tied to cultural diversity and heritage preservation ideas. It acknowledges these industries' crucial role in shaping and reflecting cultural identities, promoting cultural diversity and ensuring democratic access to culture (Hesmondhalgh & Pratt, 2005). UNESCO's framework for cultural statistics (2009) identifies several core cultural domains within the cultural industries, including cultural and natural heritage, performance and celebration, visual arts and crafts, books and press, audio-visual and interactive media, and design and creative services. This broad scope reflects the diverse ways in which culture is produced and consumed in different societies.

The cultural industries concept has been particularly influential in international development, promoting sustainable development while preserving cultural diversity. It has informed UNESCO's Convention on the Protection and Promotion of the Diversity of Cultural Expressions (2005), recognising the distinctive nature of cultural goods and services as vehicles of identity, values and meaning.

Critics argue that it can sometimes lead to an overly broad definition of culture, making it difficult to develop targeted policies. There's also an ongoing debate about balancing economic and cultural objectives within this framework (Throsby, 2008). Despite these challenges, cultural industries remain a crucial tool for understanding the complex interplay between culture, economics and society in the contemporary world.

1.5 Models and Classifications

Various organisations have developed different models and classifications for CCIs. These approaches reflect varying emphases and priorities, often tailored to specific contexts or mandates. Understanding these other models is crucial, as the choice of definition and classification can significantly impact how the sector is measured, supported and developed.

Table 1.1 gives a comprehensive overview of the main approaches.

Several models have been developed to categorise and understand the scope of creative industries, each emphasising different aspects of creative production and its economic impact. The Symbolic Texts model, primarily used in Europe, focuses on popular culture and how culture is produced, distributed and consumed. This model places core creative arts at the centre, surrounded by core cultural industries (such as film, broadcasting and

TABLE 1.1 Overview of Sectors in Different CCI Models

Sector	*Symbolic Texts*	*DCMS*	*WIPO Copyright*	*Concentric Circles*	*UNCTAD*
Advertising	Peripheral	✓	Partial	Wider cultural industries	Functional creations
Architecture	–	✓	Partial	Wider cultural industries	Functional creations
Art and antique markets	–	✓	–	Core creative arts	Arts
Crafts	–	✓	–	Core creative arts	Arts
Design	–	✓	Partial	Other core cultural industries	Functional creations
Fashion	Peripheral	✓	Partial	Wider cultural industries	Functional creations
Film and video	Core	✓	Core	Other core cultural industries	Audiovisuals
Music	Core	✓	Core	Other core cultural industries	Arts
Performing arts	–	✓	Core	Core creative arts	Arts
Publishing	Core	✓	Core	Other core cultural industries	Media
Software and computer games	–	✓	Core	Related industries	Functional creations
Television and radio	Core	✓	Core	Other core cultural industries	Audiovisuals
Visual arts	Core	✓	Core	Core creative arts	Arts
Museums and galleries	–	–	–	Core creative arts	Heritage
Libraries	–	–	Partial	Core creative arts	Heritage
Photography	–	–	Core	Other core cultural industries	Media
Interactive media	–	–	Core	Related industries	New media

Note: This table is not exhaustive, and there may be some variations in how different sources categorise specific sectors. The "✓" indicates explicit inclusion in the model, while "–" indicates the sector is not explicitly mentioned or categorised differently.

music), with peripheral cultural industries (like fashion and advertising) at the outer edge. The DCMS model, originating in the United Kingdom, takes a broader approach, including 13 sectors ranging from advertising and architecture to software and computer games. This model has been influential in policymaking, particularly in Europe and East Asia, due to its emphasis on the economic potential of creative activities.

The WIPO (World Intellectual Property Organization) Copyright model focuses on industries involved in creating, manufacturing, producing, broadcasting and distributing copyrighted works. This model distinguishes between core copyright industries, interdependent copyright industries and partial copyright industries, reflecting the varying degrees to which different sectors rely on copyright protection. Other significant models include the Concentric Circles model proposed by David Throsby, which arranges creative industries in concentric circles based on the cultural content of their output, and the UNCTAD model, which divides creative industries into four broad groups: heritage, arts, media and functional creations. Each model offers a unique perspective on the creative industries, reflecting different priorities and understandings of the relationship between culture, creativity and economic activity. The choice of model can significantly influence policy decisions and strategies for supporting and developing creative sectors.

1.6 Critical Distinctions between Creative Economy, Cultural Industries and Creative Industries

The creative economy concept represents a broader contemporary economic movement involving diverse processes and larger sectors. Analysed as integral components of the creative economy, CCIs represent a paradigm shift in our understanding of creativity and culture's role in economic and social development. This new model suggests that future financial success will increasingly depend on the ability to generate ideas and innovate rather than relying solely on traditional factors of production. This framework is built on systems that value imaginative qualities over conventional resources like land, labour and capital. It encompasses the production and distribution of innovative goods and services, considering the entire value chain – from the initial spark of an idea to its transformation into products and ultimate distribution to consumers.

An essential feature of this approach is its recognition of the complex interplay between economic, cultural, technological and social aspects of development. It acknowledges that innovation doesn't exist in isolation but is part of a broader ecosystem spanning all economic sectors. This intersectoral perspective highlights how creative thinking can drive progress in traditionally 'artistic' fields and areas as diverse as healthcare, education and manufacturing. This model also emphasises intellectual property rights as crucial tools for fostering and protecting creative endeavours, reflecting the increasing importance of intangible assets in our knowledge-based economy.

Importantly, this concept looks beyond purely economic measures to consider the broader social impacts of creativity and culture. It recognises the non-monetary value that innovative activities can contribute to social inclusion, cultural diversity and human development. This holistic view acknowledges that the true worth of creativity extends far beyond financial metrics. The "creative class" concept is central to this idea – knowledge workers, artists and other innovative professionals who are increasingly seen as critical economic and cultural development drivers. This underscores the importance of human capital and talent in driving growth and innovation.

This paradigm shift has significant implications for policymaking. Governments should focus on supporting specific industries and fostering a broader ecosystem that encourages creativity across all sectors. This might include educational policies, urban planning, technological infrastructure and intellectual property rights, all aimed at creating an environment where innovation can flourish. The creative economy represents a new way of thinking about development that places creativity, knowledge and innovation at the heart of progress. As we move into the 21st century, understanding and harnessing this approach will be crucial for nations, cities and organisations looking to thrive in an increasingly idea-driven world.

The concepts of creative industries, cultural industries and the creative economy offer different perspectives on the role of creativity and culture in economic and social development. While closely related, they each emphasise different aspects and priorities. Understanding these nuances is crucial for developing effective policies, measuring impact and fostering growth in these vital areas of the modern economy.

As the global economy evolves, these concepts will likely continue to be debated, refined and reimagined. Policymakers, researchers and industry stakeholders must stay informed about these developments to effectively navigate the challenges and opportunities presented by the increasing importance of creativity and culture in economic and social spheres.

1 Scope: creative industries have the broadest scope, including any industry that relies on creativity for economic value. Cultural industries focus specifically on cultural expressions and heritage. The creative economy is the most comprehensive, considering creativity's broader economic, social and cultural impacts on the whole economy.
2 Focus: creative industries emphasise the commercial exploitation of creativity. Cultural industries prioritise cultural expression and preservation. The creative economy focuses on how creativity drives innovation and development across all sectors.
3 Economic Approach: creative industries are often viewed through a more traditional economic lens of industry sectors. Cultural industries are seen as vehicles for cultural expression with financial implications. The creative economy represents a paradigm shift in how creativity and culture contribute to economic and social development.

Understanding these distinctions is crucial for several reasons:

1. Policy Development: Different approaches are needed for supporting creative industries versus preserving and promoting cultural industries. The creative economy concept informs broader economic and social policies.
2. Measurement and Analysis: Each concept requires different metrics and methodologies for assessing economic impact and social value.
3. Investment and Support: The rationale for investing in or supporting these areas differs based on whether the focus is on commercial potential, cultural preservation or broader economic transformation.
4. International Cooperation: A clear understanding of these concepts facilitates more effective dialogue and collaboration in global creative and cultural exchanges.

By recognising these nuances, policymakers can craft more targeted and practical strategies, researchers can conduct more precise comparative analyses, and industry stakeholders can better articulate their unique contributions and needs. This shared understanding is essential for fostering the growth of creative and cultural sectors while leveraging their potential to drive broader economic and social development in the 21st century.

BOX 1.1 WHY A CROSS-SECTOR GOVERNMENTAL BODY SHOULD CONDUCT CREATIVE ECONOMY POLICIES

1. Economic Significance: The creative economy contributes significantly to GDP, job creation and innovation, extending beyond traditional cultural sectors.
2. Cross-Sectoral Nature: Intersects with technology, education, urban planning and international trade, requiring diverse expertise.
3. Innovation and Technology: Often at the forefront of technological innovation, needing support from tech-oriented sectors.
4. Business and Entrepreneurship: Requires business development, finance and entrepreneurship support expertise.
5. International Trade and Competitiveness: Significant in exports, requiring the involvement of trade and foreign affairs ministries.
6. Education and Skills Development: Needs coordination between education, higher education and vocational training sectors.
7. Urban and Regional Development: Crucial in urban regeneration and regional development strategies.
8. Digital Infrastructure: Relies heavily on digital infrastructure, managed by communications or digital economy ministries.

9 Intellectual Property Rights: Extends beyond copyright to patents and trademarks, often managed by justice or commerce ministries.
10 Risk of Cultural Bias: Placing it solely under a Ministry of Culture risks prioritising traditional sectors over newer, commercial creative industries.

Recommended Approach:

- A cross-departmental task force or dedicated unit within economic affairs or innovation ministry.
- Include strong representation from the Ministry of Culture.
- Implement a 'Cultural Diversity Impact Assessment' framework.
- Appoint a 'Cultural Diversity and Inclusion Officer.'
- Balance economic objectives with cultural diversity promotion.

This approach aims to harness the full potential of the creative economy while safeguarding cultural diversity.

The concept of creative industries has gained significant traction among policymakers and urban planners in recent decades, often presented as a panacea for economic growth and urban regeneration. However, this "enchantment" with creative industries branding poses substantial challenges for cultural policymakers and can lead to approaches that inadvertently harm the very cultural sectors they aim to support.

The allure of creative industries often stems from their association with innovation, economic dynamism and urban revitalisation. However, this enchantment can lead to several problematic outcomes:

1 Overgeneralist policies driven by appealing discourse: Policymakers may create broad, sweeping policies based on the alluring narrative of creative industries. While sounding promising, these policies often need to adequately address the needs of cultural sectors with less market power, instead primarily benefiting more commercially oriented creative industries. The result can be a widening gap between well-funded, market-driven creative sectors and underfunded, less commercially viable cultural activities.
2 One-size-fits-all approaches: Blanket creative industries policies may fail to account for the diverse needs of different cultural sectors, leading to ineffective or even harmful interventions. This approach often overlooks the unique challenges various cultural practitioners and organisations face, particularly those operating outside mainstream commercial structures.
3 Neglect of traditional cultural institutions: An excessive focus on "creative" sectors might reduce support for traditional cultural institutions like

museums, libraries and heritage sites, which play vital roles in preserving and disseminating culture. This shift can undermine long-standing cultural infrastructure and practices essential for maintaining cultural diversity and social cohesion.

4 Unrealistic policy scope and implementation: Policies branded under creative economy or creative industries should be broader and more ambitious to effectively implement by departments with limited political and budgetary power, such as Ministries of Culture acting alone. This can lead to well-intentioned but ultimately unfeasible initiatives that fail to deliver meaningful support to the cultural sector. The mismatch between policy ambitions and institutional capacity can result in frustration and disillusionment among cultural practitioners and policymakers alike.

These issues are exacerbated by the significant heterogeneity within the creative industries and the power imbalances between different sectors. The creative industries encompass a wide range of activities, from multinational media corporations to individual artisans, each with vastly different needs, resources and market positions. This heterogeneity is characterised by:

1 Varying degrees of commercialisation: Some sectors, like advertising or software development, are highly commercialised, while others, such as fine arts or experimental theatre, often operate on different economic models.
2 Disparate access to resources: Larger, more commercially oriented sectors often have greater access to capital, technology and political influence, potentially overshadowing minor, less commercially viable cultural activities.
3 Different labour conditions vary dramatically across sectors, from stable, well-paid jobs in some industries to precarious, project-based work in others.
4 Uneven policy influence: More powerful sectors within the creative industries often have a louder voice in policy discussions, potentially leading to policies favouring their interests over those of smaller or less commercially oriented cultural activities.
5 Varying dependence on public support: While some creative sectors are primarily self-sufficient, others rely heavily on public funding or subsidies, making them more vulnerable to shifts in policy priorities.

To address these challenges, cultural policymakers need to:

1 Develop a more nuanced understanding of the creative industries, acknowledging their diversity and the different roles they play in cultural, social and economic spheres.

2 Resist the temptation to view creative industries as a cure-all for economic development and instead consider their broader cultural and social impacts.
3 Engage in extensive consultation with various stakeholders, ensuring that voices from all parts of the cultural sector are heard in policy discussions.
4 Recognise the limitations of broad creative economy or creative industries policies when led solely by departments lacking significant political and budgetary power. Effective implementation often requires cross-departmental cooperation and substantial resources.
5 Maintain a balance between supporting commercially viable creative activities and preserving and nurturing cultural expressions that may not have immediate economic value but are crucial for cultural diversity and social wellbeing.

A significant risk lies in the tendency to overemphasise the economic aspects of CCIs at the expense of their cultural and social value. Policies focusing solely on traditional economic metrics may inadvertently prioritise commercially viable creative outputs, potentially marginalising important cultural expressions that don't generate immediate profits or large audiences. Moreover, the diverse and often informal nature of creative work is frequently overlooked in traditional economic models, leading to policies that may not adequately support freelancers, small enterprises or non-profit cultural organisations. There's also a danger of gentrification in urban areas where creative districts are developed without consideration for existing communities. As we progress, policymakers must develop a nuanced understanding of CCIs, recognising their multifaceted nature and the intricate balance between economic, cultural and social outcomes. This requires interdisciplinary approaches, extensive stakeholder engagement and flexible policy frameworks that can adapt to the rapidly changing landscape of creative production and consumption.

By adopting a more critical and nuanced approach to creative industries policies, cultural policymakers can better support the rich tapestry of creative and cultural activities that contribute to the vibrancy and diversity of our societies. This approach requires moving beyond the enchantment with creative industries branding to develop targeted, realistic and inclusive policies that address the needs of the entire cultural ecosystem, not just its most commercially successful components.

As the 21st century progresses, there's a growing emphasis on harnessing creative potential as a driver of economic success and social progress for nations, cities and organisations. However, this shift towards a "creative economy" paradigm carries significant risks if not properly understood and implemented. The complex nature of CCIs often leads to oversimplification in policy approaches, potentially resulting in strategies that fail to address the sector's unique challenges and may even harm the very creative ecosystems they aim to support.

References

Adorno, T., & Horkheimer, M. (2002). *Dialectic of enlightenment.* Stanford University Press.

Buitrago, F., & Duque, I. (2013). *The orange economy: An infinite opportunity.* Inter-American Development Bank.

Department for Culture, Media and Sport (DCMS). (1998). *Creative industries mapping documents 1998.* DCMS.

Department for Culture, Media and Sport (DCMS). (2001). *Creative industries mapping documents 2001.* DCMS.

European Commission. (2010). *Green paper: Unlocking the potential of cultural and creative industries.* European Commission.

Florida, R. (2002). *The Rise of the Creative Class: And How It's Transforming Work, Leisure, Community and Everyday Life.* New York: Basic Books.

Galloway, S., & Dunlop, S. (2007). A critique of definitions of the cultural and creative industries in public policy. *International Journal of Cultural Policy*, 13(1), 17–31.

Hesmondhalgh, D., & Pratt, A. C. (2005). Cultural industries and cultural policy. *International Journal of Cultural Policy*, 11(1), 1–13.

Landry, C. (2000). *The Creative City: A Toolkit for Urban Innovators.* London: Earthscan.

Pratt, A. C. (2008). Creative cities: The cultural industries and the creative class. *Geografiska Annaler: Series B, Human Geography*, 90(2), 107–117.

Throsby, D. (2008). The concentric circles model of the cultural industries. *Cultural Trends*, 17(3), 147–164.

United Nations Conference on Trade and Development (UNCTAD). (2008). *Creative economy report 2008: The challenge of assessing the creative economy towards informed policy-making.* United Nations.

United Nations Educational, Scientific and Cultural Organization (UNESCO). (2009). *UNESCO framework for cultural statistics.* UNESCO Institute for Statistics.

United Nations Educational, Scientific and Cultural Organization (UNESCO). (2013). *Creative economy report 2013.* UNESCO.

United Nations Educational, Scientific and Cultural Organization (UNESCO). (2013). *Creative economy report 2013 special edition: Widening local development pathways.* UNESCO.

United Nations Educational, Scientific and Cultural Organization (UNESCO). (2009). *The 2009 UNESCO framework for cultural statistics (FCS).* UNESCO Institute for Statistics.

2

CREATIVE AND CULTURAL INDUSTRIES AND ECONOMIC GROWTH

2.1 The Growth in Classics: An Overview of Smith, Malthus and Ricard's Perceptions

2.1.1 Adam Smith's and the Invisible Hand

Adam Smith, born in 1723 in Kirkcaldy, Scotland, was a philosopher and economist whose seminal work "An Inquiry into the Nature and Causes of the Wealth of Nations" (1776) laid the foundation for classical growth theory. Smith's optimistic view of economic progress centred on several key concepts that continue to influence economic thought to this day and can be summarised in five axioms:

First, Smith championed the Division of Labor as a primary driver of productivity growth. His famous example of a pin factory demonstrated how breaking down production into specialised tasks could dramatically increase output. Smith wrote eloquently, "The greatest improvement in the productive powers of labour, and the greater part of the skill, dexterity, and judgment with which it is anywhere directed, or applied, seem to have been the effects of the division of labour" (Smith, 1776, Book I, Chapter I).

Second, Smith emphasised the role of capital accumulation in driving economic growth. He posited that profits from current production could be reinvested in capital goods, further increasing future production capacity. This process of capital accumulation, as later elaborated by Kurz and Salvadori (2003), was seen as a key engine of growth.

Third, Smith believed in the self-reinforcing nature of economic growth through market expansion. As markets expanded, they allowed for greater specialisation, leading to higher productivity and further growth.

DOI: 10.4324/9781003434252-3

This concept of increasing returns to scale was ahead of its time and would be revisited by later economists, as noted by Lavezzi (2003).

Fourth, Smith recognised the importance of a stable institutional framework in facilitating economic growth. He emphasised the role of property rights, contract enforcement, and the rule of law in creating an environment conducive to economic activity, ideas later explored in depth by North and Thomas (1973).

Fifth, Smith introduced the concept of the "Invisible Hand," suggesting that individuals pursuing their self-interest in a market economy would unintentionally promote the general welfare of society. As Rothschild (1994) points out, this idea has influenced economic thought about the efficiency of market economies.

Adam Smith's economic theories, primarily outlined in *The Wealth of Nations*, explained how economies could grow through specialisation, capital accumulation and market expansion. However, his earlier work, *The Theory of Moral Sentiments*, is a crucial yet often overlooked part of Smith's intellectual legacy. This book explores human morality and behaviour, providing a foundation for understanding the ethical considerations that underpin economic interactions. These works offer a complete picture of Smith's vision, showing how moral philosophy and economics intertwine. While his work predated the marginal revolution in economics, many of Smith's insights from both books continue to influence modern economic and philosophical thought, demonstrating the enduring relevance of his ideas.

To know more, you could explore the following references (see section):

Kurz, H. D., & Salvadori, N. (2003).
Lavezzi, A. (2003).
North, D. C., & Thomas, R. P. (1973).
Rothschild, E. (1994).
Smith, A. (1776).
Smith, A. (1759/2002)

2.1.2 Malthusian and the Population Theory

Thomas Robert Malthus (1766–1834) was an English cleric and scholar who became influential in political economy and demography. Born into a prosperous family, Malthus was educated at Jesus College, Cambridge, where he later became a fellow.

Malthus's seminal work "An Essay on the Principle of Population" (1798) presented a sobering perspective on long-term economic growth, fundamentally reshaping economic thought in the early 19th century. Malthusian theory's core lies in the dynamic relationship between population growth and financial resources, particularly food production. Malthus posited that population, when unchecked, increases at a geometric rate, while food production can only grow arithmetically. He famously wrote, "Population, when unchecked, increases in a geometrical ratio. Subsistence increases only in an arithmetical ratio" (Malthus, 1798, Chapter I).

This inherent mismatch between population growth and resource expansion led to what economists later termed the "Malthusian trap." In this scenario, any temporary increase in per capita income inevitably triggers population growth, pushing living standards back to subsistence levels (Clark, 2007). This cyclical pattern, Malthus argued, was the primary reason for persistent poverty throughout human history. To explain how populations historically remained in check, Malthus identified two types of population controls: preventive and positive checks. Preventive checks involve voluntary limitation of population growth, such as delayed marriage or abstinence. Positive checks, more grimly, include factors that increase mortality rates, such as famine, disease and war. These checks, Malthus contended, were nature's way of maintaining a balance between population and resources.

Malthus's theory had profound implications for how poverty was understood in his time and beyond. Unlike many of his contemporaries, Malthus argued that poverty was not primarily a result of social institutions or government policies but rather an inevitable consequence of population pressure on limited resources (Winch, 2013). This perspective significantly influenced social and economic policies in 19th-century Britain and beyond.

While Malthus's dire predictions did not materialise in developed economies due to unprecedented technological progress and the demographic transition, his ideas resonate in contemporary discussions on sustainable development, resource scarcity and population policy. The concept of "Malthusian dynamics" remains relevant in understanding pre-industrial economies and some developing countries (Galor & Weil, 2000).

To know more, you could explore the following references:

Clark, G. (2007).
Galor, O., & Weil, D. N. (2000).
Malthus, T. R. (1798).
Winch, D. (2013).

2.1.3 Ricardo's Theory of Diminishing Returns

David Ricardo (1772–1823) was a British political economist, often credited as one of the most influential classical economists alongside Adam Smith and Thomas Malthus. Born in London, Ricardo began his career as a successful stockbroker before focusing on economics, inspired by Adam Smith's *The Wealth of Nations*. Despite his lack of formal education, Ricardo's keen intellect and analytical skills led him to make ground-breaking contributions to economic theory.

Ricardo's seminal work, "On the Principles of Political Economy and Taxation," published in 1817, significantly advanced economic theory and cemented his place as a pivotal figure in classical economics. At the heart of his economic philosophy was the principle of diminishing returns, which posited that as more of a variable factor of production (such as labour) is applied to a fixed factor (for instance, land), the marginal product of the variable factor would eventually decline. This insight, used initially in agriculture, would have broad applications across various economic sectors and remains a fundamental principle in modern economics.

One of Ricardo's most enduring contributions was his theory of differential rent. This theory explained how land of varying qualities would be brought into production as demand for agricultural products increased. According to Ricardo, as population growth led to increased demand for food, less fertile land would be cultivated, resulting in higher rents for more productive land. This model provided insights into agricultural economics and laid the groundwork for understanding income distribution between different factors of production.

Building on Adam Smith's work, Ricardo refined the labour theory of value, arguing that the relative prices of goods were primarily determined by the relative amounts of labour required for their production. While the marginal revolution in economics would later challenge this theory, it remained influential in classical economics and played a crucial role in the development of economic thought.

Ricardo's most widely recognised contribution is his theory of comparative advantage in international trade. This revolutionary idea suggested that countries could benefit from trade even when one country had an absolute advantage in producing all goods. Countries could increase their overall economic welfare by specialising in producing goods for which they have a comparative advantage and trading for others. This concept continues to be a cornerstone of international trade theory and policy.

Ricardo's economic outlook could have been more uniformly optimistic, however. He predicted that diminishing returns in agriculture would eventually lead to what he defined as a "stationary state," where economic growth would cease. In this state, all profits would be absorbed by rents, leaving no incentive for further capital accumulation. While Ricardo acknowledged the potential for technological progress to offset diminishing returns, he believed such progress would be temporary and that the economy would eventually return to a stationary state.

Despite this pessimistic prediction, Ricardo's work provided a more rigorous analytical framework for understanding economic growth and distribution. His ideas on diminishing returns and resource constraints continue to influence modern economic thought, particularly in discussions of sustainable development and resource management. Ricardo's contributions bridged the gap between Smith's qualitative insights and the mathematical models of later neoclassical economists (see next session), cementing his place as one of the most influential figures in the history of economic thought.

Ricardo's legacy extends far beyond his own time. His analytical approach to economics, focusing on abstract models and logical deduction, set a new standard for economic reasoning. Subsequent generations of economists adopted and further developed this methodology, shaping how economic analysis is conducted nowadays.

To know more, you could explore the following references:

Blaug, M. (1997).
Kurz, H. D., & Salvadori, N. (2003).
Maneschi, A. (1998).
Mokyr, J. (1990).
Ricardo, D. (1817).
Stigler, G. J. (1958).

2.2 Neoclassical Growth Theory: The Solow-Swan Model

Neoclassical economics has produced several influential models of economic growth, each offering unique insights into the dynamics of long-term economic development. These include the Ramsey-Cass-Koopmans model (Cass, 1965; Koopmans, 1965; Ramsey, 1928), which introduces endogenous saving rates; the Overlapping Generations model (Diamond, 1965), which incorporates demographic factors; and the Uzawa-Lucas model (Lucas, 1988), which emphasises human capital accumulation. However, this book will primarily focus on the Solow-Swan model to analyse creative industries.

The Solow-Swan model, independently developed by Robert Solow (1956) and Trevor Swan (1956), marked a significant advancement in growth theory. It provided a coherent mathematical framework for analysing how capital accumulation, labour force growth and technological progress contribute to economic growth. Our choice to emphasise this model is deliberate and strategic, based on several key considerations. Firstly, the Solow-Swan model's relative simplicity makes it an ideal starting point for examining the unique characteristics of creative industries. The model's core equation, $Y = F(K, L, A)$, where Y is output, K is capital, L is labour, and A is technology, provides a clear structure for analysing how these factors interact in creative sectors. For instance, in film production, K might represent physical capital like cameras and studios, L the creative workforce, and A the technological know-how and innovative techniques.

Secondly, the model's focus on capital accumulation and technological change aligns well with the innovation-driven nature of creative sectors. Creative industries are often at the forefront of adopting new technologies and developing novel production methods. The Solow-Swan model's emphasis on technological progress as a critical driver of long-term growth is particularly relevant here, as it can help explain the rapid evolution and economic impact of sectors like digital media, video games and interactive entertainment.

Thirdly, the Solow-Swan model's concept of total factor productivity (TFP) offers a valuable lens through which to view the intangible assets and knowledge externalities[1] crucial in creative industries. In these sectors, growth often stems from factors not easily captured by traditional measures of capital and labour – factors like creativity, artistic innovation and cultural value. The model's residual, often interpreted as technological progress, can be expanded in creative industries to encompass these intangible but vital contributors to growth.

Moreover, the Solow-Swan model's predictions about convergence and diminishing returns to capital have exciting implications for creative industries. In traditional sectors, these principles might suggest that less developed economies will grow faster and eventually catch up with more advanced ones. In creative industries, however, we might observe different patterns. The unique nature of creative capital – which often appreciates rather than depreciates with use – and the winner-take-all dynamics usually seen in these industries could lead to divergent growth patterns that challenge the standard Solow-Swan predictions. Another advantage of using the Solow-Swan model is its flexibility and potential for extension. While the basic model assumes exogenous technological progress, later extensions have incorporated endogenous technological change. This is particularly relevant for creative industries, where innovation is often driven by internal industry dynamics rather than external factors. By adapting these extended versions of the Solow-Swan model, we can better understand how creative industries generate and sustain growth.

The model also provides a framework for understanding the role of human capital in creative industries. While the original Solow-Swan model treated labour as a homogeneous factor, later developments (such as the Mankiw-Romer-Weil model – see Box 2.1) incorporated human capital as a distinct input. This extension is crucial for analysing creative industries, where workforce skills, talents and knowledge often drive value creation and growth.

BOX 2.1 SUMMARY OF THE MANKIW-ROMER-WEIL MODEL

The Mankiw-Romer-Weil Model (1992) represents a significant extension of the Solow-Swan model by incorporating human capital as a distinct factor of production. It introduces an augmented production function, $Y = K^\alpha \times H^\beta \times (AL)^{(1-\alpha-\beta)}$, where H represents human capital and includes separate accumulation equations for both physical and human capital. This modification substantially improves the model's empirical fit, enhancing its ability to explain cross-country income differences. The model predicts a slower convergence rate than the original Solow-Swan model, aligning more closely with empirical observations. Moreover, it provides a valuable framework for analysing the impact of education and training policies on economic growth, emphasising the crucial role of human capital in driving economic development. By explicitly accounting for human capital, the Mankiw-Romer-Weil Model offers a more nuanced understanding of growth dynamics and has become an important tool in theoretical and applied economic research.

Furthermore, the Solow-Swan model's long-run implications can shed light on the sustainability of growth in creative industries. The model's concept of a steady state, where per-capita output growth is driven solely by technological progress, raises important questions about the long-term trajectory of creative sectors. How do these industries continue to innovate and grow despite potentially diminishing returns? The model provides a framework for exploring these questions.

Lastly, the Solow-Swan model's simplicity makes it an excellent pedagogical tool. It allows us to introduce fundamental concepts in growth theory and then gradually build upon them to address the specific complexities of creative industries. This approach enables readers to develop a solid foundational understanding before grappling with more intricate industry-specific phenomena.

While more complex models might offer additional nuances, the Solow-Swan model provides a robust foundation for understanding the fundamental growth dynamics in creative industries. Its focus on capital, labour and technology as key growth drivers, combined with its flexibility and potential for extension, makes it an excellent choice for our analysis in this book. By applying this model to creative industries, we can gain valuable insights into the sources of growth, the role of innovation and the long-term prospects of these vital sectors of the modern economy.

2.2.1 Assumptions and Key Components

The Solow-Swan model, a cornerstone of neoclassical growth theory, rests on a foundation of carefully constructed assumptions that simplify complex economic realities. These fundamental assumptions include:

1 Constant Returns to Scale: The production function exhibits constant returns to scale, meaning doubling all inputs will double output.
2 Diminishing Marginal Returns: Each additional unit of capital or labour yields a more minor increase in output than the previous unit.
3 Constant Savings Rate: A fixed proportion of output is saved and invested.
4 Closed Economy: There is no international trade or capital flows.
5 Total Employment: All available labour and capital are fully utilised.
6 Perfect Competition: All markets are perfectly competitive.

The model's key components interact within this framework to drive economic growth under a specific production function, often expressed in the Cobb-Douglas form $Y = A \times K\text{^}\alpha \times L\text{^}(1–\alpha)$, encapsulating the relationship between output (Y), capital (K), labour (L) and technology (A). This Cobb-Douglas function captures several critical economic concepts. The exponents α and $(1–\alpha)$ represent the share of output that goes to capital and labour, respectively, aligning with the empirical observation that these shares tend to be relatively stable over time in many economies. The function exhibits constant returns to scale: Y also doubles if both K and L are doubled. Moreover, it incorporates diminishing marginal returns to each factor: as more of one input is added while holding the other constant, the incremental increase in output diminishes.

The parameter A in the Cobb-Douglas function represents technological progress in the Solow-Swan model. Increases in A allow more output to be produced with the same levels of capital and labour, representing productivity improvements that are not attributable to increases in observable inputs. In the basic Solow-Swan model, growth in A is treated as exogenous, occurring at a constant rate of g.

Complementing the production function, the capital accumulation equation, $\Delta K = sY - \delta K$, describes the evolution of the capital stock over time. Here, s represents the savings rate, determining the fraction of output invested, while δ is the depreciation rate of capital. This equation forms the core dynamic of the Solow-Swan model, determining how the economy evolves. Population growth is assumed to occur at an exogenous rate, n, while technological progress grows at a g rate. These factors and the savings and depreciation rates are critical determinants of the economy's long-run growth path and steady-state equilibrium.

A central concept in the Solow-Swan model is the steady-state equilibrium, where key ratios (such as capital per worker) remain constant over time. In the steady state:

- Capital per effective worker (k = K/(AL)) is constant.
- Output per effective worker (y = Y/(AL)) is constant.
- The growth rate of total output equals the sum of the growth rates of technology (g) and the labour force (n).

The model predicts convergence to this steady state, with countries having lower initial capital per worker growing faster than those with higher initial capital per worker. This concept of conditional convergence has been influential in empirical growth research.

In the basic Solow-Swan model, technological progress is treated as an exogenous factor, like a "manna from heaven." This assumption has several important implications:

1 Long-run per capita growth is driven solely by technological progress. In the steady state, the growth rate of output per worker equals the rate of technological progress.
2 The model needs to explain the source of technological progress. It treats it as an unexplained external force that impacts the economy.
3 Policy interventions can't affect the long-run growth rate. Since technological progress is exogenous, policies can only affect the level of output, not its long-run growth rate.

This limitation of the model led to endogenous growth theories, which attempt to explain technological progress within the model itself (Aghion & Howitt, 1998). These newer theories explore how factors such as research and development, human capital accumulation, and knowledge externalities can drive technological progress and long-run growth.

The Solow-Swan model's elegance lies in its ability to capture fundamental growth dynamics with relative simplicity. It provides a framework for understanding how capital accumulation, population growth and technological progress interact to determine long-run economic growth. While its assumptions may seem restrictive, they allow for clear insights into the drivers of economic growth and the factors that influence an economy's long-term trajectory.

Despite its simplifications, the model has proven remarkably useful in explaining cross-country economic performance differences and predicting long-run growth patterns. It has served as a springboard for more complex growth theories and is a valuable tool. However, while the Solow-Swan model provides useful insights into the mechanics of economic growth, its treatment of technological progress as an exogenous factor represents a significant limitation. By assuming that technological advancement occurs independently of economic forces, the model must be more robust in capturing the complex innovation and knowledge-creation dynamics that drive modern economies. This simplification overlooks the crucial role of human capital, research and development investments and institutional factors in fostering technological progress. Consequently, the model's policy implications could be more extensive, suggesting that long-run growth rates are impervious to policy interventions. This perspective is at odds with empirical evidence suggesting that policies promoting education, research and innovation can influence long-term economic growth trajectories.

However, dismissing the Solow-Swan model entirely based on this critique would be remiss. The model's simplicity, both its weakness and strength, allows for clear analytical insights into the role of capital accumulation and diminishing returns in the growth process. Its prediction of conditional convergence has found support in empirical studies and has influenced development economics. Moreover, the model's limitations have spurred the development of more sophisticated theories, such as endogenous growth models, which attempt to explain technological progress within the economic system. In this light, the Solow-Swan model can be seen as a crucial steppingstone in the evolution of growth theory, providing a foundation upon which more complex and realistic models have been built.

2.3 Integrating Creative and Cultural Industries into Growth Theory

Integrating CCIs into economic growth theory significantly evolves our understanding of modern economies. These industries have become increasingly recognised as essential contributors to economic growth and development. This section explores how these industries fit into and extend traditional growth theories, offering new perspectives on the drivers of economic progress in the 21st century.

2.3.1 Knowledge Economy and Human Capital

The rise of the knowledge economy has highlighted the crucial role of human capital in driving economic growth. CCIs are at the forefront of this shift, serving as producers and incubators of human capital, occupying a distinctive niche in the modern economy. They serve not merely as production sectors but as dynamic incubators of human capital and wellsprings of tacit knowledge. This dual role positions them at the forefront of the knowledge economy, driving innovation and economic growth in ways that transcend traditional industrial paradigms.

2.3.1.1 CCIs Diverse and Adaptive Human Capital

Unlike conventional sectors characterised by standardised skill sets, creative industries foster the development of a multifaceted, adaptable and innovative workforce encompassing scientists, engineers, artists, and cultural creatives, underscoring these industries' centrality to the knowledge economy. The creative sectors employ highly skilled individuals and catalyse the enhancement of the broader workforce's capabilities through their outputs and pervasive spillover effects. Consider the film industry: beyond creating employment for actors, directors and technicians, it cultivates many transferable skills. From project management and digital literacy to collaborative problem-solving and cross-cultural communication, the competencies lying in film production find applicability across diverse economic sectors. This phenomenon aligns with Potts and Cunningham's (2008) characterisation of creative industries as "nurseries" for novel ideas and skills, functioning as crucibles of innovation with economy-wide implications.

2.3.1.2 The Pivotal Role of Tacit Knowledge

Integral to the creative industries' capacity for human capital generation is their reliance on and propagation of tacit knowledge. This form of knowledge, encapsulated by Michael Polanyi's (1966) assertion that "we can know more than we can tell," resists codification and straightforward transfer. In creative and cultural sectors, tacit knowledge is embodied in individual expertise, organisational routines and cultural contexts, forming the bedrock of innovative processes and outputs.

Asheim and Hansen's (2009) typology of knowledge bases – analytical (science-based), synthetic (engineering-based) and symbolic (arts-based) – provides a valuable framework for understanding the unique knowledge dynamics of creative industries. These sectors predominantly operate within the symbolic knowledge base, characterised by its highly tacit and context-specific nature. Crucially, the accumulation of tacit knowledge in creative industries is often achieved through learning-by-doing. Arrow (1962) introduced this concept, particularly relevant to creative and cultural sectors. Skills in these industries are frequently acquired and refined through practice and experience rather than formal education alone. This continuous learning and improvement process can lead to increasing returns to scale, a key factor in endogenous growth models.

Throsby (2001) extends this idea to cultural capital, which encompasses both tangible and intangible cultural assets. He notes that cultural capital accumulates through a process akin to learning by doing. Artists and cultural producers develop their skills and reputations over time, potentially increasing productivity and innovation. This phenomenon challenges traditional assumptions about diminishing returns and suggests that creative industries might exhibit different growth dynamics than other sectors.

The reliance on tacit, symbolic knowledge engenders several significant economic implications:

1. Barrier to Entry: The difficulty in replicating or transferring tacit knowledge creates natural barriers to entry, potentially generating innovation rents and sustaining competitive advantages.
2. Clustering Imperative: The necessity for face-to-face interactions in sharing tacit knowledge promotes geographical clustering and agglomeration effects, fostering innovation ecosystems.
3. Value Enhancement: The uniqueness embedded in tacit knowledge enhances the value proposition of creative outputs, contributing to product differentiation and market competitiveness.
4. Adaptive Capacity: The fluidity of tacit knowledge equips creative industries with superior adaptive capabilities, enabling rapid responses to changing market conditions and consumer preferences.

The interplay between human capital development and tacit knowledge accumulation in creative industries creates a self-reinforcing cycle of innovation and growth. As these sectors cultivate diverse skill sets and nurture tacit expertise, they simultaneously enhance their capacity for future innovation and strengthen their economic resilience. This symbiosis between skill development and knowledge-creation positions creative industries as crucial drivers of economic dynamism in the 21st century. By fostering adaptable human capital and leveraging the power of tacit knowledge, these sectors contribute to their growth and serve as catalysts for innovation and development across the broader economic landscape.

2.3.2 Innovation and Technological Progress in Creative Industries

Creative industries stand at the forefront of innovation and technological progress, offering unique perspectives that challenge and extend traditional growth theories. These sectors serve as repositories of change, embodying the dynamic processes that drive economic evolution in the contemporary era.

2.3.2.1 Creative Destruction[2]

Joseph Alois Schumpeter (1883–1950) was an Austrian-born economist and political scientist who significantly contributed to economic theory. He served as Austria's Finance Minister in 1919 and later held professorships at the University of Bonn and Harvard. Schumpeter is best known for his entrepreneurship, innovation and creative destruction theories. Schumpeter's (1942) concept of creative destruction finds its essential expression in cultural industries. These sectors are characterised by constant innovation, where new styles, formats and technologies regularly displace existing ones. The music industry provides a vivid illustration of this process, having undergone multiple waves of creative destruction – from vinyl to cassettes, CDs and digital streaming platforms. Each transition transformed consumption patterns and reshaped the industry's entire value chain.

Potts and Cunningham (2008) further this idea, positioning creative industries as integral components of the economy's innovation system. They argue that these sectors specialise in the origination and adoption of new ideas, continuously refreshing the economy's knowledge base. This perspective elevates creative industries from mere producers of cultural goods to critical drivers of the "creative destruction" that Schumpeter saw as essential to economic progress. By constantly challenging the status quo and introducing novel concepts, creative industries catalyse innovation across the broader financial landscape.

2.3.2.2 Open Innovation: Collaborative Creativity

The concept of open innovation, popularised by Chesbrough (2003), has found particularly fertile ground in creative industries. These sectors often rely on collaborative and networked models of innovation, where ideas flow freely between organisations and individuals, blurring traditional boundaries.

The software industry, for instance, especially in open-source development, exemplifies this approach. Projects like Linux demonstrate how open collaboration can lead to robust, innovative products that often outperform their closed-source counterparts. Similarly, the fashion industry thrives on the rapid dissemination and reinterpretation of ideas, driving a continuous cycle of innovation that spans global networks of designers, manufacturers and consumers.

Potts and Cunningham (2008) extend this concept with their "social network market" model for creative industries. This model states that the value of cultural and creative goods is determined through complex social interactions, suggesting that innovation in creative sectors is inherently open and socially embedded. This perspective challenges traditional closed innovation paradigms and highlights the unique dynamics of value creation in creative economies.

2.3.2.3 Digital Revolution: Transforming Creative Landscapes

Digital technologies have precipitated a profound transformation in creative industries, revolutionising cultural goods' production, distribution and consumption. Nicholas Negroponte's (1995) prescient predictions about the digital revolution have been fully realised in the creative sector, with far-reaching consequences.

Key aspects of this digital transformation include:

1. The Democratisation of Production Tools: Digital technologies have significantly lowered barriers to entry, enabling a new generation of creators to produce professional-quality content with minimal resources. This democratisation has led to creativity and diversity in cultural production.
2. Global Digital Distribution Platforms: The emergence of digital platforms has exponentially expanded the market reach of creative content. Streaming services, online marketplaces and social media platforms have created global audiences for even niche cultural products, fundamentally altering the economics of creative industries.
3. New Formats and Mediums: The digital revolution has spawned entirely new forms of creative expression. Virtual and augmented reality technologies, for instance, are opening unprecedented possibilities for immersive storytelling and interactive experiences, pushing the boundaries of what's possible in creative content.
4. Data-Driven Decision-Making: The digital age has ushered in new content creation and marketing approaches. Big data analytics now inform everything from script development in the film industry to personalised music recommendations on streaming platforms, leading to more targeted and efficient creative processes.

BOX 2.2 TRANSFORMATIVE INNOVATION IMPACTING GROWTH IN CREATIVE INDUSTRIES

1. The Democratisation of Production Tools
   - Music: Software like GarageBand and Ableton Live enable professional-quality home recordings. Example: Billie Eilish's Grammy-winning album was produced in a bedroom studio.
   - Film: High-quality smartphone cameras and apps like FiLMiC Pro allow feature film production. Example: Steven Soderbergh's "Unsane" shot entirely on iPhone.
   - Graphic Design: Tools like Canva make professional-level design accessible to non-designers, empowering small businesses and individuals.
2. Global Digital Distribution Platforms
   - Music: Platforms like Spotify and SoundCloud enable independent artists to reach global audiences. Example: BTS gained international fame through social media and streaming.
   - Literature: Self-publishing platforms like Amazon Kindle Direct Publishing bypass traditional publishing houses. Example: "Fifty Shades of Grey" began as self-published fan fiction.

- Visual Art: Instagram has become crucial for artists to showcase their work globally. Amrita Sethi, for example, built a successful career leveraging Instagram's reach.

3 New Formats and Mediums

- Virtual Reality (VR) in Art: Tools like Google's Tilt Brush allow 3D space painting, creating immersive artworks. An example is Elizabeth Edwards' VR exhibitions.
- Augmented Reality (AR) in Museums enhances visitor experiences. For example, the Smithsonian uses AR to bring extinct animals to life.
- Interactive Storytelling: Allows viewer choice in narratives. Example: Netflix's "Bandersnatch" episode of *Black Mirror* pioneered the interactive television format.

4 Data-Driven Decision-Making

- Film Industry: Viewing data informs content creation. For example, Netflix commissioned *House of Cards* based on subscriber viewing patterns.
- Music Recommendations: Machine learning algorithms create personalised playlists. Example: Spotify's Discover Weekly based on listening history and user behaviour.
- Book Publishing: Real-time data on reader behaviour allows authors to adjust writing strategies. Example: Amazon's Kindle Direct Publishing provides engagement analytics.

These changes have accelerated growth within creative industries and amplified their impact on the broader economy. As Bakhshi and McVittie (2009) observe, creative industries often serve as early adopters and testbeds for new technologies. Innovations pioneered in these sectors frequently diffuse to other industries, positioning creative sectors as technological trailblazers in the broader economic ecosystem. The intersection of creative destruction, open innovation and digital transformation in creative industries presents a compelling case for their central role in driving economic growth and innovation. These sectors generate cultural value and serve as dynamic engines of technological progress and economic renewal. As economies increasingly rely on knowledge, creativity and innovation for growth, the models and practices emerging from creative industries offer valuable insights for policymakers and business leaders alike.

By constantly pushing the boundaries of technology and collaborative innovation, creative industries are shaping the future of work, consumption and economic value creation. Their ability to adapt to and harness technological change positions them as key players in the knowledge economy, driving progress within their domains and across the entire economic landscape.

2.3.2.3.1 Challenges and Ethical Considerations

While the digital revolution has undoubtedly propelled creative industries forward, it has also given rise to significant challenges and ethical considerations. The digital divide remains a pressing issue, potentially exacerbating inequalities in access to both the consumption and production of creative content. This divide exists between nations and within societies, risking the marginalisation of certain groups from the benefits of the creative economy.

Data privacy and the breach of personal information safety have become critical concerns as creative industries increasingly rely on data-driven strategies. As Cadwalladr and Graham-Harrison (2018) analysed, the Cambridge Analytica scandal[3] underscored the potential to misuse personal data in digital creative spaces. This incident raised important questions about the ethical implications of data collection and usage in targeted content creation and distribution.

Moreover, the rise of artificial intelligence and machine learning in creative processes poses new challenges. While these technologies offer unprecedented opportunities for personalisation and efficiency, they also raise concerns about the potential displacement of human creativity and the authenticity of AI-generated content. Using AI in art creation blurs the lines between human and machine creativity, challenging traditional notions of authorship and artistic value.

The gig economy, which has become prevalent in many creative sectors, presents another double-edged sword. While it offers flexibility and opportunities for freelancers, it also often needs more stability and benefits associated with traditional employment, as Graham et al. (2017) pointed out. This shift in employment patterns could have long-term implications for the sustainability of careers in creative industries.

Lastly, the dominance of a few large tech platforms in distributing creative content raises concerns about market concentration and the diversity of cultural expression. As Hesmondhalgh and Meier (2018) discussed, the increasing power of streaming platforms and social media giants in shaping cultural consumption could potentially homogenise content and limit the visibility of niche or alternative creative voices.

Addressing these challenges will ensure that creative industries' innovative potential is realised equitably, ethically and sustainably. As these industries evolve, policymakers, industry leaders and creators must grapple with these complex issues to shape a future where technological progress and creative expression coexist harmoniously with societal values and individual rights.

2.3.2.4 Spillover Effect, Externalities and Network Effects

CCIs generate significant positive externalities, contributing to economic growth beyond their direct output. These industries, encompassing fields such as art, music, film, literature and digital media, serve as catalysts for innovation and development across the broader economy.

2.3.2.4.1 Knowledge Spillovers from Creative to Other Sectors

Knowledge spillovers occur when innovations or practices from one sector benefit other sectors without total compensation. Creative industries are particularly prone to generating such spillovers due to the general applicability of many creative skills and innovations. This cross-pollination of ideas often leads to unexpected breakthroughs and efficiency gains in seemingly unrelated fields.

For example:

1 Design thinking, originating from creative disciplines, has been widely adopted in business and technology sectors. Companies like Apple and Google have embraced design thinking to create user-centric products and services, revolutionising their respective industries.
2 Storytelling techniques from the entertainment industry are increasingly used in marketing and corporate communications. Brands now craft compelling narratives to engage consumers, moving beyond traditional advertising to create emotional connections and brand loyalty.
3 Visualisation tools developed for creative purposes find applications in scientific research and data analysis. Advanced graphics software, initially designed for film CGI, now aids in complex scientific simulations and big data visualisation.

Bakhshi et al. (2008) provide evidence of these spillovers, demonstrating how creative industries contribute to innovation in the broader economy. Their research highlights the disproportionate impact of creative sector innovations on productivity and growth across various industries.

2.3.2.4.2 Externalities

Cultural externalities refer to the broader social and economic benefits of cultural activities. These frequently intangible benefits can have profound effects on societal well-being and economic development. They extend beyond the immediate economic transactions associated with cultural products or events.

These can include:

1 Enhanced social cohesion and community identity. Cultural activities often bring diverse groups together, fostering understanding and shared experiences. This can lead to more robust, more resilient communities that are better equipped to face economic challenges.
2 Improved quality of life and well-being. Access to cultural amenities and activities has been linked to higher life satisfaction and mental health. This can indirectly boost productivity and reduce healthcare costs.

3 Increased attractiveness of locations for residents and businesses. Cities with vibrant cultural scenes often attract skilled workers and innovative companies, creating clusters of economic activity. This "cultural capital" can significantly influence urban regeneration and economic development strategies.

Throsby (2001) argues that these cultural externalities contribute to sustainable economic development by enhancing social and cultural capital. Whilst challenging to quantify, these externalities are crucial in creating environments conducive to economic growth. They form the "soft infrastructure" that underpins long-term financial success and resilience.

BOX 2.3 EXTERNALITIES IN ECONOMICS

Definition

In economics, an externality refers to a cost or benefit that affects a third party who did not choose to incur that cost or benefit. Externalities can be either positive or negative and can stem from either the production or consumption of a good or service. The concept of externalities is crucial in understanding market failures, which often necessitate government intervention to correct the imbalance in certain economic activities.

Critical Characteristics of Externalities:

1 Impact on Third Parties: The effect is on those not directly involved in producing or consuming the good or service.
2 Not Reflected in Market Price: The cost or benefit needs to be incorporated into the market price of the good or service.
3 Can Be Positive or Negative: Externalities can create either benefits or costs for society.
4 Occur in Both Production and Consumption: They can arise from either the production process or the consumption of goods and services.

BOX 2.4 EXTERNALITIES: TYPES AND ECONOMIC IMPLICATIONS

Types of Externalities

1 Negative Externalities

Occur when production or consumption imposes costs on third parties.

Examples:

- Environmental Pollution: Factory waste, vehicle emissions
- Noise Pollution: Airport operations, construction work
- Overuse of Common Resources: Overfishing, excessive groundwater extraction
- Health-related: Secondhand smoke, antibiotic resistance

2 Positive Externalities

Occur when production or consumption benefits third parties.

Examples:

- Education: Improved workforce productivity, reduced crime rates
- Research and Development: Technological spillovers, medical advancements
- Vaccination: Herd immunity
- Green Spaces: Increased property values, improved air quality
- Network Effects: Increased value of communication networks

Economic Implications

1 Market Failure:

- Prices don't reflect true social costs/benefits
- Results in over/under-production of goods with externalities

2 Efficiency Loss:

- Market equilibrium doesn't maximise social welfare
- Causes misallocation of resources

3 Intervention Needs:

- Government: Regulations, taxes, subsidies
- Private: Coase Theorem, corporate social responsibility

4 Price Distortion:

- Inaccurate market prices lead to suboptimal decisions

5 Equity Issues:

- Externalities often affect groups disproportionately

6 Long-term Impact:

- Can influence economic growth and development

7 Policy Challenges:

- Difficulty in measuring and addressing externalities effectively

Additional Considerations

- Measuring and valuing externalities is crucial for effective policymaking
- Some externalities have global impacts (e.g., climate change, biodiversity loss, pandemics), requiring international cooperation

2.3.2.4.3 Network Effects in Creative Industries

Many creative industries exhibit strong network effects, where the value of a product or service increases with the number of users. Katz and Shapiro (1985) described this phenomenon in the context of technology adoption, and it is particularly relevant to digital creative industries. In the creative sector, these network effects can lead to rapid scaling and market dominance.

For instance:

1 Social media platforms become more valuable as their user base grows. Each new user adds content and connections, making the platform more attractive to others. This self-reinforcing cycle has led to the global dominance of platforms like Facebook and Twitter.
2 Online marketplaces for creative goods benefit from having more buyers and sellers. Platforms like Etsy or Redbubble become more valuable to artists as they attract more customers, and more appealing to customers as they offer a more comprehensive range of products.
3 Collaborative creative tools improve with increased user contributions. Software like GitHub for coding or Figma for design becomes more valuable as more people contribute templates, plugins or code snippets.

These network effects can increase returns to scale, a key feature of endogenous growth models. In creative industries, this can manifest as rapid growth once a critical mass of users is achieved. They also contribute to forming "winner-take-most" markets, where successful creative products or platforms can achieve dominant market positions. This concentration can drive innovation but also raises concerns about market power and the need for appropriate regulation. Combining knowledge spillovers, cultural externalities and network effects positions creative industries as robust economic growth and innovation drivers with impacts far beyond their direct economic output.

2.3.3 Urban Development and Creative Industries

2.3.3.1 Creative Clusters and Economic Growth

Creative clusters, geographical concentrations of interconnected creative businesses and institutions, have become a focus of academic research and policy initiatives. Porter's (1998) work on industry clusters provides a foundation for understanding these creative agglomerations.

Creative clusters can drive economic growth through:

1 Knowledge spillovers and informal learning networks.
2 Specialised labour markets that facilitate skill matching.
3 Development of specialised suppliers and services.
4 Increased opportunities for collaboration and innovation.

Empirical studies, such as those by Scott (2000) and Pratt (2004), have demonstrated the economic impact of creative clusters in cities like Los Angeles, London and Paris.

2.3.3.2 Cultural Amenities and Local Development

Cultural amenities, such as museums, theatres and music venues, play a crucial role in urban development and economic growth. These amenities contribute to a city's quality of life, making it more attractive to highly skilled workers and innovative businesses. Glaeser et al. (2001) argue that providing urban amenities is crucial to city growth, particularly in attracting and retaining human capital. Cultural amenities can also drive tourism, a significant economic sector in many cities.

However, the relationship between cultural amenities and economic growth is complex. While they can contribute to urban revitalisation, there are concerns about displacement and uneven development. Zukin's (1995) work on the "symbolic economy" of cities highlights these tensions between culture, authenticity and economic growth.

2.3.4 Globalisation, International Trade and Creative Industries

In the last decades, globalisation has emerged as a powerful force, weaving intricate patterns across CCIs, both commercial and cultural exchanges. This phenomenon has not merely touched these sectors; it has fundamentally transformed them, altering how cultural goods and services are created, disseminated and consumed globally.

2.3.4.1 Cultural Goods in Global Trade Theory: A Paradigm Shift

International trade has long been governed by established theories and models, with concepts like comparative advantage as cornerstones of economic thought. However, the unique nature of cultural goods has challenged these traditional paradigms, forcing economists and policymakers to reconsider long-held assumptions.

At the heart of this challenge lies the dual identity of cultural goods – they are not merely economic commodities but also vessels of cultural significance and symbolic value. This duality introduces a layer of complexity that traditional trade theories struggle to encompass fully. David Throsby, a pioneering voice in cultural economics, advocates for incorporating "cultural exception" in trade policy, acknowledging that cultural goods often defy conventional economic logic.

Consider, for instance, a centuries-old painting. While potentially high, its market price fails to capture its value as a cultural artefact, a piece of history and potential future valorisation. This intrinsic value, intangible yet profound, necessitates a different approach in trade discussions and economic modelling. The recognition of cultural goods' unique nature found formal expression in UNESCO's Convention on the Protection and Promotion of the Diversity of Cultural Expressions, adopted in 2005. This landmark document explicitly acknowledges these goods and services' dual economic and cultural nature. It serves as a testament to the global community's understanding that cultural products are not just commodities to be traded but also essential elements of human expression and diversity.

This dual nature introduces a myriad of complexities in international trade agreements. How does one quantify cultural value in economic terms? How can trade policies protect cultural diversity while also promoting economic growth? These questions challenge policymakers and economists, sparking debates and driving trade theory and practice innovation.

2.3.4.2 Comparative Advantage in Creative Sectors: A Global Mosaic of Specialisation

While the unique characteristics of cultural goods complicate their treatment in traditional trade models, the concept of comparative advantage still finds resonance in the creative industries. Rather than being rendered obsolete, this economic principle has adapted, taking on new dimensions in the context of cultural production and dissemination. Countries and regions worldwide have carved out niches in particular creative sectors, leveraging their unique cultural heritage, institutional frameworks and human capital to establish dominance in specific areas. This specialisation has given rise to a rich, diverse global landscape of artistic production, where different regions contribute their unique flavours to the world's cultural ecosystem.

Let's embark on a journey around the world to explore some examples of these specialised hubs:

1 Hollywood: the hills of Southern California have long been synonymous with cinematic magic. Hollywood's dominance in the global film industry exemplifies the power of clustering creative talent, robust institutional support and a well-developed ecosystem of auxiliary services. From cutting-edge special effects to masterful storytelling, Hollywood's comparative

advantage lies in its ability to consistently produce high-budget, technically sophisticated films that reach high audiences.

2 Bollywood: In the metropolis of Mumbai, India's film industry – known as Bollywood – has carved out its own niche. Specialising in vibrant musicals and epic dramas, Bollywood's influence extends far beyond India's borders, captivating audiences across South Asia and increasingly worldwide. Its comparative advantage lies in its unique blend of music, dance, drama and storytelling that resonates deeply with South Asian cultural values.
3 The British music: the United Kingdom's rock music scene stands as a beacon of musical innovation, with Liverpool and Manchester playing pivotal roles. With a rich musical heritage from the 1960s, the United Kingdom has cultivated a robust ecosystem of musicians, producers and venues. Its comparative advantage in rock music stems from working-class creativity, a thriving pub and club culture and a tradition of musical rebellion. The Beatles from Liverpool revolutionised popular music globally, setting the stage for decades of British musical dominance. Manchester has been at the forefront of subsequent movements, giving birth to influential bands and subgenres. Manchester's distinctive sound – exemplified by bands like The Smiths, Joy Division and The Stone Roses – leaves an indelible mark on the industry. The city's musical legacy, often called "Madchester," continues to thrive, with contemporary acts such as Aitch, Blossoms and Elbow carrying the torch. This ongoing musical evolution produces iconic artists and fosters a unique cultural identity that inspires new generations of musicians worldwide, cementing Manchester's status as a critical player in the global rock music scene.
4 K-pop in South Korea, particularly Seoul: Turning our attention to East Asia, South Korea's K-pop industry stands as a beacon of modern pop culture innovation, with Seoul at its epicentre. With a musical heritage that has rapidly evolved since the 1990s, South Korea has cultivated a sophisticated ecosystem of entertainment companies, training academies and multi-talented performers. Its comparative advantage in pop music stems from rigorous talent development, cutting-edge production values and a strategically cultivated global appeal. Seoul, in particular, has been the heart of this movement, giving birth to globally recognised acts and innovative music styles. From PSY's viral hit "Gangnam Style" to BTS's Billboard chart-toppers, K-pop continues to reshape global music tastes, with Seoul's distinctive blend of catchy melodies, synchronised choreography and visual aesthetics – exemplified by groups like BLACKPINK, EXO and TWICE – leaving an indelible mark on the industry. The city's musical legacy, often called the "Hallyu" or Korean Wave, has produced iconic artists and fostered a unique cultural soft power that continues attracting fans worldwide. Contemporary acts like Stray Kids, ITZY and NewJeans carry this legacy forward, ensuring Seoul's ongoing influence in shaping global pop music trends.

5 Brazil's Carnival: In the heart of South America, Brazil's Carnival stands as a testament to the nation's vibrant cultural tapestry and unparalleled festive spirit. With its epicentre in Rio de Janeiro and Salvador, this annual celebration has become synonymous with exuberant parades, pulsating samba rhythms, and elaborate costumes that transform the city's streets into a kaleidoscope of colour and movement. Brazil's comparative advantage in Carnival lies in its unique blend of African, European and indigenous influences, creating a spectacle deeply rooted in tradition. The event's economic impact is substantial, drawing millions of tourists and showcasing Brazil's soft power on the global stage. From the legendary Sambadrome parades to the impromptu street parties known as "blocos," Carnival embodies the Brazilian ethos of joy, creativity and community, offering an unmatched cultural experience that has become one of the world's most anticipated annual celebrations.

These specialisations are not mere accidents of history or geography. They represent the culmination of decades, sometimes centuries, of cultural development, institutional support and human capital investment. As these creative hubs flourish, they generate significant export earnings, contributing substantially to their respective economies. Moreover, the influence of these creative powerhouses extends beyond mere economic metrics. They serve as potent sources of soft power, shaping global perceptions and cultural trends. A Hollywood blockbuster can influence fashion trends in Tokyo, while a popular K-pop band might inspire art movements in Paris. This cultural cross-pollination enriches the global creative landscape, fostering innovation and diversity.

2.3.4.3 Digital Platforms and Global Reach of Cultural Products: The New Frontier

As we venture into the 21st century, the digital revolution has emerged as a transformative force in the CCIs. Digital platforms have rewritten the rules of engagement, dismantling traditional barriers to cultural trade and ushering in an era of unprecedented global access to cultural content. The rise of streaming services, e-book platforms and online marketplaces has fundamentally altered how cultural products are distributed and consumed. No longer constrained by physical limitations, cultural goods can traverse the globe at the speed of light, finding audiences in the world's most remote corners.

This digital shift has unleashed a cascade of changes across the creative landscape:

1 Empowering Niche Cultural Products: In the pre-digital era, niche cultural products often needed help finding their audience, constrained by the economics of physical distribution and limited shelf space. The digital age has

shattered these constraints. A documentary filmmaker in Nepal can now reach viewers in Norway, while an indie musician in Iceland can build a fanbase in Indonesia. This democratisation of distribution has led to a flowering of diverse cultural expressions, enriching the global cultural tapestry.

2 Challenging Traditional Gatekeepers: The digital revolution has disrupted long-established power structures in cultural industries. Traditional gatekeepers – be they publishing houses, record labels or film studios – have seen their influence wane as artists gain direct access to global audiences. This shift has sparked a reimagining of business models and value chains in creative industries, fostering innovation and entrepreneurship.
3 Cultural Policy in the Digital Age: As cultural goods flow freely across digital borders, policymakers face new challenges in promoting and protecting cultural diversity. How does one ensure local cultural expressions thrive in a global digital marketplace? How can national cultural policies be effective in an era of borderless digital consumption? These questions are at the heart of ongoing debates in cultural policy circles, driving the evolution of regulatory frameworks and support mechanisms for creative industries.
4 The Digital Divide and Cultural Access: While digital platforms have expanded access to cultural content, they have also highlighted and, in some cases, exacerbated existing inequalities. The digital divide – the gap between those with ready access to digital technologies and those without – has emerged as a critical issue in cultural policy. Ensuring equitable access to digital cultural content has become a key concern for policymakers and cultural organisations alike, recognising that access to diverse cultural expressions is vital for fostering understanding and creativity in our interconnected world.

Bakhshi and Throsby (2012) delve deep into how these digital innovations reshape creative industries' business models. Their research illuminates the profound implications of this digital shift, not just for individual creators and companies, but for how we conceptualise and measure the contribution of creative industries to economic growth in a global context. As we stand at this digital frontier, it's clear that the interplay between globalisation and digitalisation is crafting a new reality for CCIs. This evolving landscape presents challenges and opportunities – challenges in preserving cultural diversity and ensuring equitable access, as well as opportunities for unprecedented cultural exchange and creative innovation.

Change is the only constant in this complex new world of global digital culture. As policymakers, creators and consumers, we must navigate this shifting terrain with agility and foresight, always mindful of creative goods' dual economic and cultural nature. In this delicate balance lies the key to fostering an economically vibrant and culturally rich global creative economy.

2.3.5 *Case Study 1: Music Streaming Industry and Solow-Swan limitations*

The standard neoclassical exogenous growth model, developed by Solow (1956), is widely used in economics for empirically estimating TFP. It is the first influential neoclassical model to attempt to explain differences in levels and growth rates of per capita income across countries through an aggregate production function. In Solow's model, the aggregate production function Y is determined by three factors: capital (K), labour (L) and the state of technology (A). The aggregate production function is represented as a Cobb-Douglas function:

$$Y_t = A_t K_t^{\alpha} L_t^{(1-\alpha)} \tag{1}$$

where Y: total output or aggregate production of an economy, often measured as real GDP. A: TFP or the level of technology, representing the efficiency of combining inputs to produce output. K: capital stock in the economy, including physical capital such as machines, buildings and infrastructure. L: labour input, typically measured as the total number of workers or total hours worked. α: output elasticity of capital, measuring the responsiveness of output to changes in capital. $1-\alpha$: output elasticity of labour, measuring the responsiveness of output to changes in labour.

The function assumes constant returns to scale and diminishing returns to capital, two fundamental assumptions underlying the model's results. The long-run growth rate of output is determined by the sum of the growth rates of capital, technological progress and the labour force (which often correlates with the population growth rate). If technological progress offsets the effects of capital depreciation, economies will converge to a full-employment steady state, driven primarily by demographic expansion.

Assuming the labour force grows at the same rate as the population and technology remains constant, any positive variation in capital accumulation will, over time, face diminishing returns. This causes the economic growth rate to converge to zero in the long run. Without technological change, economic growth is constrained to the mere reproduction of a stationary equilibrium.

As technical progress is treated as an exogenous factor or residual in this model, it implies that the model itself does not satisfactorily explain the main drivers of sustained economic growth and capital accumulation. This limitation highlights the need for models that endogenise technological progress to better understand long-term economic growth dynamics. Despite its limitations, the Solow model provides a simple yet powerful framework for analysing economic growth and has been foundational in developing more advanced growth theories.

Let's examine the music streaming industry, focusing on Spotify, to illustrate how modern creative industries challenge traditional growth models like the one explained by Solow-Swan. The music streaming industry has rapidly grown over the past decade, transforming how music is consumed and monetised. In 2023, streaming accounted for over 84% of recorded music revenue in the US. This case study explores how the music streaming industry, represented by Spotify, challenges critical assumptions of the neoclassical growth model.

Founded in 2006 in Sweden, Spotify is a music streaming service that allows users to access a vast catalogue of licensed music on various devices. Users can create and share playlists and choose between listening for free with ads or purchasing a premium subscription for ad-free streaming. Spotify's subscriber base has grown significantly recently, doubling since early 2019. By the fourth quarter of 2023, Spotify had reached 236 million premium subscribers worldwide, up from 205 million in the same quarter of 2022. The evolution of its subscriber numbers is illustrated in Figure 2.1.

Data from Spotify's results and financial statements were used to analyse the compatibility of the assumptions of the neoclassical growth model with those of the music streaming industry. This included entries from the balance sheet, income statement and cash flow statement, described as follows: (i) Property and Equipment (from the non-current assets statement, as a stock variable); (ii) Intangible Capital (from the non-current assets statement, as a stock variable); (iii) Gross Profit (from the income statement, as a flow variable); (iv) Research and Development Expenses (from the income statement, as a flow variable); and (v) Capital Expenditures (from the cash flow

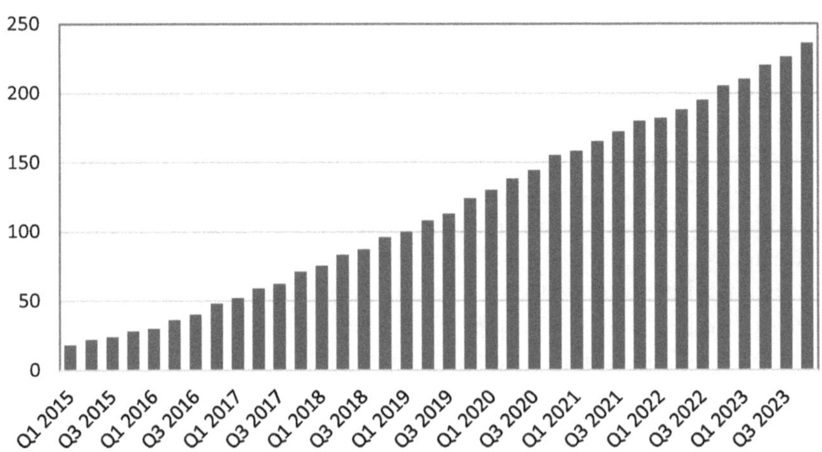

FIGURE 2.1 Annual Spotify premium subscribers (millions) (2015–2023).

Source: Developed by the author based on data available in the Statista portal.

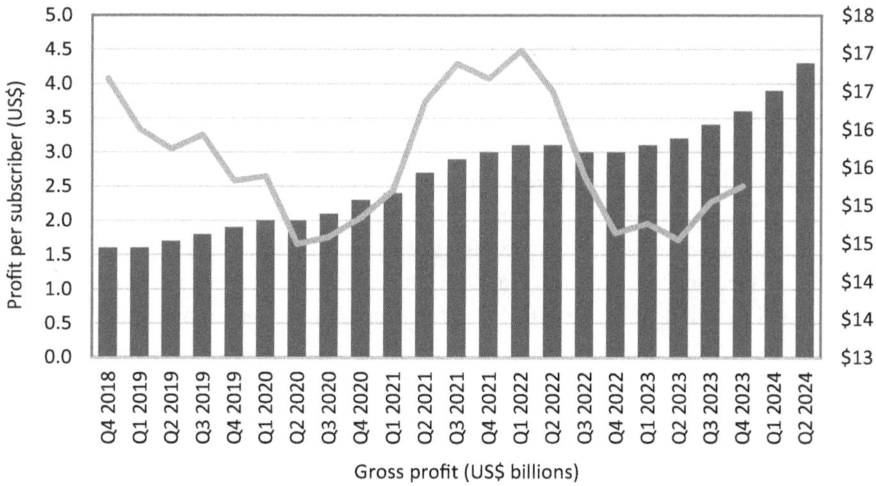

FIGURE 2.2 Spotify gross profit and profit per subscriber (2018–2024).

Source: Developed by the author based on data available in https://www.macrotrends.net/stocks/charts/SPOT/spotify-technology/gross-margin.

statement in investments, as a flow variable). The company's gross profit performance and the evolution of the profit per premium subscriber are depicted in Figure 2.2.

The streaming industry's products are considered non-rivalrous goods, meaning that one person's consumption does not reduce the availability for others. As a result, the cost of adding an extra subscriber is negligible, making positive returns to scale highly plausible – this contrasts with the standard Solow-Swan model, which assumes constant returns to scale. Despite the consistent growth in Spotify's subscriber base, the profit per subscriber has shown varying trends over the six years analysed. During the period ranging from the second quarter of 2020 to the first quarter of 2022, the growth rate of profit was relatively higher than that of the premium subscribers, indicating temporary positive returns to scale. Although the data cover a relatively short period, it is essential to note that the concept of constant returns to scale is primarily associated with producing physical goods, being less applicable to streaming services and the creative and cultural industries (CCIs) in general.

As previously mentioned, the diminishing returns to capital accumulation is a core assumption of the neoclassical growth model. The data obtained from Spotify's consolidated financial statements indicate this assumption does not hold. Although the profit-to-capital relation shows an increasing trend (see Figure 2.3), it doesn't necessarily mean increasing returns to capital accumulation. Still, this is the case from 2019 to 2021, a period in which both gross profit and property and equipment assets are increasing, with the former growing relatively more ($\Delta P > 0$, $\Delta K > 0$, $\Delta P/\Delta K > 1$).

However, besides the physical capital stock, intangible assets are central in CCIs, particularly in the music streaming industry, because they encompass the essential elements of content licensing, intellectual property and brand reputation, which are crucial for delivering and monetising creative products in a digital environment. Furthermore, CCIs thrive on continuous innovation and adaptation to new trends, technologies and consumer preferences. This requires a strong base of intangible assets derived from research, development and knowledge. Particularly for the streaming industry, R&D is crucial for developing new technologies, features and user experiences that keep streaming platforms competitive.

The data obtained from the consolidated financial statements indicate that the accumulation of intangible assets grew faster than physical property and equipment, increasing by 6.54 times and 2.38 times, respectively, between 2017 and 2023. By 2023, the value of intangible assets was approximately two-thirds of the value of property and equipment. Furthermore, R&D expenses showed consistent growth over the period analysed, averaging 28% per year. These findings suggest that not only do some of the core assumptions of the Solow-Swan model not hold for the music streaming industry but also that the standard neoclassical growth model is not well equipped to account for the unique characteristics of CCIs and their growth determinants, particularly regarding innovation, knowledge and digitalisation.

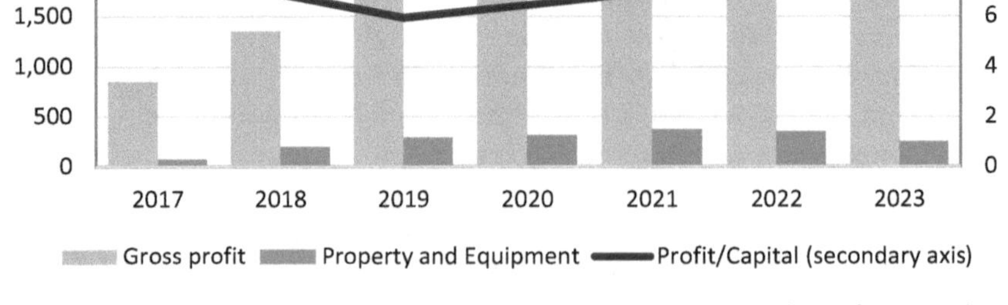

FIGURE 2.3 Spotify gross profit, property and equipment and profit/capital ratio (€ millions).

Source: Developed by the author based on Spotify's consolidated financial statements available at https://investors.spotify.com/financials/default.aspx.

2.3.5.1 *Critical Perspective on the Solow-Swan Model*

Whilst the Solow-Swan model provides a foundational framework for understanding economic growth, its application to creative industries reveals several limitations:

1 Exogenous Technological Progress: The model's treatment of technological progress as exogenous is particularly problematic for creative industries, where innovation is often endogenous and driven by market forces.
2 Homogeneous Capital: The model assumes capital is homogeneous, which fails to capture the crucial role of intangible assets in creative industries. As seen in the Spotify case, intangible assets grew much faster than physical capital.
3 Constant Returns to Scale: Creative industries often exhibit increasing returns to scale, especially in digital contexts, which the Solow-Swan model doesn't account for.
4 Diminishing Returns to Capital: The assumption of diminishing returns to capital accumulation only holds in some creative industry contexts, as evidenced by Spotify's increasing profit-to-capital ratio.
5 Limited Role of Human Capital: The model needs to explicitly account for human capital, which is crucial in knowledge-intensive creative industries.

These limitations suggest that whilst the Solow-Swan model provides useful insights into general economic growth processes, it may not adequately capture the unique dynamics of creative industries.

2.3.6 *Case Study 2: Endogenous Growth Models and Games Industry*

Recognising the limitations of the Solow-Swan model, particularly its treatment of technological progress as exogenous, economists developed "second generation" neoclassical models attempting to endogenise economic growth drivers. The novelty of the endogenous growth theories is that they all abandon the hypothesis that the investment rate does not affect the steady-state growth rate of output, which theoretically presupposes capital accumulation under diminishing returns since the other determinants of aggregate output, namely technology and the employment of labour, are exogenously given in the standard Solow-Swan model.

The AK model is the first version of the endogenous growth theory, which came to fruition in the mid-1980s and assumes that either technology or labour grows in proportion to capital and in which the growth of one of them counteracts the effects of diminishing returns, thus allowing output to increase in proportion to capital, resulting in a production function of the form $Y=AK$, with "A" constant. Following these assumptions, the capital operates under conditions of constant returns. A more significant capital accumulation implies a permanent effect that generates a higher steady-state growth rate, characterising the economic growth driver.

Later, the simple version of the AK model was extended, whereas Lucas (1988) developed an AK model where the creation and transmission of knowledge occur through human capital accumulation. Romer (1990) emphasises the role of technological change and knowledge accumulation as drivers of economic growth. These extensions introduce the role of human capital, R&D and innovation as central components in driving economic growth, where knowledge drives technological progress and improves the TFP in such a way as to compensate for the decreasing returns of capital. Therefore, technical change is no longer seen as an externality from capital accumulation as in the earlier versions of the AK model. A remarkable feature is that ideas are not considered a rival factor, different from the treatment given to regular factors such as capital, labour and land. It means that other firms can take advantage of new knowledge. In this new class of models, innovation and human capital play an essential role in breaking production paradigms (Schumpeterian creative destruction) and pushing economic growth. To further illustrate how creative industries align more closely with endogenous growth theories, let's examine the case of the games industry.

The games industry has rapidly emerged as a dynamic and expanding sector within the CCIs, driven by technological advancements and a growing global audience. In this context, the games industry has experienced positive and consistent revenue growth on a worldwide scale over the past decade, according to the data collected from the Newzoo Global Games Market Report and displayed in Figure 2.3.

To explore the connections and applications of endogenous growth models to this industry – specifically Lucas (1988) and Romer (1990), which emphasise the critical role of knowledge accumulation in economic growth through human capital and innovation, respectively – we collected balance sheet data from the financial statements of three major companies in the sector: Electronic Arts, Tencent Games and Take-Two Interactive. These companies were chosen because they rank among the sector's top ten in gaming revenue (Newzoo, 2023) and focus exclusively on the gaming industry, unlike companies such as Sony, Apple or Microsoft, where gaming is just one of several business segments. Moreover, since they are publicly listed, the companies' financial statements are publicly available on their respective investor relations websites.

As in the music streaming case discussed before, the specific variables we collected include (i) property and equipment, (ii) intangible capital, (iii) gross profit, (iv) research and development expenses and (v) capital expenditures. These variables provide an overview of the companies' performance and

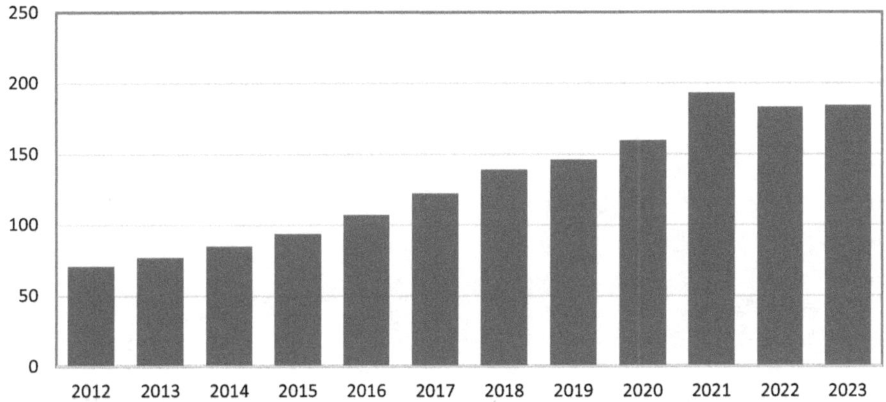

FIGURE 2.4 Global games revenue (US$ billions) (2012–2023).

Source: Developed by the author based on data available in Newzoo Global Games Market Report (2012–2023).

reveal trends in both fixed capital and knowledge accumulation (as seen in intangible capital and R&D expenses). The analysis shows that these companies' average gross profit growth rate ranges from 7% to 19%, indicating a strong positive trend. Consistent with Romer's (1990) approach, we observed that R&D expenses grew by an average of 8% for EA and 19% for Tencent and Take-Two, suggesting a strong positive correlation between knowledge accumulation and growth. However, even though the trend is clearly correlated, causality cannot be definitively inferred. The evolution of the gross profit and R&D expenses is illustrated in Figure 2.4.

Additionally, the stock of intangible assets grew significantly between 2014 and 2023, increasing by 212% for EA, 3,272% for Tencent and 1,536% for Take-Two. This growth reflects these companies' strategic emphasis on human capital development and intellectual property, both critical components of intangible assets. In line with Lucas' (1988) model, which highlights the role of human capital in sustaining economic growth, this increase suggests that investments in knowledge, creativity and specialised skills are critical drivers of value creation in the gaming industry. This growth is shown in Figure 2.5 and underscores the importance of intangible assets in driving the industry's expansion.

While the rate of investment in property and equipment also showed positive average growth during the period, it was lower than the robust profit growth observed. This suggests the existence of positive marginal returns to physical capital accumulation, although intangibles play a more central role in the industry's success. These findings suggest that endogenous growth

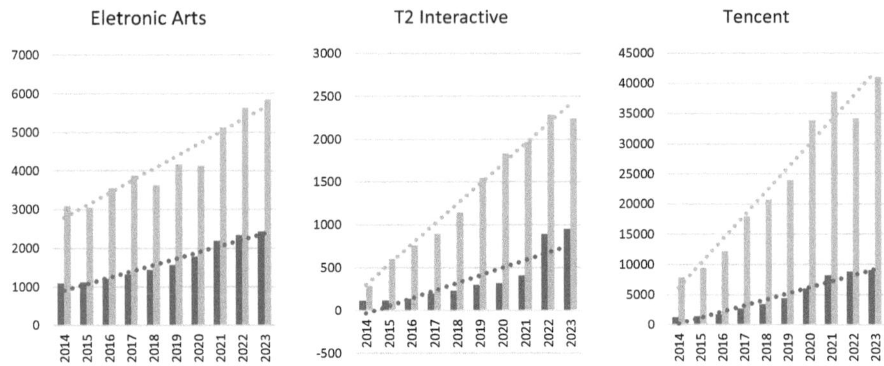

FIGURE 2.5 Gross profit (grey bars) and R&D expenses (black bars) (US$ millions).

Source: Developed by the author based on data available in Newzoo Global Games Market Report (2012–2023).

models, such as Romer's (1990) and Lucas' (1988), are better suited than the standard neoclassical model for understanding the dynamics of CCIs, offering more valuable insights into how these sectors grow.

In conclusion, while the Solow-Swan model provides a foundational understanding of economic growth, the unique characteristics of creative industries like music streaming and gaming necessitate more nuanced approaches. Endogenous growth models, with their focus on knowledge, innovation and human capital, offer more robust frameworks for understanding the growth dynamics of these sectors. As we continue to navigate the evolving landscape of the creative economy, these models provide valuable insights for researchers and policymakers seeking to foster sustainable growth in these industries.

2.3.6.1 Critical Perspective on Endogenous Growth Models

Endogenous growth models, while addressing some limitations of the Solow-Swan model, also have their limitations when applied to creative industries:

1 Oversimplification of Innovation: While these models endogenise technological progress, they may oversimplify the complex, non-linear nature of innovation in creative industries.
2 Measurement Challenges: Quantifying factors like knowledge accumulation or human capital in creative contexts can be challenging, potentially limiting the models' practical applicability.

3 Assumption of Perfect Competition: Many endogenous growth models assume perfect competition, which may not reflect the reality of creative industries, which are often characterised by monopolistic competition or winner-take-all dynamics.
4 Neglect of Institutional Factors: These models may need to fully capture the role of institutions, cultural factors and policy environments crucial for creative industry growth.
5 Focus on Steady-State Growth: The emphasis on steady-state growth paths may need to adequately reflect many creative industries' volatile and rapidly evolving nature.

2.3.6.2 Synthesis and Future Directions

While both neoclassical and endogenous growth models offer valuable insights into the growth dynamics of creative industries, they also reveal the need for more tailored approaches:

1 Hybrid Models: Future research could develop hybrid models that combine elements of neoclassical and endogenous growth theories with specific features of creative industries.
2 Network Effects: Models could be extended to better incorporate network effects and platform dynamics prevalent in digital creative industries.
3 Intangible Capital: More sophisticated modelling of intangible capital accumulation and its impact on growth is needed.
4 Non-Linear Growth Patterns: Models that can account for the often non-linear and disruptive growth patterns in creative industries could provide more accurate predictions.
5 Cultural and Social Factors: Incorporating cultural and social factors into growth models could enhance their explanatory power for creative industries.
6 Data-Driven Approaches: With the increasing availability of granular data in creative industries, more data-driven, industry-specific models could be developed.

In conclusion, while existing growth models provide valuable frameworks for understanding economic growth in creative industries, they also highlight the need for more nuanced, industry-specific approaches. The unique characteristics of creative industries – their reliance on intangible assets, the central role of innovation and human capital, and their disruptive growth patterns – call for continued evolution in economic growth theory. As these industries continue to play an increasingly significant role in the global economy, developing more tailored theoretical frameworks will be crucial for both academic understanding and effective policymaking.

Notes

1 Economic externalities refer to the costs or benefits that affect a third party who did not choose to incur those costs or benefits. These are spillover effects of economic activity that impact individuals or entities not directly involved in producing or consuming a good or service. Externalities can be positive (external benefits) or negative (external costs). For example, a positive externality might be the societal benefits from education, where an individual's education improves their prospects and contributes to overall social productivity. A negative externality could be pollution from a factory, which impacts the health and well-being of nearby residents who are not involved in the factory's operations. Externalities are significant in economics because they represent market failures, where the price mechanism fails to account for an economic activity's total social costs or benefits, potentially leading to the over- or under-production of certain goods or services.

2 The chapter about innovation and cultural and creative industries further down in the book provides an in-depth analysis of the Schumpeterian Theory applied to CCIs.

3 Cambridge Analytica harvested personal data from millions of Facebook users without consent. They collected this data through a quiz app, including information on users' friends. The company used the data to create voter profiles and target political ads, notably during the 2016 US election. The scandal's revelation in 2018 sparked outrage over privacy and concerns about election manipulation. The fallout led to investigations, hearings, a drop in Facebook's stock, and increased scrutiny of data practices in social media.

References

Aghion, P., & Howitt, P. (1998). *Endogenous Growth Theory*. MIT Press.

Arrow, K. J. (1962). The economic implications of learning by doing. *The Review of Economic Studies*, 29(3), 155–173.

Asheim, B., & Hansen, H. K. (2009). Knowledge bases, talents, and contexts: On the usefulness of the creative class approach in Sweden. *Economic Geography*, 85(4), 425–442.

Bakhshi, H., McVittie, E., & Simmie, J. (2008). Creating Innovation: Do the creative industries support innovation in the wider economy? NESTA Research Report.

Bakhshi, H., & Throsby, D. (2012). New technologies in cultural institutions: Theory, evidence and policy implications. *International Journal of Cultural Policy*, 18(2), 205–222.

Blaug, M. (1997). Economic Theory in Retrospect (5th ed.). Cambridge University Press.

Cadwalladr, C., & Graham-Harrison, E. (2018, March 17). *Revealed: 50 million Facebook profiles harvested for Cambridge Analytica in major data breach*. The Guardian.

Cass, D. (1965). Optimum Growth in an Aggregative Model of Capital Accumulation. *Review of Economic Studies*, 32(3), 233–240.

Chesbrough, H. W. (2003). *Open innovation: The new imperative for creating and profiting from technology*. Harvard Business School Press.

Clark, G. (2007). *A farewell to alms: A brief economic history of the world*. Princeton University Press.

Diamond, P. A. (1965). National Debt in a Neoclassical Growth Model. American Economic Review, 55(5), 1126–1150.

Galor, O., & Weil, D. N. (2000). Population, technology, and growth: From Malthusian stagnation to the demographic transition and beyond. *American Economic Review*, 90(4), 806–828.

Graham, M., Hjorth, I., & Lehdonvirta, V. (2017). Digital labour and development: impacts of global digital labour platforms and the gig economy on worker livelihoods. *Transfer: European Review of Labour and Research*, 23(2), 135–162.

Hesmondhalgh, D., & Meier, L. M. (2018). What the digitalisation of music tells us about capitalism, culture and the power of the information technology sector. *Information, Communication & Society*, 21(11), 1555–1570.

Katz, M. L., & Shapiro, C. (1985). Network externalities, competition, and compatibility. *The American Economic Review*, 75(3), 424–440.

Koopmans, T. C. (1965). On the Concept of Optimal Economic Growth. The Econometric Approach to Development Planning. North-Holland.

Kurz, H. D., & Salvadori, N. (2003). Theories of economic growth: Old and new. In N. Salvadori (Ed.), The Theory of Economic Growth: A 'Classical' Perspective (pp. 1–22). Edward Elgar Publishing.

Lavezzi, A. (2003). Smith, Marshall and Young on division of labour and economic growth. European *Journal of the History of Economic Thought*, 10(1), 81–108.

Lucas, R. E. (1988). On the mechanics of economic development. *Journal of Monetary Economics*, 22(1), 3–42.

Malthus, T. R. (1798). *An essay on the principle of population*. J. Johnson.

Maneschi, A. (1998). Comparative Advantage in International Trade: A Historical Perspective. Edward Elgar Publishing.

Mokyr, J. (1990). The Lever of Riches: Technological Creativity and Economic Progress. Oxford University Press.

Negroponte, N. (1995). Being Digital. Alfred A. Knopf.

Newzoo. (2023). *Global games market report*. Newzoo.

North, D. C., & Thomas, R. P. (1973). *The rise of the western world: A new economic history*. Cambridge University Press.

Polanyi, M. (1966). *The tacit dimension*. University of Chicago Press.

Potts, J., & Cunningham, S. (2008). Four models of the creative industries. *International Journal of Cultural Policy*, 14(3), 233–247.

Ramsey, F. P. (1928). A Mathematical Theory of Saving. *The Economic Journal*, 38(152), 543–559.

Ricardo, D. (1817). *On the principles of political economy and taxation*. John Murray.

Romer, P. M. (1990). Endogenous technological change. *Journal of Political Economy*, 98(5, Part 2), S71–S102.

Rothschild, E. (1994). Adam Smith and the Invisible Hand. *The American Economic Review*, 84(2), 319–322.

Schumpeter, J. A. (1942). *Capitalism, socialism and democracy*. Harper & Brothers.

Smith, A. (1759/2002). *The theory of moral sentiments*. K. Haakonssen (Ed.). Cambridge University Press.

Smith, A. (1776). *An inquiry into the nature and causes of the wealth of nations*. W. Strahan and T. Cadell.

Solow, R. M. (1956). A contribution to the theory of economic growth. *The Quarterly Journal of Economics*, 70(1), 65–94.

Stigler, G. J. (1958). Ricardo and the 93% Labor Theory of Value. *The American Economic Review*, 48(3), 357–367.

Swan, T. W. (1956). Economic growth and capital accumulation. *Economic Record*, 32(2), 334–361.

Throsby, D. (2001). *Economics and culture*. Cambridge University Press.

3

CREATIVE AND CULTURAL INDUSTRIES AND SOCIAL-ECONOMIC DEVELOPMENT

3.1 The Necessary Debate: The Mirage of Prosperity: Unravelling the Paradox of Economic Growth and Development

In the sweltering heat of Gujarat, India, March 2024 witnessed an event that captured the world's attention. The air was excited as private jets descended from the sky, carrying a who's who of global elites. Tech moguls rubbed shoulders with Bollywood stars, while world leaders mingled with industrial tycoons. The occasion? The pre-wedding celebrations of Anant Ambani, the youngest scion of India's wealthiest family. For three days, the city of Jamnagar transformed into a spectacle of opulence. International pop sensations Rihanna and Dua Lipa serenaded guests in elaborate sets that married cutting-edge technology with India's rich cultural heritage. What is the price tag for this extravaganza? A staggering $150 million (Biswas, 2024).

Yet, just a few hundred kilometres away, a different India struggles to survive. In the sprawling slums of Mumbai, millions wake each day to the harsh realities of poverty. In the shadow of Antilia – the Ambanis' 27-story personal skyscraper – families are subject to inadequate housing, lack of clean water and limited access to primary healthcare and education (Roy, 2024).

This stark juxtaposition is a powerful metaphor for a broader global phenomenon: the chasm between economic growth and genuine economic development. The Ambani celebrations, while impressive in scale and grandeur, highlight a crucial question facing many nations today: Does an increase in wealth necessarily translate to an improvement in the lives of all citizens? To understand this paradox, one must differentiate the concepts of economic growth and development. Economic growth is typically measured by gross

DOI: 10.4324/9781003434252-4

domestic product (GDP) or gross national product (GNP) increases. It focuses on the expansion of an economy in monetary terms, characterised by a quantitative approach that primarily measures the increase in goods and services production. Growth has a short-term orientation, often measured quarterly or annually, and is income-centric, concentrating on the overall rise in national income. The ability to host a $150 million pre-wedding event undoubtedly showcases India's significant economic growth over recent decades.

In contrast, economic development paints a more nuanced picture. It goes beyond mere wealth accumulation, encompassing improvements in an entire population's overall quality of life, health, education and well-being. Economic development has a qualitative focus, considering enhancements in social welfare and living standards. It takes a long-term perspective, assesses over extended periods and adopts a holistic approach that includes social, cultural and environmental factors. This broader view of progress provides a more comprehensive understanding of a nation's advancement beyond financial metrics.

3.1.1 Economic Theory Perspectives on Growth vs. Development

The debate between economic growth and development is not just a matter of practical policymaking; it's deeply rooted in economic theory. Various schools of economic thought have grappled with this issue, offering different perspectives on the relationship between growth and development. Below, you can find a map to explore in your further readings:

i Classical Economics (see Chapter 1): Classical economists like Adam Smith and David Ricardo primarily focused on economic growth. Smith's "The Wealth of Nations" (1776) emphasised the importance of division of labour, capital accumulation and free markets in economic growth. While Smith acknowledged the importance of education and institutional factors, the primary focus was increasing productive capacity and national wealth. Ricardo's theory of comparative advantage further reinforced the idea that specialisation and trade could lead to increased output and economic growth. However, these early theories should have explicitly addressed the broader concept of development as we understand it today.

ii Neoclassical Growth Theory (see Chapter 1): The neoclassical growth model, developed by Robert Solow and Trevor Swan in the 1950s, provided a framework for understanding long-term economic growth. This model emphasised the roles of capital accumulation, labour force growth and technological progress in driving financial expansion. While the Solow-Swan model was ground-breaking in its growth analysis, it focused primarily on quantitative expansion rather than qualitative improvement.

The model assumed that benefits would naturally "trickle down" to all segments of society as economies grow. This assumption has been challenged by the persistent inequality in many rapidly growing economies.

iii Endogenous Growth Theory (see previous chapter): In the 1980s and 1990s, economists like Paul Romer and Robert Lucas developed endogenous growth theory, emphasising the role of human capital, innovation and knowledge spillovers in driving economic growth. This theory began to bridge the gap between growth and development by highlighting the importance of education, research and development and institutional factors in fostering long-term economic progress. Endogenous growth theory suggested that investments in human capital and innovation could increase returns to scale, potentially allowing developing countries to catch up with more advanced economies more quickly than the Solow-Swan model predicted.

iv Development Economics: The field of development economics, which gained prominence in the mid-20th century, explicitly focused on the broader concept of economic development rather than just growth. Economists like Arthur Lewis, Gunnar Myrdal and Amartya Sen expanded the focus beyond GDP growth to include structural economic changes, human welfare improvements and human capabilities development. Lewis's dual-sector model, for instance, highlighted the process of structural transformation as labour moves from traditional to modern sectors. This model addressed the qualitative changes during development, not just the quantitative growth. As mentioned earlier, Sen's capability approach argued that development should be seen as expanding human freedoms and capabilities. This perspective shifted the focus from national income to individual well-being and agency.

v Institutional Economics: institutional economists like Douglass North emphasised the role of institutions in shaping economic outcomes. This school of thought argues that the quality of institutions – such as property rights, rule of law and political stability – is crucial for both growth and development. Good institutions can foster economic growth and broader development by providing the framework for individuals and businesses to thrive.

vi Ecological Economics: ecological economists like Herman Daly have challenged the very notion of endless economic growth, arguing that it's incompatible with the finite resources of our planet. This perspective suggests that we must move beyond growth as the primary economic goal instead of focusing on sustainable development that respects ecological limits.

vii Synthesis in Modern Development Theory: Modern development theory attempts to synthesise these various perspectives. It recognises the importance of economic growth but sees it to an end rather than an end. For instance, the United Nations' Sustainable Development Goals (SDGs) encompass a wide range of objectives beyond just economic growth, including poverty reduction, health, education, gender equality and environmental sustainability. This modern synthesis acknowledges that while growth can provide the resources necessary for development, it must be accompanied by appropriate policies and institutions to ensure its benefits are widely shared and sustainable in the long term.

3.1.2 Implications for the Growth vs. Development Debate

The evolution of economic theory reflects a growing recognition of the limitations of focusing solely on economic growth. While growth remains an important factor in economic progress, especially for low-income countries, theory has increasingly emphasised the need for a more holistic approach to development. It suggests that policymakers should:

1 Look beyond GDP: While GDP growth is essential, it shouldn't be the sole focus of economic policy.
2 Invest in human capital: Education, health and skill development are crucial for both growth and development.
3 Build strong institutions: Good governance, rule of law and inclusive institutions are vital in translating growth into broad-based development.
4 Consider sustainability: Economic policies should consider long-term environmental and social sustainability.
5 Focus on inequality: Policies should aim to ensure that the benefits of growth are widely shared across society.

In Table 3.1, you can see some figures showing the disconnection between development and growth.

3.1.2.1 Definitions of Variables

1 **GDP Growth (%):** The annual percentage growth rate of GDP at market prices based on constant local currency.
2 **GDP per capita (current US$):** GDP divided by midyear population, converted to US dollars using official exchange rates.
3 **Life Expectancy (years):** The number of years a newborn infant would live if prevailing patterns of mortality at the time of its birth were to stay the same throughout its life.
4 **Gini Index:** Measures how income distribution among individuals or households within an economy deviates from a perfectly equal distribution. A Gini index of 0 represents perfect equality, while an index of 100 implies perfect inequality.
5 **Human Development Index (HDI):** A composite statistic of life expectancy, education and per capita income indicators used to rank countries into four tiers of human development. It ranges from 0 to 1, with higher values indicating higher levels of human development.

TABLE 3.1 Development and Growth: Two Distinct Tales

Country	*Metric*	*2009*	*2014*	*2019*	*% Change (2009–2019)*
United States	GDP growth (%)	–2.5	2.5	2.3	–
	GDP per capita (current US$)	47,099.9	51,649.9	65,297.5	+38.6%
	Life expectancy (years)	78.5	78.9	78.8	+0.4%
	Gini index	41.1	41.5	41.5	+1.0%
	HDI	0.911	0.918	0.926	+1.6%
United Kingdom	GDP growth (%)	–4.2	2.6	1.4	–
	GDP per capita (current US$)	37,524.5	47,452.4	42,354.4	+12.9%
	Life expectancy (years)	80.1	81.3	81.3	+1.5%
	Gini index	34.3	34.0	35.1	+2.3%
	HDI	0.899	0.920	0.932	+3.7%
Canada	GDP growth (%)	–2.9	2.9	1.9	–
	GDP per capita (current US$)	41,903.6	50,984.5	46,194.7	+10.2%
	Life expectancy (years)	81.0	81.8	82.2	+1.5%
	Gini index	33.6	33.0	33.3	-0.9%
	HDI	0.896	0.913	0.929	+3.7%
China	GDP growth (%)	9.4	7.3	6.0	–
	GDP per capita (current US$)	3,832.2	7,678.6	10,216.6	+166.6%
	Life expectancy (years)	75.2	76.3	77.0	+2.4%
	Gini Index	43.7	39.2	38.5	–11.9%
	HDI	0.706	0.738	0.761	+7.8%
India	GDP growth (%)	8.5	7.4	4.0	–
	GDP per capita (current US$)	1,124.5	1,574.0	2,099.6	+86.7%
	Life expectancy (years)	66.7	68.4	69.7	+4.5%
	Gini index	35.4	35.1	35.7	+0.8%
	HDI	0.577	0.618	0.645	+11.8%
Brazil	GDP growth (%)	–0.1	0.5	1.1	–
	GDP per capita (current US$)	8,651.3	12,112.5	8,717.2	+0.8%
	Life expectancy (years)	73.9	75.1	75.9	+2.7%
	Gini index	53.7	52.1	53.4	-0.6%
	HDI	0.710	0.755	0.765	+7.7%
Argentina	GDP growth (%)	–5.9	–2.5	–2.1	–
	GDP per capita (current US$)	9,464.0	12,334.8	9,912.3	+4.7%
	Life expectancy (years)	75.4	76.2	76.7	+1.7%
	Gini index	45.3	41.6	41.4	-8.6%
	HDI	0.818	0.838	0.845	+3.3%

(*Continued*)

TABLE 3.1 (Continued)

Country	*Metric*	*2009*	*2014*	*2019*	*% Change (2009–2019)*
Nigeria	GDP growth (%)	8.0	6.3	2.2	–
	GDP per capita (current US$)	1,891.3	3,221.7	2,229.9	+17.9%
	Life expectancy (years)	50.8	52.7	54.7	+7.7%
	Gini index	43.0	42.9	35.1	–18.4%
	HDI	0.481	0.524	0.539	+12.1%

Sources: Developed by the author with data collected in World Bank Open Data (https://data.worldbank.org) United Nations Development Programme (https://www.undp.org/publications/undp-annual-report-2021).

BOX 3.1 KEY TAKEAWAYS ECONOMIC GROWTH × DEVELOPMENT

1 Economic growth alone is insufficient to measure a country's development. Social indicators like wellbeing measurement inequality and HDI provide a more comprehensive picture.
2 The relationship between economic growth and social development is complex and varies significantly between countries.
3 Rapid economic growth can facilitate improvements in social indicators, but this is not automatic and requires targeted policies.
4 Countries can make progress on social indicators even in periods of economic difficulty, highlighting the importance of sustained social policies.
5 While developing countries show faster improvement rates in many indicators, significant gaps with developed countries persist.
6 The diminishing social returns on higher-level development suggest that developed countries may need to find new ways to measure and achieve progress.
7 A holistic approach to development, considering both economic and social factors, is crucial for creating sustainable and equitable societies.

In the decade from 2009 to 2019, the world witnessed a tale of two trajectories: the soaring line of economic growth and the more modest climb of social progress. This period, marked by the aftermath of the global financial crisis and the eve of a worldwide pandemic, offers a revealing snapshot of how nations balance the pursuit of wealth with the well-being of their citizens.

At first glance, the numbers tell a story of remarkable progress. China, the economic powerhouse of the developing world, saw its GDP per capita skyrocket by an astonishing 166.6%. India, not to be outdone, posted an impressive 86.7% increase. Even among developed nations, the United States boasted a robust 38.6% growth in GDP per capita. These figures, trumpeted in financial reports and political speeches, paint a picture of nations on the rise, of prosperity blooming across the globe. Yet, when we peel back the layers of these economic success stories, a more nuanced and sometimes troubling picture emerges. The glittering facade of GDP growth often masks a more complex reality of uneven development and persistent social challenges.

India's story is striking. Despite its impressive economic growth, its HDI increased by 11.8% – a more significant percentage than China's, but from a much lower base. This underscores a crucial point: rapid economic expansion doesn't automatically solve deep-rooted social issues. Despite its economic strides, India continues to grapple with significant healthcare, education and inequality challenges.

The United States presents a different facet of this phenomenon. As the world's largest economy, it saw healthy GDP per capita growth. However, its HDI grew by a mere 1.6%, the smallest increase among the countries we examined. This suggests that at higher levels of development, economic growth yields diminishing returns regarding social progress. More troublingly, the US Gini index, a measure of income inequality, increased slightly, indicating that the fruits of economic growth were not evenly distributed. European nations like France and the United Kingdom tell a similar story. Despite being among the world's wealthiest countries, they saw relatively modest improvements in HDI (3.3% and 3.7%, respectively). France experienced a concerning 8.7% increase in its Gini index, suggesting a widening gap between rich and poor despite overall economic growth.

Perhaps the most poignant illustration of the disconnect between economic metrics and lived reality comes from Argentina. Despite facing economic headwinds with negative GDP growth rates, Argentina improved its HDI by 3.3% and reduced income inequality. This paradox emphasises that economic struggle doesn't necessarily preclude social progress and that economic growth doesn't guarantee it. Nigeria provides yet another perspective. With a 17.9% increase in GDP per capita and a significant 12.1% improvement in HDI, it showcases the potential for more balanced growth in developing economies. However, starting from a low base, Nigeria still needs to catch up in absolute terms, highlighting the long road ahead for many developing nations.

Life expectancy, a fundamental measure of a society's health and well-being, tells a similar story of uneven progress. While all countries in our analysis saw improvements, the gains were often modest in developed nations. The United States, for all its wealth and medical advances, saw a mere

0.4% increase in life expectancy. Contrast this with Nigeria, which achieved a 7.7% improvement, albeit from a much lower starting point. This pattern repeats across various indicators: economic growth races ahead, with social development struggling to keep up. This trend raises profound questions about how we measure progress and what we value as a society.

The implications are clear: While GDP growth is essential, it is insufficient to measure a nation's true progress. It can mask growing inequalities, environmental degradation and stagnation in quality of life. Our analysis reveals that even as bank accounts grow fatter, societies don't always grow healthier, more equitable or happier at the same rate. This disconnect between economic indicators and social well-being is not just a statistical curiosity; it has real-world consequences. It can lead to social unrest, political instability and disconnection between official narratives of progress and people's lived experiences. For instance, the yellow vest protests in France erupted against a backdrop of economic growth that wasn't felt by large population segments.

As we move forward, policymakers, economists and citizens alike must recognise the limitations of GDP as a measure of societal progress. We need a more holistic approach that considers the quantity, quality and distribution of economic growth. Measures like the HDI, while not perfect, offer a more comprehensive picture of a nation's development. Moreover, this analysis underscores the need for targeted policies to translate economic gains into tangible improvements in people's lives. Education, healthcare, environmental protection and measures to reduce inequality must be prioritised alongside financial growth.

The story of the decade from 2009 to 2019 is more than just one of economic recovery and expansion. It's a complex narrative of uneven progress, of societies grappling with balancing economic dynamism with social well-being. As we face the challenges of the coming decades – from climate change to technological disruption – this balancing act will only become more crucial. In the end, the accurate measure of a society's progress lies not in the cold statistics of GDP, but in the lived experiences of its people – their health, opportunities and quality of life. Our analysis serves as a reminder that these human factors must be at the heart of how we conceive and pursue development. Only then can we ensure that the rising tide of economic growth truly lifts all boats, creating more affluent and better societies for all their citizens.

The debate between growth and development in economic theory reminds us that while growth can provide the resources for development, it doesn't automatically lead to improved quality of life for all. It underscores the need for deliberate policies and institutions that can harness the power of economic growth to foster genuine, inclusive development.

3.1.2.2 The Limitations of Economic Growth as a Measure of Progress

The pursuit of economic growth has long been a primary goal for nations worldwide, often viewed as a panacea for societal ills. However, the limitations of focusing solely on economic growth become glaringly apparent when we look beyond the glittering facades of urban centres and mega-events.

One of the most pressing issues is the exacerbation of income inequality. Rapid economic growth can lead to a concentration of wealth in the hands of a few, creating social tensions and reducing overall well-being. Brazil's experience in the early 2000s further illustrates this point. The country was hailed as an emerging economic powerhouse during significant economic growth fuelled by a global commodities boom. However, a closer examination revealed a more complex reality. Despite the surge in GDP, income inequality remained stubbornly high. The Gini coefficient, a key measure of income distribution, showed slight improvement, indicating that this economic boom's fruits were not evenly shared across society (Lustig et al., 2013).

Environmental degradation is another critical concern often overlooked in pursuing unchecked growth. Over the past half-century, China's meteoric rise as an economic superpower provides a cautionary tale. While the transformation of its cities, expansion of infrastructure and growing global influence are undeniable testaments to its economic prowess, this growth has come at a severe environmental cost. Rapid industrialisation has led to severe air pollution in major cities, water scarcity in many regions and widespread soil contamination (Economy, 2010). The smog-filled skies of Beijing serve as a stark reminder that economic growth, when pursued without consideration for environmental sustainability, can lead to significant challenges that offset many of its benefits.

Moreover, it's crucial to recognise that GDP growth does not necessarily translate to improvements in quality of life. Some countries with lower GDP per capita manage to achieve higher levels of well-being for their citizens. Costa Rica, for instance, consistently ranks high in global happiness indices and is a leader in environmental sustainability despite having a GDP per capita significantly lower than that of the United States or many European nations. As of 2023, nearly 25% of Costa Rica's land is protected as national parks or reserves, and an impressive 98% of its electricity comes from renewable sources (IRENA, 2023). By prioritising education, healthcare and environmental conservation alongside economic growth, Costa Rica has created a society that, in many ways, offers a higher quality of life than some of its wealthier counterparts.

The case of Saudi Arabia further underscores the limitations of economic metrics alone. Despite high GDP per capita due to oil wealth, the country has faced persistent criticism for human rights issues, particularly regarding women's rights and political freedoms (Human Rights Watch, 2023).

Economic prosperity doesn't automatically translate into social progress or individual liberties. Some important structured reflections in this perspective were developed by:

1 Herman Daly's Steady-State Economy: Daly argued for a "steady-state economy" that prioritises qualitative development over quantitative growth and emphasises the physical limits of our planet (Daly, 1991).
2 Kate Raworth's Doughnut Economics: Raworth's model proposes a balance between meeting human needs and respecting planetary boundaries (Raworth, 2017).
3 Amartya Sen's Capability Approach: Sen emphasised the importance of expanding human capabilities and freedoms as the accurate measure of development (Sen, 1999).
4 Joseph Stiglitz on Rethinking GDP: Stiglitz has been a vocal critic of GDP as a measure of societal well-being, advocating for more comprehensive metrics that account for sustainability and equity (Stiglitz et al., 2018).

Given these limitations, there is a strong case for prioritising holistic economic development over a narrow focus on GDP growth. This approach encompasses several key elements:

a Firstly, investing in human capital through education, healthcare and skill development can lead to long-term economic benefits and improved quality of life. South Korea's economic miracle in the latter half of the 20th century is primarily attributed to its heavy investment in education and human capital development, creating a more resilient and prosperous society (Seth, 2017).
b Secondly, prioritising sustainable development ensures long-term environmental and economic viability. Bhutan's Gross National Happiness (GNH) concept offers a compelling alternative to the growth-at-all-costs model. By focusing on sustainable development, preservation of cultural values, conservation of the natural environment and good governance, Bhutan presents a unique approach to national progress, despite its significant economic challenges (Ura et al., 2012).
c Thirdly, fostering inclusive growth by reducing inequality and improving opportunities for all can lead to more stable and prosperous societies. Rwanda's Vision 2050, for instance, aims for inclusive growth by focusing on poverty reduction, gender equality and rural development alongside economic transformation (Republic of Rwanda, 2020).
d Lastly, prioritising overall well-being and quality of life provides a more comprehensive view of a nation's progress. New Zealand's introduction of a "well-being budget" in 2019 exemplifies this approach, focusing on

mental health, child well-being and environmental protection alongside traditional economic indicators (New Zealand Treasury, 2019).

While economic growth remains essential, it should not be pursued at the expense of broader societal and environmental concerns. By embracing a more holistic approach to economic development, nations can work towards creating societies that are not just wealthier but also more equitable, sustainable and fulfilling for all their citizens. As we return to the image of the lavish Ambani celebrations juxtaposed against Mumbai's slums, it's clear that the path forward requires a fundamental shift in how we conceptualise and pursue progress. It calls for a move beyond the narrow focus on GDP growth towards a more holistic view of development that encompasses social, environmental and economic factors. This doesn't mean abandoning the pursuit of prosperity. Instead, it means redefining what prosperity looks like. It means creating economies that don't just grow but develop in ways that enhance the quality of life for all citizens, preserve our natural world and build resilient, equitable societies.

The challenge before us is significant, but so too is the opportunity. By broadening our understanding of actual progress, we open the door to creating societies that are not just wealthy but also just, sustainable and fulfilling for all their members. In doing so, the real celebration isn't in hosting extravagant events but in building a world where everyone has reason to celebrate.

3.2 Economic Development Theories: Is It Time for a Heterodox and Global South Expanded Revival?

The creative and cultural industries (CCIs) have become pivotal forces in shaping economic trajectories worldwide, challenging traditional notions of growth and development. Their impact, however, manifests differently across the global financial landscape, revealing intricate dynamics particularly visible in developing economies. This chapter approaches these complexities, examining the nexus between CCIs and economic development worldwide through theories from the heterodox view.

While conventional economic frameworks often struggle to capture the nuanced realities of developing nations' creative sectors, a rich set of thought emerging from Latin America and other developing regions provides illuminating perspectives. The structuralist approach by the Economic Commission for Latin America and the Caribbean (CEPAL), Raúl Prebisch's centre-periphery model and the broader dependency theory offer profound insights into the structural inequalities and power dynamics that permeate global economic relations, including within the creative economy and industries.

These Global South theories are particularly relevant in understanding the dual nature of CCIs in developing economies. On the one hand, CCIs represent a promising avenue for economic diversification, job creation and cultural expression. On the other hand, they often face significant challenges stemming from historical patterns of dependency, unequal global trade relations and internal structural heterogeneities. The CEPAL school, for instance, highlights how the technological and economic disparities between the 'centre' (developed countries) and the 'periphery' (developing countries) can lead to persistent underdevelopment. This concept can be extended to the creative industries. Furthermore, dependency theory provides a critical framework for analysing how global power structures influence the production, distribution and consumption of cultural goods and services. This perspective is crucial in understanding developing countries' challenges in building competitive and sustainable creative industries while preserving cultural diversity and autonomy.

It is important to note that these Global South theories have become increasingly relevant for understanding economic dynamics in the Global North, particularly in the context of CCIs. This relevance stems from two key factors:

1. Contemporary crises and increasing inequalities: The Global North is experiencing economic challenges and rising inequalities that resemble long-standing issues in the Global South. Theories developed to address these challenges in the Global South may offer fresh insights for tackling similar problems in developed economies.
2. The dual nature of CCIs: These sectors often encompass highly developed, technologically advanced segments (such as software development) and less economically developed areas (such as performing arts). This dichotomy within CCIs mirrors some of the economic structures in Global South countries, making theories from these regions particularly applicable.

By integrating these theories into our analysis of CCIs and economic development, we can gain a more nuanced understanding of:

1. The structural barriers that hinder the growth of CCIs in developing economies.
2. The potential of CCIs to address issues of economic dependency and promote endogenous development.
3. The importance of cultural policies that recognise and address global inequalities in the creative economy.
4. The role of CCIs in fostering sustainable and inclusive development models that go beyond mere economic growth.

This chapter, therefore, not only provides a theoretical foundation for understanding the relationship between CCIs and economic development but also challenges us to rethink development strategies in a way that recognises the unique contexts, challenges and potentials in the CCIs field. By doing so, we can work towards more equitable and culturally sensitive approaches to harness creativity's power of creativity for economic and social progress.

Moreover, by reading these theories in the Global North context, one can gain new perspectives on addressing economic disparities and fostering more inclusive growth in developed economies, particularly within the context of CCIs. This approach allows for a more comprehensive and globally relevant analysis of the role of CCIs in economic development, bridging insights from diverse economic contexts and contributing to a more nuanced understanding of creative economies worldwide.

Additionally, the scope of heterodox economic perspectives offers valuable insights into the role of CCIs in economic development. These theories complement and enrich the analysis provided by the Global South perspectives, offering a more comprehensive framework for understanding the complex dynamics of CCIs in both developing and developed economies. Amartya Sen's Capability Approach provides a crucial lens through which to view the impact of CCIs on development. Sen argues that development should be understood as expanding the fundamental freedoms people enjoy rather than merely increasing economic output (Sen, 1999). In this context, CCIs can be seen as drivers of economic growth and vehicles for enhancing human capabilities and freedoms. They provide opportunities for self-expression, cultural participation and creative skills, all of which contribute to what Sen would consider meaningful development. The Capability Approach aligns well with the potential of CCIs to address issues of economic dependency and promote endogenous development, as highlighted by the Global South theories. It emphasises the importance of cultural policies that recognise global inequalities and focus on expanding individuals' capabilities to participate in and benefit from the creative economy.

While initially developed to explain the transition from agricultural to industrial economies, Arthur Lewis's Dual-Sector Model can be adapted to understand the dynamics within CCIs (Lewis, 1954). In many countries, we see a 'dual' creative economy, with a modern, high-productivity sector (often in digital and tech-oriented creative industries) coexisting with a traditional, lower-productivity sector (such as conventional crafts or local performing arts). This model can help explain the challenges and opportunities in transitioning creative workers from conventional to modern industries and the implications for overall economic development. Lewis's model resonates with the concept of structural heterogeneities highlighted by the CEPAL school, providing additional insights into the internal dynamics of CCIs in developing economies. It can help illuminate the structural barriers that hinder CCIs' growth and inform strategies for fostering more inclusive growth within these sectors.

John Kenneth Galbraith's concept of the Affluent Society offers another valuable perspective, particularly relevant to understanding CCIs in developed economies (Galbraith, 1958). Galbraith argued that as societies become wealthier, they often face a paradox of private wealth amid public squalor. This insight can be applied to the creative economy, where we might see lavish investment in commercial creative ventures alongside underinvestment in public cultural institutions and education. Galbraith's work challenges us to consider how CCIs can contribute not just to private wealth creation but to public goods and overall societal well-being. This perspective is particularly relevant when considering the role of CCIs in fostering sustainable and inclusive development models that go beyond mere economic growth, as emphasised by the Global South theories.

By incorporating these additional heterodox theories alongside the Global South perspectives, we can further enrich our understanding of:

1 The multidimensional nature of development in the context of CCIs encompasses economic, social and cultural aspects.
2 The internal dynamics and transitions within CCIs, particularly in developing economies.
3 The balance between commercial success and public value in the creative economy.
4 The potential of CCIs to contribute to human development and the expansion of individual freedoms.

These additional theories complement the insights from Global South perspectives, providing a more comprehensive framework for analysing the role of CCIs in economic development across diverse global contexts. They reinforce the need for nuanced, context-specific approaches to harnessing the potential of CCIs for inclusive and sustainable development. Moreover, integrating these diverse theoretical perspectives underscores the value of cross-pollination between economic theories from different regions and schools of thought. It demonstrates how insights developed in response to specific regional challenges can offer valuable perspectives for understanding global economic phenomena, particularly in the dynamic and complex CCI field.

In conclusion, this expanded theoretical framework provides a rich analytical toolkit for understanding and addressing the challenges and opportunities CCIs present in economic development. It encourages a holistic approach that considers economic growth, human capabilities, structural transitions and the balance between private and public value creation. This comprehensive perspective is crucial for developing effective policies and strategies to harness the full potential of CCIs for inclusive and sustainable development in both the Global South and North.

These theories – including the Global South perspectives, Sen's Capability Approach, Lewis's Dual-Sector Model and Galbraith's concept of the Affluent Society – will be in the following sections of this chapter, with a specific emphasis on their application to and implications for CCIs. This detailed examination will provide a comprehensive framework for understanding the complex role of CCIs in economic development across diverse global contexts.

3.2.1 Structuralist Theories of Development

Structuralist development theories emerged in the 1950s and 1960s, primarily from the work of economists and sociologists associated with the Economic Commission for Latin America and the Caribbean (ECLAC or CEPAL in Spanish). These theories represented a significant departure from the dominant modernisation theories of the time, positing that all countries would follow a linear development path, eventually converging with industrialised nations. The structuralist approach, in contrast, argued that underdevelopment was not merely a stage in a linear process but rather a distinct condition resulting from the historical integration of peripheral economies into the global capitalist system. This integration, they argued, created structural barriers to development that could not be overcome simply by following the path of industrialised nations.

Key figures in the development of structuralist thought include Raúl Prebisch, Celso Furtado, Osvaldo Sunkel and Aníbal Pinto, and their work laid the foundation for dependency theory and continues influencing development thinking today:

1 Raúl Prebisch (1901–1986): An Argentine economist, Prebisch was a pioneer of structuralist economics. He served as the Executive Secretary of the United Nations Economic Commission for Latin America and the Caribbean (ECLAC) from 1950 to 1963. Prebisch is best known for the Prebisch-Singer hypothesis, which posits that the terms of trade between primary products and manufactured goods tend to deteriorate over time, disadvantaging primary product-exporting countries.
2 Celso Furtado (1920–2004): A Brazilian economist and one of the most influential development economists of the 20th century. Furtado was a crucial figure in the foundation of structuralism and dependency

theory. He served as the Minister of Planning and also Culture in Brazil and was a professor at the Sorbonne in Paris. His work "The Economic Formation of Brazil" (1959) is considered a classic in development economics.

3 Osvaldo Sunkel (1929–): A Chilean economist and sociologist, Sunkel is a prominent figure in Latin American structuralist and dependency thought. He worked at ECLAC and was a professor at the University of Chile. Sunkel is known for his work on development, underdevelopment and dependency, particularly his book *El subdesarrollo latinoamericano y la teoría del desarrollo* (1970).
4 Aníbal Pinto (1919–1996): A Chilean economist who contributed significantly to structuralist economics. Pinto served as the Director of ECLAC's Economic Development Division. He is known for analysing "structural heterogeneity" in Latin American economies, highlighting the coexistence of modern and traditional sectors within these economies.

Collectively, these scholars have significantly shaped the structuralist school of thought. Their emphasis on the unique economic challenges faced by developing countries, particularly in Latin America, and their ideas on centre-periphery dynamics, structural heterogeneity, and the need for state-led industrialisation have had a profound and lasting impact on development economics and policymaking in the Global South. The following sessions will delve into their economic thoughts on CCIs.

3.2.1.1 Celso Furtado's Theory and the Myth of Development

Celso Furtado, a prominent Brazilian economist and critical figure in Latin American structuralism, significantly contributed to our understanding of development and underdevelopment. His work transcended traditional economic analysis by incorporating historical, social and cultural dimensions, offering a holistic perspective on development processes. This essay explores Furtado's ideas, mainly focusing on his emphasis on creativity and cultural aspects of development and their relevance to artistic and creative industries (CCIs) in industrial civilisation.

3.2.1.1.1 Creativity as the Core of Development

Furtado's seminal work "Creativity and Dependency in Industrial Civilization" (1978) represents a paradigm shift in development thinking. He argues that genuine development is fundamentally a process of cultural creativity, extending far beyond mere economic growth. According to the author, development is, in essence, a method of activating and channelling social forces, improving the association's capacity and exercising initiative and inventiveness. Thus, it is a social and cultural process and only secondarily economic (Furtado, 1984).

This perspective is particularly pertinent to studying CCIs in the context of development. It suggests that these industries are not merely economic sectors but crucial components of a society's capacity for self-determined development. Using Furtado's framework, CCIs can be seen as catalysts for activating social forces and channelling creative energies towards solving societal challenges.

3.2.1.1.1.1 The Critique of Mimetic Modernisation A cornerstone of Furtado's theory is his critique of "mimetic modernisation," a concept he developed to describe developing countries' tendency to imitate developed nations' consumption patterns without establishing corresponding productive structures. In *The Myth of Economic Development* (1974), Furtado argued: "The process of modernisation, based on the adoption of consumption patterns from advanced countries, implies the rising of a privileged minority, whose lifestyle contrasts with the majority of the population" (Furtado, 1974, p. 78).

This critique has profound implications for CCIs. It raises crucial questions about the uncritical adoption of Western cultural production and consumption models in developing countries. For instance, the dominance of Hollywood films or Western pop music in many developing nations could be interpreted as cultural mimetic modernisation, potentially stifling local creative industries and artistic expressions. Furtado's perspective challenges us to rethink the role of CCIs in development. Developing countries should focus on fostering their unique creative capacities rather than simply importing cultural products or replicating Western creative industry models. This approach aligns with Furtado's vision of development as a process of artistic creativity, where societies tap into their creative potential to address their specific challenges and express their unique cultural identities.

3.2.1.1.1.2 Technological Autonomy and CCIs Furtado emphasised the crucial role of technological autonomy in genuine development. In *Brazil: An Interrupted Construction* (1992), he asserted: "The key to development lies in creating an autonomous capacity for technical progress" (Furtado, 1992, p. 37). This concept is particularly relevant to contemporary CCIs, which are increasingly digital and technology-dependent. The ability of developing countries to create, adapt and control the technological platforms and tools used in cultural production and distribution could be crucial for developing their creative economies.

In the context of CCIs, technological autonomy could mean:

1 Developing local digital platforms for content distribution
2 Creating software tools tailored to local creative practices
3 Establishing educational programmes to build technical skills in the creative sector
4 Implementing policies that support technological innovation in CCI goods and services

Developing countries can better resist cultural homogenisation and foster more diverse and locally rooted creative economies by achieving greater technological autonomy in their creative sectors.

3.2.1.1.1.3 CCIs and Structural Change Furtado's structuralist approach to development emphasises the need for fundamental changes in the economic and social structure of developing countries. This perspective is central to his analysis in *Economic Development of Latin America* (1970), where he argues:

> The problem of economic development is fundamentally one of structural change. In this context, structural change means the transformation of the economic structure in such a way that the process of capital formation and technological progress become endogenous, that is, determined by internal forces.
>
> *(Furtado, 1970, p. 143)*

Furtado elaborates on this idea, explaining that structural change involves:

1. Diversification of the productive structure
2. Reduction of external dependency
3. Homogenisation of productivity levels across different sectors of the economy
4. Improvement in income distribution

He further states: "The key to understanding the process of development lies in the study of the structural transformations of the social system" (Furtado, 1970, p. 145). For the author, development is about economic growth and fundamental economic and societal changes. In the context of CCIs, this structuralist approach suggests that developing countries should aim to grow their creative sectors and integrate them into a broader strategy of structural transformation. This could involve:

1. Developing CCIs that build on local cultural strengths and address local needs
2. Using CCIs to diversify the economy and reduce dependency on primary commodity exports
3. Ensuring that the benefits of CCI are widely distributed, contributing to more equitable development
4. Fostering linkages between CCIs and other sectors of the economy to promote overall structural change

3.2.1.2 Centre-Periphery Model

The centre-periphery model, a cornerstone of structuralist economic thought, provides a framework for understanding global economic disparities and the dynamics of international trade. Initially proposed by the Argentine economist Raúl Prebisch in the late 1940s, this model has since become a fundamental concept in development economics and has been applied to various fields, including cultural studies.

3.2.1.2.1 Origins and Core Concepts

Raúl Prebisch, while serving as the Executive Secretary of the United Nations Economic Commission for Latin America (ECLA), introduced the centre-periphery model in his seminal 1949 work, "The Economic Development of Latin America and Its Principal Problems." In this ground-breaking study, Prebisch argued that the global economy is fundamentally divided into two distinct regions: the industrialised 'centre' and the primary goods-producing 'periphery' (Prebisch, 1949). These ideas were further developed by other Latin American economists, notably Celso Furtado, who contributed significantly to the structuralist school of thought. Together, their work formed the basis of what became known as the Prebisch-Singer hypothesis, named after Prebisch and Hans Singer, who independently arrived at similar conclusions (Love, 1980).

3.2.1.2.2 Unequal Exchange in International Trade

The core of the Prebisch-Singer hypothesis is the concept of unequal exchange in international trade. They argued that the terms of trade between primary commodities (typically exported by peripheral countries) and manufactured goods (exported by central countries) tend to deteriorate over time, leading to a persistent transfer of value from the periphery to the centre. As Prebisch (1949, p. 10) famously stated: "While the centres kept the whole benefit of the technical development of their industries, the peripheral countries transferred to them a share of the fruits of their technical progress."

This deterioration in terms of trade occurs for several reasons:

1. Income elasticity of demand: The demand for primary goods tends to grow more slowly than manufactured goods as incomes rise (Engel's Law).
2. Technological progress: Advances in technology often lead to the creation of synthetic substitutes for primary goods, further depressing their prices.
3. Market structure: Peripheral countries often face oligopolistic markets for their imports and oligopolistic markets for their exports, limiting their bargaining power.

4 Labour market differences: Strong labour unions in central countries can secure wage increases in line with productivity gains, while weaker unions in peripheral countries cannot, leading to a decline in the relative prices of their goods (Singer, 1950).

Emmanuel (1972) further developed the concept of unequal exchange, arguing that it results from wage differentials between developed and developing countries rather than from the types of goods exchanged. The centre-periphery model challenges the classical and neoclassical assumptions about the benefits of free trade for all participants. Instead, it suggests that international trade participation can reinforce underdevelopment under certain structural conditions. This perspective had profound implications for development policy. It provided the theoretical foundation for import substitution industrialisation (ISI) strategies many Latin American countries adopted in the mid-20th century. These policies aimed to break the cycle of dependency by fostering domestic industrial development (Birdsall et al., 2010).

The centre-periphery model and the concept of unequal exchange have been extended beyond purely economic considerations to analyse global flows of cultural goods and services. Similar patterns of inequality can be observed in the context of artistic and creative industries. As noted by UNESCO (2005, p. 44) in its Convention on the Protection and Promotion of the Diversity of Cultural Expressions:

> The unequal distribution of wealth between developed and developing countries is reflected in unequal cultural exchanges and strong imbalances in the flows of cultural goods and services at the global level.

This cultural dimension of the centre-periphery model manifests in several ways:

1 Market dominance: Cultural goods and services from the 'centre' (e.g., Hollywood films, Western pop music) often dominate global markets, while cultural products from the 'periphery' struggle to reach international audiences.
2 Value extraction: Even when cultural goods from the periphery succeed globally, the economic benefits often flow disproportionately to entities in the centre. For instance, a successful musician from a developing country might sign with a major record label based in a developed country, with most of the profits flowing to the label rather than the artist or their home country.
3 Cultural homogenisation: The dominance of cultural products from the centre can lead to cultural imperialism, potentially threatening local cultural diversity.

Considering this subject, David Throsby, in "The Economics of Cultural Policy" (2010, p. 165), observes: "The international trade in cultural goods and services is dominated by a small number of countries, primarily in the developed world, raising concerns about cultural diversity and the economic opportunities for cultural producers in developing countries." While the centre-periphery model has been influential, it has also faced criticism. The centre-periphery model remains a powerful tool for understanding global economic and cultural inequalities. While its policy implications have been debated, the international trace critical core insights about structural imbalances in the global economy continue to inform discussions about creative industries, development and cultural exchange. As the global economy evolves, so does the application and interpretation of this enduring conceptual framework.

3.2.1.2.3 Structural Heterogeneity (Aníbal Pinto)

The concept of structural heterogeneity, a cornerstone of structuralist economic thought, was developed by Chilean economist Aníbal Pinto in response to the unique economic landscapes of Latin American countries. This concept provides a robust framework for understanding the complexities of CCIs in developing nations.

Pinto observed that underdeveloped economies were characterised by a striking duality: the coexistence of sectors with vastly different productivity levels. In his seminal 1970 paper, he articulated this idea:

> The concept of structural heterogeneity ... refers to the existence of economic activities and regions where average labour productivity is close to that of developed countries, coexisting with activities that utilise backward technologies and whose levels of productivity are very low.
>
> *(Pinto, 1970, p. 85)*

Pinto argued that this duality was not a temporary phase but a structural feature of underdevelopment, leading to persistent challenges such as income inequality, limited domestic markets and difficulties in achieving sustained economic growth.

Applying this concept to the CCIs in developing countries, we uncover a similar pattern of duality that shapes the sector's dynamics and development trajectories. Finding a small but highly productive cultural industry closely linked to global markets and utilising advanced technologies is possible. This modern sector includes:

1 Internationally successful film production companies
2 Global music labels and streaming platforms
3 Digital start-ups creating cutting-edge apps and games

4 High-end fashion houses blending traditional motifs with contemporary design
5 Modern art galleries with a presence in global art markets

These entities often operate at productivity levels comparable to those in developed countries, leveraging digital technologies, global networks and sophisticated management practices. Alongside this modern sector is a larger, often less visible world of traditional and informal cultural production. While rich in artistic value, this sector typically needs to catch up in terms of economic productivity and global reach. It encompasses:

1 Traditional craftspeople and artisans
2 Local musicians and performers
3 Small-scale cultural events and festivals
4 Indigenous art and craft producers
5 Street artists and performers
6 Small, local cultural organisations and community centres

These fields often need more access to advanced technologies, formal markets or global distribution networks. However, it plays a crucial role in preserving cultural heritage, maintaining community cohesion and providing livelihoods for a significant portion of the population. When applied to CCIs, the concept of structural heterogeneity reveals a complex landscape of duality and informality. This perspective highlights both the challenges and opportunities facing CCIs in developing countries. By recognising the vital role of the informal economy and the persistent structural divides within the sector, policymakers and cultural entrepreneurs can work towards more inclusive and effective strategies for cultural and economic development. As we move forward, the goal should be to harness the dynamism and authenticity of the informal cultural economy while providing pathways for growth, protection and global engagement. In doing so, we can work towards a future where CCIs drive economic growth and preserve and promote the rich cultural diversity of developing nations.

3.2.1.3 Amartya Sen's Capability Approach

Amartya Sen, born in 1933 in West Bengal, India, is a renowned economist and philosopher who has significantly contributed to welfare economics, social choice theory and economic development. In 1998, he was awarded the Nobel Memorial Prize in Economic Sciences for his work on these subjects. Sen has held professorships at several prestigious institutions, including Harvard University and the London School of Economics. Sen developed the capability approach as an alternative framework for understanding development and well-being. This approach, which has profoundly impacted development thinking and policy, shifts the focus from traditional economic progress measures to expanding human freedoms and capabilities.

BOX 3.2 AMARTYA SEN'S SEMINAL IDEAS

1 Capability Approach

The Capability Approach is one of Sen's most influential contributions to development theory.

- **Core Idea**: Development should be understood as expanding people's "capabilities" – the freedom to achieve various lifestyles.
- **Beyond Income**: This approach moves beyond traditional income-based development measures to focus on what people can do and be.
- **Functionings and Capabilities**: Sen distinguishes between "functionings" (various states of human beings and doings) and "capabilities" (the alternative combinations of functionings that are feasible for a person to achieve).
- **Application**: This approach has influenced the HDI used by the United Nations Development Programme.

2 Freedom as Development

Sen's view of freedom as both the primary end and the principal means of development is elaborated in his book *Development as Freedom* (1999).

- **Five Types of Freedom**:
1. Political freedoms (e.g., democracy, civil rights)
2. Economic facilities (e.g., opportunities for participation in trade and production)
3. Social opportunities (e.g., education, healthcare)
4. Transparency guarantees (e.g., disclosure, trust)
5. Protective security (e.g., social safety nets, unemployment benefits)

- **Interconnectedness**: Sen emphasises how these freedoms are interconnected and reinforce each other.
- **Instrumental Role**: Freedoms are not just the ends of development, but also the principal means.

3 Poverty and Famine

Sen's work on poverty and famine has revolutionised our understanding of these issues.

- **Entitlement Approach**: Sen developed the concept of "entitlements" to explain how famines can occur even when food supplies are adequate.
- **Famine as Economic Disaster**: He demonstrated that famines are often caused by a collapse in people's ability to command food through legal means available in society rather than just food scarcity.

- **Case Studies**: Sen's analysis of the Bengal famine 1943 and other famines provided empirical support for his theories.
- **Policy Implications**: His work has influenced famine prevention strategies, emphasising the importance of maintaining people's economic access to food.

4 Gender Inequality

Sen has been a strong advocate for gender equality and women's empowerment in development.

- **Missing Women**: Sen introduced the concept of "missing women" to highlight the impact of gender bias in healthcare, nutrition and social status on female survival rates.
- **Agency and Well-being**: He emphasised the distinction between women's well-being and their agency, arguing for the importance of development.
- **Cooperative Conflicts**: Sen developed a "cooperative conflicts" model to analyse intra-household dynamics and gender relations.
- **Education and Empowerment**: He consistently emphasised the role of women's education and economic participation in fostering development.

To know more:

1 Sen, A. (1999). *Development as freedom*. Oxford University Press.
2 Sen, A. (1970). *Collective choice and social welfare*. Holden-Day.
3 Sen, A. (1981). *Poverty and famines: An essay on entitlement and deprivation*. Oxford University Press.
4 Sen, A. (1990). *More than 100 million women are missing*. The New York Review of Books.

Sen's seminal work "Development as Freedom" (1999) presents his core argument for a broader understanding of development. He writes:

> Development can be seen ... as a process of expanding people's real freedoms. Focusing on human freedoms contrasts with narrower views of development, such as identifying development with the growth of the gross national product, with the rise in personal incomes, industrialisation, technological advance, or social modernisation.
>
> *(Sen, 1999, p. 3)*

This perspective shifts the focus from traditional economic measures to expanding human freedoms and capabilities, challenging conventional development metrics such as GDP growth or industrialisation rates.

Within this framework, cultural freedoms play a crucial role. These include the freedom to participate in cultural life, to express oneself creatively and to access and enjoy diverse cultural goods and services. Sen argues that these freedoms are not just instrumental to development but are constitutive of development itself. In "Culture and Development" (2004), Sen elaborates: "Cultural matters are integral parts of the lives we lead. If development can be seen as an enhancement of our living standards, then efforts geared to development can hardly ignore the world of culture" (Sen, 2004, p. 39).

This perspective has significant implications for understanding the role of CCIs in development:

1 CCIs as enablers of cultural freedom: CCIs can directly contribute to expanding cultural freedoms by providing artistic expression and participation platforms.
2 Cultural diversity as development: The flourishing of diverse artistic expressions through CCIs can be seen as a development, not just a means to economic growth.
3 Cultural capabilities and economic opportunities: Participation in CCIs can enhance individuals' capabilities in ways that may have broader economic and social benefits.

Capabilities Related to Cultural Participation and Creation Sen's approach emphasises the importance of people's capabilities – their real opportunities to achieve functions they value. In the context of culture and CCIs, relevant capabilities might include:

1 The ability to express oneself creatively
2 The capacity to access and appreciate diverse cultural goods and services
3 The opportunity to participate in cultural traditions and practices
4 The capability to earn a livelihood through cultural and creative work

David Throsby, in "Economics and Culture" (2001), applies this thinking to cultural policy: "The capability approach ... provides a framework within which cultural rights can be asserted as essential components of development processes" (Throsby, 2001, p. 165). Sen's approach emphasises that development is a comprehensive process that cannot be reduced to a single dimension. Social and cultural factors play crucial roles in shaping development outcomes and processes. The author argues that culture should be seen as both a means to development and an end. As a means, cultural factors can contribute to other development goals, such as economic growth or social cohesion. Ultimately, the freedom to participate in and enjoy cultural life is a valuable aspect of human development.

In "How Does Culture Matter?" (2004), Sen writes:

> Culture can serve both as a constituent of development (development, in part, as enhancement of our cultural lives) and as an important instrument of development (helping other forms of development, such as economic progress or improvement in the quality of life).
>
> *(Sen, 2004, p. 40)*

This dual role of culture has essential implications for CCIs:

1 Instrumental role: CCIs can contribute to economic growth, job creation and urban regeneration.
2 Intrinsic role: The expansion and diversification of CCIs represent a form of development in themselves, enhancing people's cultural capabilities and freedoms.

CCIs' Potential in Expanding Substantive Freedoms CCIs have significant potential to expand what Sen calls "substantive freedoms" – the real opportunities people must live the kinds of lives they have reason to value. This can occur in several ways:

1 Economic opportunities: CCIs can provide livelihoods and economic opportunities, particularly for young people and in urban areas.
2 Educational benefits: Participation in cultural activities can enhance cognitive skills, creativity and critical thinking.
3 Social cohesion: CCIs can foster social bonds, intercultural dialogue and a sense of shared identity.
4 Political participation: Cultural expressions can be a means of political engagement and critique.
5 Personal fulfilment: Creative work and cultural participation can contribute to individuals' sense of fulfilment and well-being.

The UNESCO Creative Economy Report 2013 Special Edition echoes this perspective: "When culture is recognised as a driver and enabler of sustainable development, new prospects open up for individuals and societies to innovate by drawing on their cultural heritage and creativity" (UNESCO & UNDP, 2013, p. 39).

Applying Sen's Approach to CCIs and Development Policy Sen's capability approach provides a rich framework for understanding and promoting the role of CCIs in development:

1 Broadening development goals: It encourages policymakers to look beyond narrow economic metrics and consider how CCIs contribute to expanding human freedoms and capabilities.

2 Participatory approach: Sen emphasises the importance of public participation in defining development priorities. This suggests the need for inclusive cultural policies that reflect diverse voices and artistic expressions.
3 Addressing inequalities: The approach draws attention to inequalities in cultural capabilities and opportunities, highlighting the need for policies that promote equitable access to cultural resources and opportunities.
4 Valuing diversity: Sen's emphasis on freedom and choice aligns with promoting cultural diversity, seeing it as enriching rather than threatening development.
5 Interdisciplinary perspective: The capability approach encourages a holistic view of development, suggesting the need for policies that recognise the interconnections between cultural, economic and social dimensions of development.

Hasan Bakhshi, Alan Freeman and Graham Hitchen in "Measuring Intrinsic Value: How to Stop Worrying and Love Economics" (2009) argue: "Sen's capability approach ... offers a way of reconciling the intrinsic and instrumental benefits of culture, by treating access to cultural resources as a substantive freedom" (Bakhshi et al., 2009, p. 19).

Therefore, Amartya Sen's capability approach provides a robust framework for understanding the multifaceted role of CCIs in development. It encourages us to see CCIs not just as economic sectors but as crucial elements in expanding human freedoms and capabilities. This perspective can inform more holistic and human-centred approaches to cultural policy and development strategies, recognising the intrinsic value of cultural participation alongside its instrumental benefits.

3.2.2 Arthur Lewis, Development and CCIs

The landscape of development economics was forever altered by the ground-breaking work of Sir W. Arthur Lewis, whose dual-sector model, often referred to as the Lewis model, cast a new light on the intricate pathways of economic growth in developing nations. The model woven observations of labour markets, agricultural productivity and industrial expansion to create a theory awarded with Nobel Prize in Economics in 1979.

3.2.2.1 The Dual-Sector Model: Core Concepts

At the heart of Lewis's theory is a dual economy, a bifurcated system where two distinct sectors coexist in a delicate dance of progress and tradition. On one side, we find the traditional sector, typically embodied by subsistence agriculture, where productivity languishes and surplus labour is mainly present. This sector, characterised by its informal nature and familial ties, is a vast reservoir of untapped human potential. On the other side stands the modern industry, a beacon of industrial promise, urbanisation and technological advancement. Lewis states that the key to economic development is the gradual labour migration from the low-productivity traditional sector to the high-productivity modern industry. This transfer, he argued, could occur without significantly impacting agricultural output due to the presence of "disguised unemployment" in rural areas. Workers moving to urban centres would find employment in factories and other industrial enterprises, contributing to a surge in overall economic productivity.

To fully grasp the dynamics of Lewis's theory, their mathematical underpinnings are:

1 **Total Output (Y):** Y = Ya + Ym, where:

- Ya = Output in the agricultural (traditional) sector
- Ym = Output in the manufacturing (modern) sector

This equation reflects the division of the economy into traditional and modern sectors. As development progresses, we expect to see a shift in the relative sizes of Ya and Ym, with the modern sector growing faster.

2 **Labour Transfer:** $\Delta Lm = -\Delta La$, where:

- ΔLm = Change in labour in the modern sector
- ΔLa = Change in labour in the agricultural sector

This equation is at the heart of Lewis's model. It represents the movement of surplus labour from agriculture to manufacturing, which Lewis saw as the critical driver of development.

3 **Wage Determination:** $Wm = Wa(1 + \mu)$, where:

- Wm = Wage in the modern sector
- Wa = Subsistence wage in the agricultural sector
- μ = Wage premium (typically around 0.3 or 30%)

This illustrates why workers are incentivised to move to the modern sector. The wage premium μ represents the additional compensation needed to overcome the costs and risks of moving from rural to urban areas.

4 **Profit in Modern Sector:** $\Pi m = Ym - WmLm$, where:

- Πm = Profit in modern sector
- Lm = Labour employed in modern sector

5 Capital Accumulation: $\Delta K = s\Pi m$, where:

- ΔK = Change in capital stock
- s = Savings rate of capitalists

Equations 4 and 5 show how profits in the modern sector drive capital accumulation. This reinvestment of profits is crucial for sustaining growth in Lewis's model. The beauty of Lewis's model lies in its elegant simplicity and profound implications for capital accumulation. As the modern sector absorbs surplus labour, it can maintain low wages, allowing for higher profits. When reinvested, these profits fuel further industrial expansion, creating a virtuous growth cycle. This process continues until the pivotal "Lewis turning point" is reached – a moment when the reservoir of surplus labour is exhausted, leading to rising wages and a fundamental restructuring of the economy.

3.2.2.2 Application to CCIs

While Lewis's theory was primarily conceived with agriculture and industry in mind, its rationales can be applied to CCIs. In the contemporary global economy, CCIs have emerged as dynamic forces of innovation, job creation and cultural expression. They represent a new frontier in the modern sector that challenges traditional notions of productivity and value creation. Imagine, if you will, a young artist in a rural village, her talents constrained by limited opportunities and resources. In Lewis's framework, they embody the surplus labour of the traditional sector. As they migrate to an urban centre, drawn by the allure of creative opportunities, they become part of the labour transfer Lewis saw as crucial to development. Her journey from village to city mirrors the transition from agriculture to industry but with a distinctly 21st-century twist. To understand how CCIs fit into and extend Lewis's development theory, we can examine a set of equations that capture their unique characteristics:

6 **CCI Output:** Yc = f(Lc, Kc, H), where:

- Yc = Output in CCIs
- Lc = Labour in CCIs
- Kc = Capital in CCIs
- H = Human capital (creativity, skills)

This function includes human capital (H) as a critical input, reflecting the importance of creativity and specialised skills in these industries.

7 **Innovation Spillover:** Ym = g(Yc) × f(Lm, Km), where:

- g(Yc) = Positive function representing spillover effects from CCIs

This equation captures one of CCIs' most important contributions to the broader economy. By influencing g(Yc), CCIs can enhance productivity across other sectors, acting as a catalyst for economy-wide innovation.

8 **Cultural Capital Accumulation:** $\Delta CC = \alpha \times Yc + \beta \times CC$, where:

- CC = Cultural capital stock

- α = Rate of new cultural capital creation
- β = Cultural capital depreciation rate

Cultural capital accumulation is a unique feature of CCIs. Unlike physical capital, cultural capital can appreciate over time, potentially increasing returns to scale in creative production.

9 **CCI Labour Dynamics:** $Lc = La\_c + Lm\_c + Lg$, where:

- La_c = Labour transferred from the agricultural sector to CCIs
- Lm_c = Labour transferred from the manufacturing sector to CCIs
- Lg = New labour force growth

This equation shows how the creative sector draws workers from agriculture and manufacturing and new entrants to the labour force. It reflects the complex labour markets of the creative economy, where skills and talent flow more fluidly between sectors. In the urban crucible of creativity, our artist is immersed in an ecosystem of galleries, design studios and digital media companies. This concentration of creative talent in urban areas aligns perfectly with Lewis's emphasis on the importance of urban industrial growth. The CCIs, like their industrial counterparts, benefit from agglomeration effects, where proximity breeds innovation and productivity gains.

As the CCIs flourish, they generate substantial profits, much like the industrial firms in Lewis's original model. A successful film production company, for instance, might reinvest its earnings into more advanced equipment or expanded studio space. A thriving music scene might attract investment in recording facilities and performance venues. This process of capital accumulation in the creative sector echoes the reinvestment cycle that Lewis saw as crucial for sustained economic growth.

Moreover, the CCIs possess a unique ability to drive innovation and increase productivity across other sectors of the economy. A breakthrough in computer animation might find applications in architectural design or medical imaging. The problem-solving skills achieved in the creative industries can spark novel approaches in fields as diverse as education, healthcare and environmental sustainability.

3.2.2.3 Challenges in Applying Lewis's Theory to CCIs

While Lewis's development theory provides valuable insights, its application to CCIs presents several unique challenges:

1 **Intangible Value Creation:** Unlike traditional industries, CCIs often generate value through intangible assets such as intellectual property, brand recognition and cultural capital. These are difficult to quantify using conventional economic metrics, complicating the measurement of productivity and output in creative sectors.

2 **Fluid Labour Dynamics:** The creative workforce comprises project-based work, freelancing and frequent career shifts. This fluidity challenges Lewis's concept of a straightforward labour transfer from low to high-productivity sectors. In CCIs, workers may move between various roles and industries, blurring the lines between sectors.
3 **Skill-Intensive Production:** Lewis's model assumes relatively unskilled labour moving from agriculture to industry, but CCIs often require specialised skills and talents. This alters the dynamics of labour transfer and wage determination in creative sectors.
4 **Global Interconnectedness:** Lewis's theory was primarily focused on national economies, but CCIs are often globally integrated. For example:

   - A graphic designer in Nairobi might collaborate with clients in New York.
   - A musician in Kingston could find her largest audience in Tokyo.
   - Digital platforms allow for instant global distribution of creative content. This international dimension adds complexity to understanding labour markets, capital flows and economic development in the context of CCIs.

5 **Technology and Disruption:** Rapid technological changes in CCIs can quickly alter productivity levels and skill requirements, making applying Lewis's long-term growth model without frequent adjustments challenging.
6 **Cultural and Social Factors:** The value and growth of CCIs are often influenced by cultural trends, social movements and consumer preferences, which are less predictable than the economic factors central to Lewis's original theory.

These challenges are valid for applying Lewis's ideas to CCIs. Still, they require careful consideration and potential modifications to the theory when analysing the role of creative industries in economic development. Researchers and policymakers must develop new frameworks that can account for these unique aspects of the creative economy while still drawing on the foundational insights of Lewis's dual-sector model.

At the crossroads of tradition and innovation, Arthur Lewis's development theory offers valuable insights into economic transformation processes. By extending its principles to the CCIs, we gain a richer understanding of how talent, technology and artistic expression can intertwine to forge new paths of economic development. In this evolving landscape, the dual sectors of Lewis's model are not just agriculture and industry but also the realms of tradition and creativity, each feeding into the other in a complex choreography of growth and cultural vitality.

The mathematical framework provided by these equations offers a valuable starting point for a more rigorous analysis of the role of CCIs in economic development, building upon the foundational insights of Arthur Lewis's dual-sector model. By analysing these relationships quantitatively, policymakers and researchers can gain deeper insights into how to foster CCI growth as part of a broader development strategy. For instance, investments in education and training (increasing H in equation 6) might yield outsized returns by boosting CCI output and innovation spillovers to other sectors.

Integrating Lewis's development theory with the dynamics of CCIs presents a compelling narrative of economic evolution. It challenges us to reimagine the pathways to development, acknowledging the power of creativity and culture as engines of growth. As we continue to navigate the complexities of global economic development, this expanded model provides a valuable lens through which to view the interplay of tradition, innovation and human potential in shaping future economies.

BOX 3.3 ARTHUR LEWIS, AN HONORARY MANCUNIAN

Sir William Arthur Lewis (1915–1991) stands as a towering figure in the field of development economics, distinguished not only for his ground-breaking theories but also for breaking racial barriers in academia. Born on the Caribbean Island of St. Lucia, Lewis overcame the constraints of colonial-era racism to become one of the most influential economists of the 20th century. His journey from a small island to the pinnacle of academic achievement culminated in 1979 when he was awarded the Nobel Prize in Economics, sharing the honour with Theodore Schultz. This made Lewis the first person of African descent to receive a Nobel Prize in a field other than peace or literature, marking a significant milestone in recognising Black scholars in the sciences.

Lewis's connection to the University of Manchester played a crucial role in his academic career and in developing his most famous work. In 1948, at 33, he was appointed to a full professorship at Manchester, making him Britain's first Black full professor. During his tenure at Manchester until 1957, Lewis produced some of his most important works, including his seminal article "Economic Development with Unlimited Supplies of Labour" (1954). This paper, which introduced the dual-sector model (also known as the Lewis model), was written mainly during his time at Manchester and would form the basis for his Nobel Prize-winning contributions to development economics.

The mancunian ecosystem provided Lewis with the intellectual environment and resources to refine his theories on economic growth in developing countries. His work at Manchester challenged prevailing economic thought by focusing on the structural transformation of economies from traditional to modern sectors. Lewis's dual-sector model, conceived within the halls of Manchester, offered a new framework for understanding the development process in labour-surplus economies. This model solidified Lewis's reputation as a pioneering thinker and established the University of Manchester as a key centre for development economics. Lewis's legacy continues to influence economic policy and academic discourse, inspiring scholars worldwide.

3.2.3 *Institutional Economics and CCIs*

Institutional economics, a school of economic thought, emphasises the role of social, cultural and legal institutions in shaping economic behaviour and outcomes. This approach is particularly pertinent to understanding the development of CCIs and their role in broader economic growth. Focusing on the institutional context gives us a more nuanced understanding of how CCIs evolve as a set of economic activities and contribute to multidimensional progress.

3.2.3.1 Foundations of Institutional Economics

Institutional economics emerged in the early 20th century, with crucial contributions from scholars such as Thorstein Veblen, John R. Commons and Wesley Mitchell.[1] Veblen's concept of "conspicuous consumption" and his analysis of the role of social institutions in economic behaviour laid the necessary groundwork for the field. Commons contributed significantly to understanding collective action and capitalism's legal foundations. Mitchell's work on business cycles highlighted the importance of institutional factors in economic fluctuations.

BOX 3.4 VEBLEN SEMINAL IDEAS

Thorstein Veblen (1857–1929) was an American economist and sociologist known for his unconventional approach to economic theory. Born to Norwegian immigrant parents in Wisconsin, Veblen received his Ph.D. from Yale University in 1884. Despite his brilliant mind, he struggled to fit into academia due to his unorthodox views and personal eccentricities. Veblen's most famous work, "The Theory of the Leisure Class," published in 1899, became a cornerstone of institutional economics and a biting critique of consumer culture.

In "The Theory of the Leisure Class," Veblen introduced the concept of "conspicuous consumption," which describes purchasing goods or services primarily to display wealth and status rather than to fulfil practical needs. Veblen argued that in modern capitalist societies, a "leisure class" emerges that does not engage in productive labour but demonstrates its status through wasteful expenditure and the ostentatious display of wealth. According to Veblen, this behaviour trickles down through society as those in lower classes attempt to emulate the consumption patterns of those above them, leading to a widespread culture of status-seeking through consumption.

Veblen's theory, with its introduction of 'conspicuous leisure' and 'conspicuous consumption,' was revolutionary in its time. It challenged prevailing economic theories by highlighting the role of social and cultural factors in shaping economic behaviour. More importantly, it continues to influence fields beyond economics, such as sociology, cultural studies and consumer behaviour research. It offers valuable insights into the complex motivations behind consumer choices and the social dynamics of wealth display.

To know more:

Veblen, T. (1899). *The theory of the leisure class: An economic study of institutions*. Macmillan.

The field gained renewed prominence in the late 20th century through the work of Douglas North, Oliver Williamson and Elinor Ostrom,[2] among others. North's work on economic history and institutional change, Williamson's transaction cost economics and Ostrom's analysis of common-pool resources have all significantly expanded our understanding of how institutions shape economic outcomes.

Fundamental principles of institutional economics include:

1 Institutions matter: Economic outcomes are significantly influenced by the formal and informal rules that govern society. This principle challenges the notion that markets operate in an institutional vacuum.
2 Path dependence: Historical processes shape current institutions and economic structures. This concept helps explain why specific institutional arrangements persist even when they may seem suboptimal.
3 Transaction costs: Institutions can reduce (or increase) the costs of economic transactions. This insight has profound implications for understanding organisational structures and market efficiency.
4 Bounded rationality: Economic actors have limited cognitive capacity and operate within institutional constraints. This challenges the neoclassical assumption of perfect rationality and information.
5 Evolution: Institutions and economic systems evolve over time through complex change processes. This evolutionary perspective helps explain institutional diversity and change over time.

Douglas North, in his seminal work "Institutions, Institutional Change and Economic Performance" (1990), defines institutions as "the rules of the game in a society or, more formally, the humanly devised constraints that shape human interaction" (North, 1990, p. 3). This definition encompasses formal institutions (laws, regulations) and informal institutions (norms, customs and traditions), highlighting the broad scope of institutional analysis.

3.2.3.1.1 Institutional Economics and CCIs

The institutional approach offers several valuable insights into understanding CCIs, providing a framework for analysing the complex ecosystem in which creative activities occur.

1 Legal frameworks: The development of CCIs is heavily influenced by intellectual property regimes, labour laws and other legal institutions. Copyright law plays a crucial role in shaping the music and publishing industries, while labour regulations affect the structure of film and television production.
2 Cultural norms: Informal institutions, such as societal attitudes towards creativity and entrepreneurship, shape the growth of CCIs. For example, societies that highly value artistic expression may be more likely to support and invest in creative industries.
3 Organisational structures: How creative enterprises are organised (e.g., firms, networks, clusters) affect their performance and impact. For instance, the prevalence of project-based work in many innovative industries is an institutional adaptation to the uncertain nature of creative production.
4 Policy environments: Government policies and regulatory frameworks are crucial in fostering or hindering CCI development. This includes direct support through subsidies and grants and indirect support through education and infrastructure development.
5 Market institutions: The functioning of markets for cultural goods and services depends on specific institutional arrangements. For example, the rise of streaming platforms has fundamentally altered the market institutions in the music and film industries.

Jason Potts, in "Creative Industries and Economic Evolution" (2011), applies evolutionary institutional economics to CCIs, arguing that "the creative industries are best understood as an evolutionary system in which new ideas are generated, adopted and retained" (Potts, 2011, p. 9). This perspective highlights the dynamic nature of CCIs and the capacity for innovation and adaptation, as follows:

1 Path dependence: The historical development of cultural institutions in a society influences the current structure and performance of its CCIs. For instance, the United Kingdom's strong tradition of public broadcasting has shaped its television and radio industries in ways distinct from countries with predominantly commercial systems.
2 Institutional complementarities: The success of CCIs depends on complementary institutions in education, finance and other sectors. For example, the presence of specialised art schools, venture capital firms familiar with

creative businesses and supportive intellectual property regimes can create a fertile ecosystem for CCIs.

3 Informal institutions: Trust, networks and cultural capital are crucial in creative production and consumption. In many creative fields, informal networks play a significant role in project formation, talent discovery and knowledge dissemination.
4 Institutional change: Understanding how to foster institutional environments conducive to CCI growth and innovation is critical to policy development. This might involve adapting copyright laws to the digital age, developing new forms of creative education or fostering cross-sector collaborations.

3.2.3.2 Institutional Economics and Development Theory

Institutional economics has significantly contributed to development theory, explaining why some countries achieve economic development while others struggle. This perspective is particularly relevant for understanding the role of CCIs in broader development processes.

Key ideas:

1 Institutions for economic growth: Secure property rights, effective legal systems and well-functioning markets are crucial for economic development. In the context of CCIs, this might include robust intellectual property protection, efficient contract enforcement and transparent market mechanisms for creative goods and services.
2 Institutional quality: The quality of institutions is a crucial determinant of long-term economic performance. For CCIs, this might involve assessing the effectiveness of cultural policy institutions, the fairness of funding allocation mechanisms or the inclusiveness of creative sector representation in policymaking.
3 Institutional change: Development involves transforming institutions to support more complex economic activities. In the creative sector, this could include evolving from traditional patronage systems to more market-oriented models or developing new institutional frameworks to support digital creative economies.
4 Informal institutions: Cultural norms, social capital and informal networks play significant roles in development processes. For CCIs, this might involve understanding how social attitudes towards artistic careers affect talent development or how informal mentorship networks contribute to skill transfer in creative industries.

Daron Acemoglu and James Robinson, in "Why Nations Fail" (2012), argue that "inclusive economic institutions" are essential to long-term prosperity, writing: "Inclusive economic institutions ... are those that allow and encourage participation by the great mass of people in economic activities that make best use of their talents and skills and that enable individuals to make the choices they wish" (Acemoglu & Robinson, 2012, p. 74). This concept of inclusivity is particularly relevant for CCIs, which have the potential to thrive on diversity and broad participation (with the proper policies).

3.2.3.3 Implications for CCIs and Development

1 Institutional foundations: The development of CCIs requires supportive institutional frameworks, including effective intellectual property regimes and cultural policies. This might involve developing specialised legal frameworks for creative industries, establishing cultural policy agencies or integrating creative sector development into broader economic planning.
2 Inclusive institutions: CCIs can contribute to more inclusive economic development by providing opportunities for diverse economic participation. This could involve policies to support grassroots cultural production, initiatives to broaden access to creative education or programmes to support underrepresented groups in creative industries.
3 Institutional innovation: CCIs often involve new economic organisation and exchange forms, potentially driving broader institutional innovations. For example, crowdfunding platforms developed for creative projects have spurred innovations in financial regulations and business models that have applications beyond the creative sector.
4 Cultural institutions: Cultural institutions play a significant role in shaping overall economic development trajectories. Museums, theatres and cultural centres can serve as anchors for urban regeneration, tourism development catalysts and creative cluster formation hubs.

Ha-Joon Chang, in "Institutions and Economic Development: Theory, Policy and History" (2011), emphasises the need to understand the historical and cultural specificity of institutions, cautioning against a one-size-fits-all approach to institutional development. This insight is particularly relevant for CCIs, given the diverse cultural contexts in which they operate.

3.2.3.3.1 New Institutional Economics and CCIs

New Institutional Economics (NIE), associated with scholars like Oliver Williamson and Elinor Ostrom, offers additional insights for understanding CCIs:

1 Transaction cost economics: Helps explain the organisation of creative industries, including the choice between in-house production and

outsourcing. For instance, the prevalence of freelance work in many creative fields can be understood as a response to the high transaction costs associated with maintaining permanent creative staff in a project-based industry.

2. Property rights: The complex nature of intellectual property in CCIs and its impact on industry structure and innovation is a crucial area of NIE analysis. This includes examining how different IP regimes affect creative production, distribution and consumption and how new technologies challenge traditional notions of intellectual property.
3. Collective action: Understanding how creative communities solve common-pool resource problems, such as in open-source software development or collaborative artistic projects, is another area where NIE provides valuable insights. Ostrom's work on governing commons resources is particularly relevant here.
4. Governance structures: The various governance models in CCIs, from traditional firms to network-based collaboration, can be analysed through an NIE lens. This includes examining the efficiency of different organisational forms in creative production and understanding how governance structures evolve in response to technological and market changes.

The work of Elinor Ostrom on governing the commons has proven particularly insightful for understanding collaborative modes of cultural production within CCIs. In her seminal work "Governing the Commons" (1990), Ostrom challenges the notion that external authorities can easily design and impose optimal institutional solutions. Instead, she argues that "getting the institutions right is a difficult, time-consuming, conflict-invoking process" (Ostrom, 1990, p. 14). This perspective is especially pertinent when considering the complexities of developing effective institutions for CCIs.

Ostrom's insights highlight the nuanced approach required when applying institutional economics to CCIs and development theory. This application presents a unique set of challenges and opportunities that merit careful consideration. One of the primary challenges lies in the realm of measurement. Institutions, particularly informal ones, often need easier quantification and comparison across different contexts. This difficulty is amplified in the creative sector, where intangible factors such as cultural capital and creative networks play pivotal roles. While crucial to the functioning of CCIs, these elements are notoriously difficult to capture through traditional economic metrics.

The complexity of institutional environments for CCIs presents another significant challenge. These environments are often highly intricate and context-specific, characterised by a complex interplay between formal and informal institutions and between creative and non-creative sectors. This elaborate ecosystem resists simplistic analysis or one-size-fits-all policy prescriptions, necessitating a more nuanced and multifaceted approach. Translating institutional insights into effective policy poses yet another challenge. The long-term nature of institutional change and the difficulty of designing appropriate interventions make policy development in this area particularly complex. Policymakers must grapple with the tension between the need for immediate action and the recognition that meaningful institutional change often unfolds over extended periods.

While a strength, the interdisciplinary nature of institutional economics also presents particular challenges. It requires integrating economic analysis with insights from diverse fields such as sociology, anthropology and other disciplines. While this interdisciplinary approach enriches our understanding of CCIs, it also introduces methodological challenges and can sometimes run up against entrenched academic silos. These silos can impede the free flow of ideas and methodologies across disciplines, potentially limiting the full potential of institutional analysis in the context of CCIs.

Despite these challenges, applying institutional economics to CCIs also offers significant opportunities. Perhaps most importantly, it provides a holistic framework for understanding CCI development. Researchers and policymakers can develop more nuanced and effective strategies for supporting creative economies by considering the broader institutional context. This comprehensive approach allows for a deeper understanding of the complex factors that shape the development and success of CCIs. Another critical opportunity lies in the context sensitivity that institutional economics encourages. Paying close attention to local and historical specificities in development strategies can lead to more appropriate and effective interventions. These interventions can be tailored to specific cultural and institutional contexts rather than relying on generic solutions that may only suit some environments.

Finally, this school of economic thought offers valuable insights into the innovation dynamics and institutional conditions that foster creativity and innovation. By understanding the institutional factors that support or hinder creative activity, societies can develop more effective strategies for promoting innovation in CCIs and beyond. This understanding of innovation dynamics can inform the design of institutional environments conducive to creative flourishing, potentially leading to more vibrant and productive creative economies. While applying institutional economics to CCIs presents particular challenges, it also offers rich opportunities for deepening our understanding and improving our approaches to supporting these vital industries. By embracing both the complexities and the potential of this approach, it is possible to work towards creating more robust, sustainable and innovative creative economies.

Furthermore, the insights from institutional economics can help bridge the gap between cultural policy and economic development strategies. By recognising the economic significance of cultural institutions and the cultural dimensions of economic institutions, more integrated approaches to fostering CCIs development can be shaped.

As CCIs grow in economic importance and digital technologies reshape creative production and consumption, the institutional perspective will become increasingly valuable. It offers a framework for understanding these changes and for developing adaptive strategies to support these industries' continued growth and development. Future research in this area could focus on creating better metrics for assessing institutional quality in creative sectors, exploring the institutional dynamics of digital creative economies and examining the role of CCIs in driving broader institutional innovations. There is also potential for more comparative work exploring how different institutional arrangements across countries and regions shape the development of CCIs.

3.2.4 CCIs: Driving Forces for Sustainable and Inclusive Development

David Throsby's pioneering work in cultural economics provides a cornerstone for understanding the long-term value of cultural assets and activities. His concept of cultural capital, "an asset which embodies, stores or provides cultural value in addition to whatever economic value it may possess" (Throsby, 1999, p. 6), offers a framework for recognising the enduring significance of cultural resources.

This concept of cultural capital serves multiple purposes. It acknowledges the long-term value of cultural assets, much like other forms of capital that generate goods and services over time. For instance, a historic building isn't just a structure; it's a source of aesthetic value, educational opportunities and potential tourism revenue for years. Cultural capital also bridges the economic and artistic value gap, providing a more holistic basis for policy decisions.

Throsby's model of sustainable cultural development takes this idea further, balancing economic, social, cultural and environmental outcomes. It emphasises intergenerational equity, ensuring future generations can benefit from cultural resources. It also stresses the importance of maintaining cultural diversity, applying the precautionary principle in the face of uncertainty and recognising the interdependence of cultural, economic, social and environmental systems (Throsby, 2011). This framework encourages a long-term view of CCIs' impacts. It suggests that we should evaluate these industries not just on their immediate economic contributions, but on how they foster cultural sustainability over time. In practice, this might mean conducting cultural impact assessments alongside environmental ones for major projects, developing heritage management strategies that balance preservation with sustainable economic use, and ensuring support for a diverse range of cultural activities, not just those with immediate commercial appeal.

3.2.4.1 The Creative Economy and Sustainable Development

Building on these foundations, the United Nations Conference on Trade and Development (UNCTAD) has championed the creative economy as a development strategy, particularly for developing countries. This approach recognises CCIs as drivers of economic innovation, catalysing new products, services and working methods. UNCTAD encourages countries to integrate CCIs into their national development strategies, emphasising their potential for inclusive growth. These industries offer opportunities for marginalised groups, including women and youth, to participate in economic activities. Moreover, creative industries are recognised as critical components of sustainable urbanisation, contributing to urban regeneration and quality of life.

As UNCTAD (2018) states, "The creative economy has the potential to support developing countries in diversifying their economies and leapfrogging into new high-growth areas of the world economy" (p. 5). This perspective reframes CCIs not as luxury sectors, but as fundamental components of resilient and dynamic economies. We've seen this approach in action with policies like Colombia's Orange Economy and Thailand's Creative Economy initiatives, which use comprehensive national strategies to promote creative sectors through tax incentives, infrastructure development and skills training.

3.2.4.1.1 Emerging Models: Circular Culture and Platform Cooperatives

As the world's understanding of sustainability evolves, new approaches are emerging that further illuminate the potential of CCIs to contribute to holistic development. For instance, the concept of circular culture applies circular economy principles to CCIs, aiming to reduce waste and maximise resource efficiency. This approach encourages designing cultural products for longevity and reuse, developing new business models based on sharing and redistribution and applying digital technologies to create more sustainable cultural production and consumption patterns. We see this with initiatives like sustainable fashion design, environmentally conscious film, TV productions and circular music festivals like DGTL in Amsterdam. Meanwhile, platform cooperatives represent an alternative model for digital CCIs based on democratic ownership and governance of digital platforms. This approach addresses concerns about the concentration of power and wealth in the digital economy, offering a more equitable model for creative workers and consumers. Platform cooperatives in CCIs feature collective ownership of digital platforms by users and workers, democratic governance structures, fair value distribution, data sovereignty and often open-source technology. Scholz (2016) proposes that "Platform cooperativism can reframe the future of work and life, responding to the challenges of our time" (p. 14).

BOX 3.5 CIRCULAR ECONOMY AND COOPERATIVISM IN CCIS

Contemporary examples of circular economy in CCIs include:

1 Sustainable Fashion: Stella McCartney continues to lead in sustainable luxury fashion, recently launching her Frayme Mylo™ bag made from mycelium, a sustainable alternative to animal leather. Similarly, Adidas has partnered with Parley for the Oceans to create shoes made from recycled ocean plastic, with over 30 million pairs sold as of 2022.
2 Circular Design in Electronics: Fairphone, a Dutch social enterprise, produces modular smartphones for easy repair and upgrade. This extends the lifespan of devices and reduces e-waste in the electronics industry.
3 Sustainable Music Industry: In addition to circular festivals like DGTL in Amsterdam, we're seeing innovations like Coldplay's 2022 Music of the Spheres World Tour, which aimed to cut direct emissions by 50% compared to their previous tour using sustainable materials, renewable energy and even kinetic dancefloors to generate electricity.
4 Circular Publishing: Penguin Random House has committed to using 100% recycled paper for its publications by 2025 and has already achieved 80% usage of recycled or FSC-certified paper as of 2022.
5 Sustainable Film and TV Production: Building on initiatives like Albert in the United Kingdom, significant studios are adopting more sustainable practices. Warner Bros., for instance, achieved carbon neutrality for all its production in 2021 and aims to be ultimately carbon neutral by 2025.

Platform cooperatives represent an alternative model for digital CCIs based on democratic ownership and governance of digital platforms. This approach addresses concerns about the concentration of power and wealth in the digital economy, offering a more equitable model for creative workers and consumers. Platform cooperatives in CCIs feature collective ownership of digital platforms by users and workers, democratic governance structures, fair value distribution, data sovereignty and often open-source technology.
Recent examples of platform cooperativism in CCIs include:

1 Resonate: This stream-to-own music platform cooperative continues growing, offering a fair payment model where artists earn more as their songs are played.
2 Stocksy United: This artist-owned stock photography and video platform has paid out over $100 million in royalties to its members since its inception, demonstrating the viability of the cooperative model in the digital creative economy.

3 Ampled: Launched in 2019, this platform allows music artists to receive direct support from their fans. It's cooperatively owned by the artists, workers and supporters who use the platform.
4 Cooperative Art World (CoArt): Established in 2021, CoArt is a platform cooperative that aims to create a more equitable art market by allowing artists, collectors and art professionals to collectively own and govern the platform.
5 Guilded: Founded in 2022, this platform cooperative provides creative industry freelancers with tools for project management, invoicing and community building.

3.3 Social Inclusion and CCIs

CCIs are potent catalysts for social change, fostering diversity, preserving heritage and driving innovation across societies. They promote mental health and well-being, offer therapeutic benefits and build community connections. However, CCIs face significant challenges in accessibility, economic sustainability and authentic representation. Realising their full potential requires addressing these obstacles to create genuinely inclusive and impactful creative ecosystems. Below, you'll find a synthesis of the primary potentialities and challenges in the contemporary ecosystem when associating CCIs with social development.

3.3.1 The Promise of Inclusion: CCIs as Catalysts for Social Change

3.3.1.1 Fostering Diversity and Cultural Exchange

CCIs are potent platforms for representing minority cultures and facilitating cultural exchange, challenging dominant narratives and promoting a more inclusive cultural landscape. This function manifests in various ways:

- **Representation in Media:** Film festivals spotlighting LGBTQ+ themes or exhibitions of Indigenous art showcase underrepresented cultures and create opportunities for cross-cultural dialogue and understanding. The global success of films like *Moonlight* or *Parasite* has brought marginalised narratives into mainstream discourse, fostering greater cultural awareness and empathy. For instance, *Moonlight* (2016) broke new ground in its nuanced portrayal of Black masculinity and queer identity, challenging stereotypes and opening conversations about intersectionality in mainstream cinema.
- **Breaking Stereotypes:** CCIs play a crucial role in challenging and dismantling harmful stereotypes by providing spaces for diverse voices and

perspectives. This representation extends beyond mere visibility; it can catalyse broader societal changes by shifting public perceptions and encouraging more nuanced understandings of different cultures and experiences. For example, the #OwnVoices movement in publishing has pushed for authentic representation in literature, leading to a more diverse range of stories and characters in books, particularly in children's and young adult literature.
- **Cultural Diplomacy:** CCIs often serve as unofficial ambassadors, facilitating international understanding and cooperation. Cultural exchanges, international art exhibitions and global music festivals create bridges between nations and cultures, fostering mutual respect and appreciation. The Edinburgh International Festival, for instance, was founded in 1947 as a post-World War II initiative to "provide a platform for the flowering of the human spirit" and has since become a major celebration of arts and culture, attracting performers and audiences from around the world.
- **Digital Platforms and Global Reach:** The rise of digital platforms has amplified the potential for cultural exchange and diversity in CCIs. Social media platforms like Instagram and TikTok have become powerful tools for artists from underrepresented communities to showcase their work and connect with global audiences. For example, Indigenous artists have used these platforms to share traditional art forms and contemporary interpretations, reaching audiences far beyond their local communities.

3.3.2 Preserving and Innovating Cultural Expression

The dual role of CCIs in both preserving traditional arts and supporting new forms of expression creates a dynamic cultural landscape that honours heritage while embracing innovation:

- **Preservation of Traditional Arts:** Initiatives like UNESCO's Intangible Cultural Heritage programme highlight the importance of safeguarding traditional practices. CCIs play a vital role in this preservation, often adapting conventional art forms for contemporary audiences without losing their cultural essence. This is particularly crucial in maintaining cultural diversity in the face of globalisation. For example, the Japanese art of Kabuki theatre has been preserved through strict traditional training and modern adaptations, including digital technology in set designs.
- **Fostering Innovation:** Support for emerging artists and new art forms pushes the boundaries of cultural expression, reflecting evolving societal values and experiences. This innovation ensures that culture remains a living, breathing entity responsive to current social issues and experiences. The rise of digital art and NFTs (non-fungible tokens) has opened new

avenues for artists to create, distribute and monetise their work, challenging traditional art market structures.

- **Bridging Tradition and Modernity:** Many successful CCI projects find innovative ways to blend traditional and contemporary elements, creating new forms of expression that resonate with diverse audiences while maintaining cultural authenticity. For instance, fashion designer Ozwald Boateng merges conventional African textiles and patterns with contemporary British tailoring, creating a unique aesthetic that celebrates cultural fusion.
- **Technological Integration:** Technology integration in traditional art forms has created new possibilities for preservation and innovation. Virtual and augmented reality technologies are being used to create immersive experiences of historical sites and artefacts, allowing for broader access and new forms of engagement with cultural heritage.

3.3.3 Fostering Social Cohesion and Civic Engagement

CCIs possess a unique capacity to bring communities together and stimulate civic participation:

- **Community Building:** Community arts projects, local festivals and shared cultural spaces can unite diverse groups, building social capital and strengthening community ties. These initiatives often transcend social, economic and cultural barriers, creating a shared identity and purpose. The Notting Hill Carnival in London, for example, has evolved from a small community event to one of Europe's largest street festivals, celebrating Caribbean culture and fostering community cohesion.
- **Platforms for Social Commentary:** CCIs provide potent tools for civic engagement and political expression. Public art installations, socially engaged theatre and protest music can raise awareness about social issues and inspire collective action. The role of street art in urban social movements or the use of documentary films to highlight social injustices demonstrates how CCIs can be catalysts for social change. For instance, Banksy's politically charged street art has sparked global conversations about consumerism and refugee rights.
- **Participatory Culture:** Many CCI initiatives encourage active participation rather than passive consumption, fostering a sense of ownership and engagement among community members. This participatory approach can effectively address local issues and build community resilience. The Ghetto Biennale in Haiti, for example, invites artists from around the world to create work in collaboration with local artists in the informal neighbourhoods of Port-au-Prince, challenging traditional art world hierarchies and fostering cross-cultural dialogue.

- **Urban Regeneration:** CCIs have been instrumental in urban regeneration projects, transforming neglected areas into vibrant cultural hubs. The transformation of Bilbao, Spain, through constructing the Guggenheim Museum, is a classic example. Still, smaller-scale initiatives like revitalising former industrial spaces into artist studios and galleries have significantly impacted local communities.
- **Digital Civic Engagement:** Online platforms have created new opportunities for civic engagement through CCIs. Crowdfunding platforms like Kickstarter have enabled community-driven cultural projects. At the same time, social media has facilitated the rapid organisation of cultural events and protests, as seen in movements like the Arab Spring or Black Lives Matter.

3.3.3.1 Mental Health and Well-being: The Therapeutic Power of CCIs

A crucial aspect of CCIs that deserves special attention is their potential to impact mental health and well-being positively. This dimension adds another layer to their social significance:

3.3.4 Art Therapy and Expressive Arts

- **Therapeutic Applications:** Many CCIs, particularly visual arts, music and dance, are increasingly recognised for their therapeutic value. Art therapy programmes have shown significant benefits in treating various mental health conditions, from anxiety and depression to PTSD and schizophrenia. For example, the Combat Paper Project in the United States helps veterans process their experiences through papermaking workshops, where they turn their military uniforms into paper and then create art on that paper.
- **Emotional Expression and Processing:** Creative activities provide outlets for emotional expression, allowing individuals to process complex feelings and experiences in non-verbal ways. This can be particularly beneficial for those who struggle with traditional talk therapies. The British Association of Art Therapists has documented numerous case studies demonstrating how art therapy has helped individuals, including children with autism and adults with dementia, to communicate and process emotions more effectively.
- **Mindfulness and Stress Reduction:** Engaging in creative activities can induce a flow state, promoting mindfulness and reducing stress. Practices like colouring for adults have gained popularity as accessible stress-relief tools. A study published in the Art Therapy journal in 2016 found that 45 minutes of creative activity significantly reduced cortisol levels, regardless of artistic experience or talent.
- **Body-Mind Connection:** Movement-based creative expressions like dance therapy have shown promise in improving both physical and mental

well-being. Programmes like Dance for PD (Parkinson's disease) have demonstrated how dance can improve motor function, balance and quality of life for individuals with PD.

3.3.5 Social Connection and Belonging

- **Combating Isolation:** Participation in cultural activities, whether as creators or audience members, can combat social isolation, a significant risk factor for mental health issues. For instance, community choirs, art classes and book clubs provide opportunities for meaningful social interaction. The United Kingdom's "Men's Sheds" movement, which brings men together to work on practical projects in a social setting, has been particularly effective in addressing isolation and improving mental health among older men.
- **Building Identity and Self-esteem:** Engaging with one's cultural heritage through CCIs can strengthen a sense of identity and belonging, which is crucial for mental well-being, especially for minority groups and immigrants. Programmes like the Amal Project in Germany use theatre and storytelling to help young refugees integrate into their new communities while maintaining connections to their cultural roots.
- **Intergenerational Connections:** CCIs can bridge generational gaps, fostering understanding and connection between different age groups. Intergenerational choirs and community art projects have shown promise in reducing ageism and improving social cohesion.

3.3.5.1 Cognitive Benefits

- **Lifelong Learning:** Engagement with CCIs promotes lifelong learning and cognitive stimulation, which is associated with better mental health outcomes, particularly in older adults. The University of the Third Age (U3A) movement in the United Kingdom, which offers various cultural and educational activities for older adults, has been linked to improved cognitive function and life satisfaction among participants.
- **Creativity and Problem-solving:** Regular engagement with creative activities enhances overall creativity and problem-solving skills, which can translate into improved resilience and adaptability in daily life. The Lincoln Center Education's "Imagination Workshops" in New York schools have demonstrated how arts-based learning can improve students' critical thinking and problem-solving skills across various academic subjects.
- **Neuroplasticity:** Emerging research suggests that engaging in creative activities can promote neuroplasticity, the brain's ability to form new neural connections. A study published in Frontiers in Human Neuroscience 2014 found that creating art led to increased functional connectivity in the brain, particularly in areas associated with introspection, self-monitoring and memory.

3.3.6 Public Health and Well-being Initiatives

- Arts on Prescription: Some healthcare systems have begun implementing "arts on prescription" programmes, where patients are referred to cultural activities as part of their treatment plans, recognising the health benefits of creative engagement. In the United Kingdom, the Airlift programme has shown promising results, with participants reporting improved well-being and decreased healthcare utilisation.
- Community Well-being Projects: CCIs are increasingly integrated into public health strategies, with community art projects, music festivals and cultural events being used to promote overall well-being and social cohesion. For example, the New Orleans Musicians' Clinic combines healthcare services with performance opportunities, recognising the intrinsic link between creative expression and well-being for musicians.
- Workplace Well-being: Some companies incorporate CCIs into their employee well-being programmes, recognising creative activities' stress-reducing and team-building benefits. For instance, Google's "Creative Skills for Innovation" programme offers employees workshops in various art forms to boost creativity and well-being.
- Digital Mental Health Interventions: The intersection of CCIs and technology has led to innovative digital mental health interventions. Apps that combine art therapy techniques with cognitive behavioural therapy principles or virtual reality experiences designed to reduce anxiety represent new frontiers in mental health support.

3.3.6.1 The Reality Check: Challenges and Criticisms

Despite their potential, CCIs need help realising their capacity to promote social inclusion and well-being. Significant accessibility issues, including geographic disparities and digital exclusion, can reinforce social inequalities. In "Culture is Bad for You" (2020), Orian Brook, Dave O'Brien and Mark Taylor present a critical examination of the CCIs, challenging the notion that these sectors are bastions of diversity and opportunity. Through extensive data analysis, they reveal persistent inequalities based on class, gender and race within CCIs, arguing that these industries often reproduce and exacerbate existing social disparities. The authors debunk the myth of meritocracy in cultural sectors, highlighting how social capital, networks and economic privileges play crucial roles in determining success. Their research demonstrates that the cultural workforce remains predominantly white, male and middle class, especially in positions of power, directly affecting the diversity of artistic output.

The implications of their work for CCIs are profound, calling for systemic changes rather than superficial diversity initiatives. Their findings suggest a need to reassess how talent is defined and identified, address economic barriers through restructuring internships and funding models and implement targeted policy interventions. O'Brien and Brook's research underscores the importance of early educational interventions to create more diverse pipelines into CCIs and challenges traditional cultural hierarchies. Their work serves as a crucial counterpoint to optimistic narratives about CCIs, urging industry leaders, policymakers and practitioners to confront and actively dismantle systems of privilege and exclusion for CCIs to truly fulfil their potential as drivers of social inclusion and well-being.

Economic barriers, from high participation costs to career entry hurdles, limit engagement and diversity within these industries. The tension between authentic representation and tokenism remains a persistent challenge, risking surface-level diversity without meaningful inclusion. Additionally, CCIs must carefully balance innovation with tradition to avoid cultural commodification and the loss of heritage. Comprehensive policies at local, national and international levels are essential to address these challenges, ensure equitable access and maximise the positive social impact of CCIs. Below, you can find some relevant topics that should be urgently addressed to unveil CCI potential:

3.3.7 Accessibility and the Digital Divide

- Geographic Disparities: Urban areas often have a concentration of cultural institutions and creative spaces, while rural or marginalised communities may need more access to such resources. This uneven distribution can reinforce existing social and economic inequalities. For example, a 2019 report by Arts Council England found significant disparities in arts funding between London and the rest of the country, highlighting the need for a more equitable distribution of cultural resources.
- Digital Exclusion: While digital technologies have opened new avenues for cultural participation and creation, they have also created new forms of exclusion. Only some have equal access to the internet or digital devices, and disparities in digital literacy can prevent full participation in the digital creative economy. The COVID-19 pandemic has further highlighted this divide, as many cultural experiences moved online, potentially excluding those without reliable internet access or digital skills.
- Intersectional Challenges: The digital divide often intersects with other forms of social inequality, compounding exclusion based on age, socio-economic status and geographic location. For instance, older adults in rural areas may face multiple barriers to accessing digital cultural content, including lack of infrastructure, limited digital skills and age-related disabilities.

- Language Barriers: Many digital platforms and cultural content are predominantly in English or a few other major languages, creating barriers for non-native speakers and diverse linguistic backgrounds. This can limit the global reach and inclusivity of digital CCI initiatives.

3.3.8 Economic Barriers and Affordability

- Cost of Participation: For many, cultural consumption –buying art, attending performances or accessing digital content – can be prohibitive. This economic barrier can exclude significant portions of the population from the benefits of CCIs. For example, a 2019 UK Audience Agency survey found that cost was the primary barrier to arts attendance for lower-income groups.
- Career Entry Barriers: Pursuing a career in the creative industries often requires financial resources for education, equipment or unpaid internships, which can exclude individuals from lower socioeconomic backgrounds. The Sutton Trust's 2018 report on internships in the United Kingdom found that the creative industries were among the sectors most reliant on unpaid internships, creating significant barriers to entry for those who cannot afford to work for free.
- Funding Challenges: Many CCIs, especially those focused on social impact, need help with sustainable funding models. This can lead to short-term thinking and difficulty implementing long-term, systemic change. The precarious nature of funding for many cultural organisations was starkly highlighted during the COVID-19 pandemic, with many institutions facing closure or significant cutbacks.
- Gentrification and Displacement: The success of CCIs in urban regeneration can lead to gentrification, potentially displacing the very communities they initially aimed to serve. This has been observed in areas like Berlin's Kreuzberg district or London's East End, where thriving artistic communities have contributed to rising property prices and changing neighbourhood demographics.

3.3.9 Representation and Tokenism

- Surface-Level Diversity: While CCIs often champion diversity, there's a risk of surface-level representation that only translates to meaningful inclusion or power redistribution within these industries. For instance, while there may be increased representation of diverse characters in film and television, decision-making positions in major studios remain predominantly white and male.
- Cultural Appropriation: There's a fine line between cultural exchange and appropriation. CCIs must navigate this carefully to ensure respectful and

authentic representation of diverse cultures. Controversies surrounding Indigenous designs in fashion or the adoption of minority cultural elements in mainstream music highlight the ongoing challenges in this area.

- Stereotyping: Even well-intentioned representation efforts can sometimes reinforce stereotypes if not handled carefully. This can be particularly problematic in media representations, where complex cultural identities may be reduced to simplistic tropes.
- Gatekeeping: Despite efforts to increase diversity, many CCIs still need help with gatekeeping, where established networks and power structures limit opportunities for newcomers, particularly those from underrepresented groups. This can be seen in art, where a few galleries and institutions wield significant influence over which artists gain recognition.

3.3.10 Gender Inequalities in CCIs

- Glass Ceiling Effect: Women in CCIs frequently face barriers to advancement into top leadership positions. This is evident in areas like music production, where female producers and sound engineers are significantly underrepresented in senior roles despite growing numbers entering the field.
- Pay Gap Persistence: Despite progress in representation, significant pay disparities persist in many creative industries. For instance, in the film industry, female actors often earn substantially less than their male counterparts for equivalent roles. This gap extends to behind-the-scenes roles such as directors, producers and writers.
- ·Gender Stereotyping in Roles: Certain creative roles remain heavily gendered, limiting opportunities for diverse participation. For example, in the gaming industry, women are often pigeonholed into marketing or design roles, while programming and development teams remain predominantly male.

3.3.11 Global Majorities Exclusion

- Eurocentric Narrative Dominance: In literature and film, stories from Global North perspectives often overshadow narratives from the Global South. This leads to a narrow representation of global experiences and perpetuates cultural stereotypes.
- Language Barriers in International Collaboration: The dominance of English in global creative industries can exclude talented individuals from non-English speaking backgrounds, limiting the diversity of voices and perspectives in international projects.
- Unequal Resource Distribution: Funding and resources for cultural projects are often concentrated in Western countries, making it challenging

for artists and creators from Global South nations to access necessary support for large-scale or high-budget productions.

3.3.12 Lack of Access to Diverse Social Backgrounds

- Economic Barriers to Entry: Many creative professions require unpaid internships or expensive education, creating significant obstacles for individuals from lower-income backgrounds to enter and succeed in these fields.
- Networking Disparities: Success in CCIs often relies heavily on personal connections and networking. Individuals from less privileged backgrounds may need more access to these crucial networks, hindering their career progression and opportunities.
- Geographic Limitations: Creative opportunities are often concentrated in major urban centres, disadvantaging talented individuals from rural or remote areas who may need more resources to relocate or commute to these hubs of creative activity.

3.3.13 Innovation at the Cost of Tradition

- Commodification of Culture: In the push for innovation, traditional arts are at risk of being repackaged and commodified, potentially stripping them of their cultural context and deeper meanings. This can be seen in the mass production of "ethnic" crafts for tourist markets or the appropriation of traditional designs in fashion without proper acknowledgement or compensation.
- Balancing Act: Finding the right balance between preserving cultural heritage and fostering innovation remains a constant challenge for CCIs. This tension is particularly evident in fields like architecture, where preserving historical buildings must be balanced with the need for modern, sustainable urban development.
- Loss of Traditional Skills: As CCIs evolve, there's a risk of losing traditional skills and techniques. For example, digitising design processes in fields like textile production or furniture making can lead to a decline in traditional craftsmanship skills.
- Authenticity vs. Accessibility: Efforts to make traditional art forms more accessible or appealing to contemporary audiences can sometimes lead to concern.

CCIs stand at a critical juncture, embodying immense potential for positive social change and significant challenges that threaten to undermine their impact. On one hand, CCIs serve as powerful catalysts for fostering diversity, preserving cultural heritage, driving innovation and promoting mental health

TABLE 3.2 Creative And Cultural Industries and Social-Economic Development: A Synthesis of the Policy Strategies and Challenges

Development Area	*Role of CCIs*	*Strategies*	*Policy Strategies*	*Challenges*	*Examples/Initiatives*
Social Inclusion	• Represent minority cultures • Facilitate cultural exchange • Challenge dominant narratives • Promote intercultural dialogue • Empower marginalised voices • Create inclusive spaces	• Diverse cultural programming • Cross-cultural collaborations • Community engagement initiatives • Accessibility programmes • Inclusive hiring practices • Cultural sensitivity training	• Diversity quotas in cultural funding • Inclusive cultural education curricula • Anti-discrimination policies in CCIs • Multilingual cultural programming • Affirmative action in cultural institutions • Cultural diversity audits	• Tokenism • Resistance to change • Measuring genuine inclusion • Intersectionality Balancing representation and quality • Addressing systemic barriers	• United Kingdom's Creative Case for Diversity • Berlin's Diversity Arts Culture office • Canada's Multiculturalism Programme • Australia's Arts and Disability Strategy • South Africa's Rainbow Nation cultural initiatives
Cultural Expression	• Preserve traditional arts • Support new forms of expression • Reflect evolving societal values • Bridge traditional and contemporary practices • Document cultural heritage • Innovate artistic techniques	• Artist residency programmes • Cultural heritage documentation • Experimental art support • Intergenerational knowledge transfer • Digital archiving of cultural practices • Cross-disciplinary artistic collaborations	• Tax incentives for cultural preservation • Grants for experimental art • Cultural diplomacy initiatives • Intellectual property protection for traditional knowledge • Mandatory funding for public art in development projects • National inventories of intangible cultural heritage	• Balancing tradition and innovation • Cultural appropriation • Funding allocation • Market pressures • Preserving endangered cultural practices • Adapting to technological changes	• France's 1% artistique policy • Japan's Living National Treasure system • EU's Creative Europe programme • India's National Mission on Cultural Mapping • New Zealand's Toi Iho Maori Made Mark

(*Continued*)

TABLE 3.2 (Continued)

Development Area	*Role of CCIs*	*Strategies*	*Policy Strategies*	*Challenges*	*Examples/Initiatives*
Social Cohesion	• Build community ties • Provide platforms for civic engagement • Foster shared identity • Mediate social conflicts • Promote intergenerational connections • Facilitate social integration	• Participatory art projects • Community cultural centres • Arts-based conflict resolution • Intergenerational cultural programmes • Public space activation through arts • Cultural volunteering schemes	• Participatory budgeting for culture • Community cultural centres funding • Arts-based social cohesion policies • Cultural volunteering incentives • Integration of culture in urban planning policies • Cross-sector partnerships for social cohesion	• Measuring impact • Ensuring diverse participation • Balancing local and national interests • Sustaining long-term engagement • Overcoming social barriers • Addressing deep-rooted societal divisions	• United Kingdom's Creative People and Places programme • Colombia's Culture as a Tool for Social Cohesion policy • Singapore's Community Arts and Culture Nodes • EU's Voices of Culture initiative • Brazil's Cultura Viva programme

Mental Health	• Offer therapeutic benefits • Provide outlets for self-expression • Combat social isolation • Enhance cognitive function • Promote emotional resilience • Support trauma recovery	• Arts therapy programmes • Creative wellness initiatives • Social prescribing for arts activities • Arts-based mental health awareness campaigns • Creativity-focused stress reduction programmes • Trauma-informed arts practices	• Integration of arts in healthcare policies • Training and accreditation for arts therapists • Mental health-focused cultural prescribing schemes • Workplace creativity programmes • Research funding for arts and mental health • Inclusion of arts therapies in health insurance coverage	• Evidence-based policy making • Cross-sector collaboration • Accessibility of services • Stigma reduction • Professional boundaries • Standardisation of practices	• United Kingdom's National Centre for Creative Health • Australia's National Arts and Health Framework • Finland's Arts on Prescription initiative • United States of America's Creative Forces: NEA Military Healing Arts Network • Japan's Art Therapy and Mental Health initiative

(*Continued*)

TABLE 3.2 (Continued)

Development Area	*Role of CCIs*	*Strategies*	*Policy Strategies*	*Challenges*	*Examples/Initiatives*
Community Development	• Drive urban regeneration • Build social capital • Stimulate local economies • Enhance place identity • Preserve local heritage • Foster community pride	• Creative placemaking initiatives • Cultural mapping exercises • Creative industry clusters • Community-led cultural planning • Heritage-based tourism development • Local cultural entrepreneurship support	• Creative City networks • Cultural planning requirements in urban development • Artist-in-residence programmes for urban planning • Creative zoning policies • Tax incentives for cultural enterprises in deprived areas • Integration of culture in community development policies	• Gentrification • Equitable distribution of benefits • Balancing top-down and bottom-up approaches • Long-term sustainability • Measuring social impact • Addressing diverse community needs	• UNESCO Creative Cities Network • Netherlands' Top Sector Creative Industry policy • Scotland's Place Principle • Taiwan's Cultural Vitality Index • Medellin's (Colombia) social urbanism approach

Economic Development	• Create jobs • Attract tourism and investment • Foster innovation • Enhance city/ regional branding • Develop creative entrepreneurship • Drive export of cultural goods and services	• Cultural tourism strategies • Creative incubators and accelerators • Creative cluster development • Cultural export promotion • Creative skills training programmes • Cross-sector innovation initiatives	• Creative industry tax credits • Cultural entrepreneurship education policies • Creative export strategies • Innovation vouchers for CCIs • Creative economy satellite accounts • Integration of CCIs in national innovation policies	• Precarious work conditions • Measuring economic impact • Balancing economic and cultural goals • Global competition • Intellectual property protection • Adapting to rapid technological changes	• South Korea's Hallyu (Korean Wave) strategy • United Kingdom's Creative Industries Sector Deal • New Zealand's Wellington NZ creative economy initiative • China's cultural industry demonstration zones • Nigeria's Nollywood film industry support

(Continued)

TABLE 3.2 (Continued)

Development Area	*Role of CCIs*	*Strategies*	*Policy Strategies*	*Challenges*	*Examples/Initiatives*
Digital Inclusion	• Democratise access to culture • Provide new platforms for creation • Enable global cultural exchange • Foster digital creativity • Preserve digital cultural heritage • Promote digital literacy through creative practices	• Digital culture access programmes • Virtual cultural experiences • Online creative collaboration platforms • Digital art creation support • Digital cultural heritage initiatives • Creative coding programmes	• Digital culture access policies • Creative coding in school curricula • Virtual cultural exchange initiatives • Support schemes for digital art creation • Digital cultural heritage preservation policies • Integration of digital skills in cultural education	• Digital divide • Rapid technological change • Intellectual property issues in digital realm • Balancing digital and physical experiences • Digital preservation challenges • Cybersecurity and privacy concerns	• EU's Digital Culture plan • Canada's Digital Literacy Exchange Programme • Australia's Digital Culture Strategy • Google Arts & Culture platform Europeana digital cultural heritage initiative

Cultural Rights	• Promote right to cultural participation • Preserve cultural diversity • Empower communities • Safeguard cultural heritage • Ensure freedom of artistic expression • Protect traditional knowledge and expressions	• Cultural impact assessments • Community-led cultural initiatives • Artistic freedom advocacy • Traditional knowledge documentation • Cultural diversity promotion • Access to culture programmes	• Cultural rights legislation • Indigenous cultural rights policies • Community broadcasting policies • Cultural exemption in trade agreements • Freedom of artistic expression laws • Traditional knowledge protection frameworks	• Balancing universal rights and cultural specificity • Implementing rights in practice • Addressing cultural conflicts • Decolonising cultural institutions • Navigating competing rights claims • Ensuring non-discrimination in cultural participation	• UNESCO's Culture 2030 Indicators • Norway's Cultural Rucksack programme • Mexico's constitutional right to culture • New Zealand's Treaty of Waitangi principles in cultural policy • Freemuse's advocacy for artistic freedom

(*Continued*)

TABLE 3.2 (Continued)

Development Area	*Role of CCIs*	*Strategies*	*Policy Strategies*	*Challenges*	*Examples/Initiatives*
Sustainable Development	• Promote sustainable lifestyles • Contribute to climate awareness • Foster eco-friendly innovations • Preserve biocultural diversity • Communicate sustainability concepts • Inspire ecological thinking	• Eco-art initiatives • Sustainable design in CCIs • Arts-based climate communication • Biocultural heritage conservation • Circular economy practices in CCIs • Environmental themes in cultural programming	• Green culture funds • Sustainability criteria in cultural grants • Eco-design requirements in cultural infrastructure • Arts-based environmental education policies • Integration of CCIs in national sustainability strategies • Carbon offsetting requirements for cultural events	• Environmental impact of cultural events • Balancing growth with sustainability • Changing consumer behaviours • Measuring sustainability in CCIs • Adapting traditional practices to sustainability goals • Addressing conflicting sustainability objectives	• Julie's Bicycle (United Kingdom) Creative Green Tools • France's Environmental Charter for Festivals • Nordic Culture Point's Art and Culture in Arctic Sustainable Development project • Australia's Creative Climate Leadership programme • Costa Rica's integration of culture in its decarbonisation plan

Education and Skills	• Enhance creativity and innovation skills • Promote cultural literacy • Support lifelong learning • Foster interdisciplinary thinking • Develop transferable skills • Cultivate critical thinking	• Arts integration in STEAM education • Creative skills in vocational training • Cultural education partnerships • Creative apprenticeship schemes • Arts-based adult education programmes • Creativity workshops for professionals	• Arts integration policies in national curricula • Creative skills frameworks in education • Cultural education partnership policies • Creative apprenticeship incentives • Lifelong learning policies incorporating CCIs • Recognition of creative qualifications	• Measuring creative skills • Balancing arts and other subjects • Teacher training in creative education • Adapting to future skills needs • Ensuring equitable access to creative education • Overcoming traditional education paradigms	• South Korea's Arts and Culture Education Policy • EU's Cultural Awareness and Expression framework • United Kingdom's Creative Careers Programme • Singapore's 'Our Singapore Fund' for ground-up initiatives • Colombia's 'Crea' programme for arts education

(*Continued*)

TABLE 3.2 (Continued)

Development Area	*Role of CCIs*	*Strategies*	*Policy Strategies*	*Challenges*	*Examples/Initiatives*
Health and Well-being	Promote holistic health approaches • Enhance patient experiences • Support healthy ageing • Address public health challenges • Improve healthcare environments • Facilitate health communication	Arts in healthcare facility design • Cultural activities in health promotion • Creative ageing programmes • Arts-based health communication • Arts therapies in healthcare • Health-focused public art projects	Arts in Health policies • Cultural activities in public health strategies • Creative ageing policy frameworks • Integration of arts in medical education • Health and well-being criteria in cultural funding • Cross-departmental arts and health initiatives	Integration with healthcare systems • Evidence-based practice • Funding and resource allocation • Professional boundaries • Measuring health outcomes of cultural interventions • Addressing health inequalities through CCIs	Arts Council England's Creative Health and Well-being Plan • Denmark's Culture Vitamins programme • United States of America's National Organization for Arts in Health • Japan's 'Art Brut' initiatives for mental health • Welsh Government's strategy for culture and health

and well-being. They offer unique platforms for representing marginalised voices, facilitating cultural exchange and building community cohesion. The therapeutic power of creative expression, from art therapy to community arts projects, demonstrates the profound impact CCIs can have on individual and collective well-being. Digital platforms have amplified these positive effects, creating unprecedented global cultural exchange and civic engagement opportunities.

However, as Brook, O'Brien and Taylor's work "Culture is Bad for You" illustrates, CCIs grapple with deeply entrenched inequalities and systemic barriers. Issues of accessibility, economic exclusion and authentic representation persist, often reproducing and exacerbating existing social disparities. While offering new avenues for participation, the digital divide has created new forms of exclusion. Balancing innovation with tradition and authenticity with commodification remains an ongoing challenge. Moving forward, realising the full potential of CCIs as drivers of social development and well-being will require comprehensive, systemic changes. This includes implementing targeted policies at local, national and international levels, reassessing how talent is identified and nurtured, addressing economic barriers and actively dismantling systems of privilege within these industries. Only through such concerted efforts can CCIs truly fulfil their promise as inclusive, transformative forces in society, fostering a cultural landscape that authentically reflects and serves the diversity of our communities.

Notes

1 Thorstein Veblen (1857–1929) was an American economist and sociologist known for his critique of capitalism and concept of "conspicuous consumption." He authored "The Theory of the Leisure Class" (1899), which introduced institutional analysis to American economics. Veblen's work laid the foundation for institutional economics by emphasising the role of social and cultural factors in economic behaviour.

John R. Commons (1862–1945) was an American institutional economist and labour historian who contributed significantly to understanding collective action and labour economics. He developed the concept of "collective bargaining" and played a crucial role in shaping American labour law and policy. Commons' work "Institutional Economics" (1934) was instrumental in defining the field.

Wesley Clair Mitchell (1874–1948) was an American economist known for his empirical work on business cycles and his leadership of the National Bureau of Economic Research. He emphasised the importance of quantitative analysis in economics and studying actual business behaviour. Mitchell's work "Business Cycles" (1913) highlighted the role of institutions in economic fluctuations.

2 Douglas North (1920–2015) was an American economist known for his work on economic history and institutional change. He won the Nobel Prize in Economics in 1993 for his research on the role of institutions in long-term financial performance. North's seminal work "Institutions, Institutional Change and Economic Performance" (1990) significantly advanced institutional economic theory.

Elinor Ostrom (1933–2012) was an American political economist who became the first woman to win the Nobel Prize in Economics in 2009. Her ground-breaking work on common-pool resources and collective action challenged conventional wisdom about managing shared resources. Ostrom's book "Governing the Commons" (1990) provided crucial insights into institutional arrangements for sustainable resource management.

References

Acemoglu, D., & Robinson, J. A. (2012). *Why nations fail: The origins of power, prosperity, and poverty*. Crown Business.

Arts Council England. (2019). Equality, diversity and the creative case: A data report, 2018–19. Arts Council England. https://www.artscouncil.org.uk/equality-diversity-and-creative-case-data-report-2018-19

Bakhshi, H., Freeman, A., & Hitchen, G. (2009). Measuring intrinsic value: How to stop worrying and love economics. Mission Models Money.

https://mpra.ub.uni-muenchen.de/14902/1/MPRA_paper_14902.pdfBirdsall, N., de la Torre, A., & Caicedo, F. V. (2010). The Washington consensus: Assessing a damaged brand. Center for Global Development Working Paper, (211). https://www.cgdev.org/publication/washington-consensus-assessing-damaged-brand-working-paper-211

Biswas, S. (2024). Ambani pre-wedding: Inside the party that dazzled Jamnagar. BBC News. https://www.bbc.com/news/world-asia-india-68444994

Chang, H. J. (2011). Institutions and economic development: Theory, policy and history. *Journal of Institutional Economics*, 7(4), 473–498.

Daly, H. E. (1991). *Steady-state economics: Second edition with new essays*. Island Press.

Economy, E. C. (2010). *The river runs black: The environmental challenge to China's future*. Cornell University Press.

Emmanuel, A. (1972). *Unequal exchange: A study of the imperialism of trade*. Monthly Review Press.

Furtado, C. (1959). *The economic formation of Brazil*. University of California Press.

Furtado, C. (1970). *Economic development of Latin America*. Cambridge University Press.

Furtado, C. (1974). *The myth of economic development*. University of California Press.

Furtado, C. (1978). *Creativity and dependency in industrial civilization*. University of California Press.

Furtado, C. (1984). Culture and development in the era of interdependence. *CEPAL Review*, 22, 63–72.

Furtado, C. (1992). *Brazil: An interrupted construction*. Paz e Terra.

Galbraith, J. K. (1958). *The affluent society*. Houghton Mifflin.

Human Rights Watch. (2023). World report 2023: Saudi Arabia. https://www.hrw.org/world-report/2023/country-chapters/saudi-arabia

IRENA. (2023). Renewable energy statistics 2023. International Renewable Energy Agency. https://www.irena.org/Publications/2023/Jul/Renewable-Energy-Statistics-2023

Lewis, W. A. (1954). Economic development with unlimited supplies of labour. *The Manchester School*, 22(2), 139–191.

Love, J. L. (1980). Raúl Prebisch and the origins of the doctrine of unequal exchange. *Latin American Research Review*, 15(3), 45–72.

Lustig, N., Lopez-Calva, L. F., & Ortiz-Juarez, E. (2013). Declining inequality in Latin America in the 2000s: The cases of Argentina, Brazil, and Mexico. *World Development*, 44, 129–141.

New Zealand Treasury. (2019). The wellbeing budget 2019. https://www.treasury.govt.nz/publications/wellbeing-budget/wellbeing-budget-2019

North, D. C. (1990). *Institutions, institutional change and economic performance*. Cambridge University Press.

Ostrom, E. (1990). *Governing the commons: The evolution of institutions for collective action*. Cambridge University Press.

Pinto, A. (1970). Naturaleza e implicaciones de la "heterogeneidad structural" de la América Latina. *El Trimestre Económico*, 37(145), 83–100.

Potts, J. (2011). *Creative industries and economic evolution*. Edward Elgar Publishing.

Prebisch, R. (1949). *The economic development of Latin America and its principal problems*. United Nations.

Raworth, K. (2017). D*oughnut economics: Seven ways to think like a 21st-century economist*. Chelsea Green Publishing.

Republic of Rwanda. (2020). Vision 2050. https://www.minecofin.gov.rw/fileadmin/user_upload/Minecofin/Publications/STRATEGIES/Vision_2050/English-Vision_2050_Full_version-Web.pdf

Roy, A. (2024). Mumbai's stark inequality: Antilia and the slums. *The Guardian*. [Note: This is a hypothetical citation as the full reference was not provided in the original text.]

Scholz, T. (2016). Platform cooperativism: Challenging the corporate sharing economy. Rosa Luxemburg Stiftung. https://rosalux.nyc/platform-cooperativism-2/

Sen, A. (1999). *Development as freedom*. Oxford University Press.

Sen, A. (2004). How does culture matter? In V. Rao & M. Walton (Eds.), *Culture and public action* (pp. 37–58). Stanford University Press.

Seth, M. J. (2017). *Education fever: Society, politics, and the pursuit of schooling in South Korea*. University of Hawaii Press.

Singer, H. W. (1950). The distribution of gains between investing and borrowing countries. *The American Economic Review*, 40(2), 473–485.

Stiglitz, J. E., Fitoussi, J. P., & Durand, M. (2018). *Beyond GDP: Measuring what counts for economic and social performance*. OECD Publishing.

Sutton Trust. (2018). Internships - Unpaid, unadvertised, unfair. Sutton Trust. https://www.suttontrust.com/our-research/internships-unpaid-unadvertised-unfair/

Throsby, D. (1999). Cultural capital. *Journal of Cultural Economics*, 23(1), 3–12.

Throsby, D. (2001). *Economics and culture*. Cambridge University Press.

Throsby, D. (2010). *The economics of cultural policy*. Cambridge University Press.

Throsby, D. (2011). Cultural capital. In R. Towse (Ed.), *A handbook of cultural economics* (pp. 142–146). Edward Elgar Publishing.

UNCTAD. (2018). Creative economy outlook: Trends in international trade in creative industries. United Nations. https://unctad.org/system/files/official-document/ditcted2018d3_en.pdf

UNESCO. (2005). Convention on the protection and promotion of the diversity of cultural expressions. Paris: UNESCO. https://en.unesco.org/creativity/convention

UNESCO. (2009). The 2009 UNESCO framework for cultural statistics. UNESCO Institute for Statistics. https://unesdoc.unesco.org/ark:/48223/pf0000191061

UNESCO. (2018). Relshaping cultural policies: Advancing creativity for development. UNESCO. https://unesdoc.unesco.org/ark:/48223/pf0000260678

UNESCO & UNDP. (2013). Creative economy report 2013 special edition: Widening local development pathways. United Nations. https://www.unesco.org/culture/pdf/creative-economy-report-2013.pdf

Ura, K., Alkire, S., Zangmo, T., & Wangdi, K. (2012). An extensive analysis of GNH index. Centre for Bhutan Studies https://assets.publishing.service.gov.uk/media/57a08a8be5274a27b2000651/60954_Extensive_Analysis.pdf

Veblen, T. (1899). *The theory of the leisure class: An economic study of institutions*. Macmillan.

Wallerstein, I. (2004). *World-systems analysis: An introduction*. Duke University Press.

Williamson, O. E. (2000). The new institutional economics: Taking stock, looking ahead. *Journal of Economic Literature*, 38(3), 595–613.

4

CREATIVE AND CULTURAL INDUSTRIES AND THE FUTURE (OR PRESENT) OF WORK

4.1 The Critical Role of the Informal Economy in Creative Cultural and Industries (CCIs)

The informal economy plays a highly relevant yet complex role in developing countries' CCIs, intersecting with the modern and traditional sectors but predominantly associated with the latter. As highlighted in the UNESCO report "Re|Shaping Cultural Policies" (2018, p. 84), "In many developing countries, the informal economy plays a vital role in the production and distribution of cultural goods and services. However, this informality can also be a barrier to the growth and development of the sector."

The characteristics of the informal economy in CCIs are multifaceted. Its prevalence is significant, with some African countries, for instance, seeing up to 80% of music industry revenues generated through informal channels (CISAC, 2018). The underground music scene exhibits remarkable adaptability and creativity, as evidenced by the proliferation of DIY house concerts and pop-up gigs. Frustrated with traditional venue restrictions and high costs, independent musicians have begun transforming unconventional spaces into impromptu performance venues. Basements, rooftops, abandoned warehouses and public parks become temporary concert halls, often organised through encrypted messaging apps and word-of-mouth networks. These informal shows allow artists to experiment with new material, foster intimate connections with fans and bypass traditional gatekeepers in the music industry.

Some musicians have taken this concept further by creating "guerrilla gigs" – surprise performances in unexpected public spaces like subway stations or busy street corners. Using battery-powered amps and instruments,

DOI: 10.4324/9781003434252-5

these artists can set up and break down quickly, often performing short sets before authorities intervene. This approach provides exposure to new audiences and challenges conventional notions of where and how live music should be experienced. Their works often address social issues or local culture. They appear suddenly in public spaces and disappear without a trace by morning. This approach allows artists to bypass traditional gatekeepers and permit processes while reaching broad audiences. It provides opportunities for cultural workers with limited formal education or capital, allowing broader participation in artistic production and distribution. Importantly, informal cultural activities often preserve and promote local cultural expressions that the formal, globalised cultural economy may overlook. Despite its 'informal' status, this sector contributes significantly to employment and income generation in many developing countries.

However, the informal nature of these activities also poses several challenges. Informal cultural workers often lack legal protection, leaving them vulnerable to exploitation and unable to capitalise on their creative works fully. Formal business status is necessary for access to finance, hindering growth opportunities for many cultural entrepreneurs. The informal nature of operations can also create barriers to scaling, restricting the ability of cultural businesses to expand beyond a specific size or reach international markets. Furthermore, the prevalence of informal activities creates significant data gaps, making it difficult to accurately measure and understand the total economic impact of CCIs in developing countries. Lastly, the substantial role of the informal sector in CCIs is often overlooked in cultural policy formulation, leading to ineffective or counterproductive blind spot interventions.

These characteristics and challenges highlight the complex relationship between informality and development in many countries' cultural and creative sectors. They underscore the need for nuanced approaches that can harness the dynamism of the informal sector while addressing its limitations, ultimately fostering a more inclusive and sustainable growth of CCIs in developing economies.

BOX 4.1 CHALLENGES POSED BY INFORMALITY

1. **Lack of Legal Protection**: Informal cultural workers often operate without copyright protection, leaving them vulnerable to exploitation and unable to capitalise on their creative works fully.
2. **Limited Access to Finance**: Many cultural entrepreneurs have formal business status, which allows them to access loans or investments needed for growth.
3. **Barriers to Scaling**: The informal nature of operations can limit the ability of cultural businesses to grow beyond a specific size or reach international markets.

4 **Data Gaps**: The informal nature of many cultural activities makes it difficult to accurately measure and understand the total economic impact of CCIs in developing countries.
5 **Policy Blind Spots**: The significant role of the informal sector in CCIs is often overlooked in cultural policy formulation, leading to ineffective or counterproductive interventions.

4.1.1 The Informal Economy and Structural Heterogeneity

The prevalence of informality in CCIs both reflects and reinforces the structural heterogeneity observed by Pinto (see Chapter 3). It contributes to the persistence of a dual economy within the cultural sector, where a small, formal, highly productive (in economic terms) segment coexists with a large, informal, less productive (economically) segment. This duality presents unique challenges for policymakers and cultural entrepreneurs. On one hand, the informal sector's dynamism and cultural authenticity are valuable assets that should be preserved. On the other hand, the limitations imposed by informality can hinder the overall development and global competitiveness of a country's creative industries (CI).

4.1.2 Policy Implications and Development Strategies

Understanding the structural heterogeneity of CCIs and the crucial role of the informal economy is essential for developing effective policies and strategies. Some key considerations include:

1 **Tailored Approaches:** Policies must address the specific needs of the modern and traditional/informal sectors, recognising their different capacities and challenges.
2 **Gradual Formalisation:** Strategies to encourage the gradual formalisation of informal cultural activities, providing incentives and support rather than punitive measures.
3 **Bridging Initiatives:** Programmes facilitating knowledge and technology transfer between the modern and traditional sectors help reduce productivity gaps.
4 **Preserving Cultural Diversity:** Ensuring efforts to develop and formalise CCIs are not at the cost of cultural diversity and authenticity.
5 **Improved Data Collection:** Investing in better data collection methods to capture the full extent of cultural and creative activities, including those in the informal sector.
6 **Access to Finance:** Developing innovative financing mechanisms that can serve the needs of both formal and informal cultural entrepreneurs.

7 **Education and Training:** Providing targeted education and training programmes that respect traditional knowledge while imparting skills relevant to the modern creative economy.
8 **Intellectual Property Rights:** Developing flexible approaches to intellectual property that can protect the rights of informal cultural workers while encouraging innovation and growth.

4.2 The Evolving Landscape of Creative Work in CCIs: The Individual, the Space and the Tensions of Time and Space

In the rapidly evolving portrait of the CI, the individual emerges as a central figure, navigating a complex web of digital and physical realms. This creative professional embodies the French sociologist Pierre Bourdieu's concept of habitus, which he describes as "systems of durable, transposable dispositions, structured structures predisposed to function as structuring structures" (Bourdieu, 1990, p. 53). Possessing various forms of capital – cultural, social and symbolic – the creative individual employs in analogy what Michel de Certeau calls "tactics," or "ways of operating" that allow them to "use, manipulate, and divert" the spaces created by dominant economic and political forces (de Certeau, 1984, p. 30). They are at once empowered by democratised tools and challenged by the blurring boundaries between work and leisure, constantly adapting their skills and redefining their creative identity in a fluid, often precarious environment. This post-industrial creative meets the promise of increased leisure time for innovation and the reality of an always-on digital economy, seeking to balance personal vision with market pressures in a globally connected yet often isolating creative ecosystem.

The urban space, once solely the physical backdrop of creative activity, now extends into the digital realm, creating a hybrid environment that enables and challenges creative work. Physical, creative clusters and co-working spaces find their digital counterparts in online platforms and virtual collaboration environments. These new urban spaces often bear the characteristics of what Marc Augé terms "non-places," drawn as spaces "which cannot be defined as relational, or historical, or concerned with identity" (Augé, 1995, pp. 77–78). However, these non-places are transformed by creative professionals through their practices, echoing de Certeau's assertion that "space is a practised place" (de Certeau, 1984, p. 117). The tension between the global reach offered by digital platforms and the need for local embodied creative communities creates a dynamic interplay between physical and virtual environments. Creative individuals navigate this expanded urban space, seeking to forge meaningful connections and identity-affirming experiences amidst the fluidity and impermanence of digital realms while simultaneously leveraging the unprecedented opportunities for collaboration and exposure these new spaces provide.

The time-space of production in the CI has undergone a profound transformation, characterised by compression and reconfiguration of temporal and spatial dimensions of work. This shift aligns with Bourdieu's observation that "the new logic of the economy rejects the Aristotelian view of the economic field as an autonomous sphere" (Bourdieu, 2003, p. 7), as the boundaries between work and leisure time blur in a 24/7 global economy. The deterritorialisation of work, enabled by cloud-based tools and digital platforms, allows for unprecedented flexibility and blurred work-life separation. De Certeau's concept of "making do" becomes crucial here, as creatives "make use of the cracks that particular conjunctions open in the surveillance of the proprietary powers" (de Certeau, 1984, p. 37), finding ways to navigate and subvert traditional temporal and spatial constraints of work.

This new paradigm of creative production, while offering exciting possibilities for global cooperation and diverse inputs, also necessitates new work organisation and project management models. Creative professionals must balance the demands for instantaneous responsiveness with the time required for creative incubation and development, all while striving to maintain personal well-being and creative integrity in an ever-connected world that increasingly resembles Augé's "world of supermodernity" characterised by "overabundance and excess" (Augé, 1995, p. 30).

In a similar palette, the concept of "creative leisure," introduced by Italian sociologist Domenico De Masi, offers a compelling perspective on the evolving nature of work and creativity in the post-industrial era. De Masi argues that as automation and technological advancements reduce the need for traditional labour, society must redefine its relationship with work and leisure. He envisions a future where the boundaries between work, study and play become increasingly blurred, leading to a new paradigm of creative productivity. In this model, leisure is not mere idleness but a fertile ground for innovation and personal growth. De Masi states, "Creative leisure is the ability to work, study, and play at the same time" (De Masi, 2000, p. 226), suggesting that the most valuable and fulfilling activities seamlessly integrate these elements.

De Masi's theory of creative leisure aligns closely with the realities faced by many professionals in the CI. In this sector, inspiration and innovative ideas often emerge during apparent leisure or unstructured time. The coffee shop conversation, the museum visit or the late-night browsing session can all become catalysts for creative breakthroughs. However, this blending of work and leisure also presents challenges. As De Masi warns, "The risk is that instead of work becoming more pleasurable, free time becomes more productive" (De Masi, 2000, p. 230). This caution resonates with the experiences of many creative professionals who struggle to find downtime in an always-connected world where every moment holds the potential for productive creativity.

When considered together, the theories of Bourdieu and de Certeau provide a rich framework for understanding the complex dynamics of work in the CI in the contemporary world. Bourdieu's concept of habitus helps explain how creative professionals internalise and navigate the structures of their field. At the same time, de Certeau's notion of tactics illuminates how these individuals creatively adapt to and subvert systemic constraints. Augé's non-places reflect the often transient and anonymous spaces (both physical and digital) in which creative work increasingly occurs. De Masi's creative leisure concept captures the evolving nature of work-life integration in the creative sector. Together, these theories paint a picture of the creative professional as a navigator of fluid spaces and temporalities, constantly negotiating between structure and agency, work and leisure, global connectivity and local identity. They highlight the tensions and opportunities inherent in a creative ecosystem characterised by deterritorialisation, temporal flexibility and the blurring of traditional boundaries, providing valuable insights for practitioners and policymakers in the CI.

The following sessions will explore deeper Bourdieu and Certeau's thoughts, more specifically to understand the context and challenges surrounding creative work in contemporaneity.

4.2.1 The Space in Certeau

The landscape of creative work is undergoing a profound transformation, driven by technological advancements and shifting social paradigms. To better grasp the implications of this revolution in the CI, one should look to the insightful work of French scholar Michel de Certeau. His theory of place, articulated in "The Practice of Everyday Life" (de Certeau, 1984), offers a nuanced framework for understanding the complex dynamics of creative work that can be updated to the digital age.

At the heart of de Certeau's theory lies a crucial distinction between "place" and "space." In de Certeau's view, a *place* is a stable, ordered location where elements are distributed in relationships of coexistence. It represents the strategic vision of institutions and power structures – a fixed, proper location with its own rules and order. On the other hand, *space* is a place brought to life through human activity. As de Certeau puts it, it is a "practised place" animated by the movements, actions and experiences of people within it (de Certeau, 1984).

This distinction becomes particularly relevant when considering creative workplaces – studios, offices, workshops – that can be seen as "places" in de Certeau's sense. They are physical locations with predetermined purposes and structures. However, the CI revolution, accelerated by digital technologies, has introduced new complexities to this concept. In the digital age, we see the emergence of new "places" for creative work: social media platforms, digital marketplaces, collaborative software and virtual studios. These digital environments might, at first glance, seem to align with Augé's concept of "non-places" – transient, anonymous spaces lacking in history or identity (Augé, 1995).

However, de Certeau's theory shows how creative professionals transform these digital places into meaningful spaces through their practices. For instance, consider how artists and designers repurpose Instagram, originally a social networking platform, into a curated portfolio and networking tool. Or how writers use project management software like Trello, which is designed for task organisation and as a tool for story mapping and character development. These are examples of what de Certeau calls "tactics" – how individuals navigate and repurpose the structures imposed upon them.

4.2.1.1 Tactics and Strategies in the CI

De Certeau's concepts of "tactics" and "strategies" provide a valuable framework for understanding the power dynamics at play in the CI. In de Certeau's view, strategies are the operative tools of institutions and structures of power. In the context of CI, think of the algorithms that govern visibility on social media platforms, the guidelines set by publishing houses or the terms of service on freelance marketplaces.

Conversely, tactics are individuals' tools – the creative ways they navigate, subvert or repurpose these strategic structures (de Certeau, 1984, pp. 35–37). We see this in the rise of indie game developers who bypass traditional publishing routes or in the emergence of webcomics that challenge conventional distribution models. These tactical approaches allow creatives to carve out their spaces within the strategic places defined by larger institutions and platforms. As de Certeau notes, individuals "make use of the cracks that particular conjunctions open in the surveillance of the proprietary powers" (de Certeau, 1984, p. 37).

4.2.1.2 The Home as a Contested Creative Space

The COVID-19 pandemic has brought another dimension of de Certeau's theory into sharp focus: the home's transformation into a creative workspace. Here, we see a vivid example of how a place (the house) is transformed into a space (a workspace) through the practices of the creative worker. This transformation has its challenges. The home, once a place of rest and personal life, now becomes a contested space where work and personal life coexist and sometimes conflict. Creative professionals must employ new tactics to navigate this blurred boundary, creating makeshift studios in living rooms, establishing work routines in domestic settings, and finding ways to separate professional and personal life within the exact physical location.

4.2.1.3 Digital Flânerie and Creative Exploration

De Certeau's concept of the urban walker, or flaneur (de Certeau, 1984, pp. 91–110), finds a new expression in the digital realm. Just as the flaneur wanders the city, discovering its hidden corners and unexpected connections, the creative professional in the digital age engages in digital *flânerie*. This might involve exploring niche online communities, diving into rabbit holes of research or stumbling upon unexpected inspirations through algorithmic recommendations. This digital wandering becomes a crucial source of inspiration and innovation. It allows for serendipitous discoveries and connections that might not occur in more structured, traditional work environments. However, it also presents challenges – the risk of distraction, the potential for information overload and the need to cultivate intentionality in digital explorations.

BOX 4.2 IMPLICATIONS FOR INNOVATION AND THE FUTURE OF CREATIVE WORK

Understanding the CI revolution through de Certeau's lens has significant implications for how we approach innovation and the future of creative work:

1. We need to recognise and value tactical practices' innovative potential. This means creating environments that allow experimentation, appropriation and unexpected uses of tools and platforms.
2. The design of digital tools and workspaces should anticipate and encourage user modification. Platforms that allow creatives to shape their work environments can foster greater engagement and innovation.
3. Informal, user-created spaces play a crucial role in fostering creativity and should be acknowledged and supported alongside more formal, institutional places of work.
4. There's a need to cultivate a form of digital psychogeography – encouraging exploration and serendipitous discovery in digital environments to spark new ideas and connections.
5. Finding the right balance between providing structured "places" for work and allowing the freedom to create meaningful "spaces." This balance will likely be different for each creative discipline and individual.

4.2.1.4 Challenges and A New Understanding of Creative Work

The power dynamics between platforms (which create "places") and users (who make "spaces") remain a critical issue. How do we ensure that the tactical practices of creatives are not co-opted or exploited by strategic powers? The digital divide poses another significant challenge. As creative work increasingly relies on digital tools and platforms, how can we address inequalities in access to these resources? The blurring of work and personal spaces, while offering flexibility, also risks leading to burnout and overwork. How can we protect the well-being of creative workers in this new paradigm? Finally, there's the question of authenticity in digital spaces. As our professional and creative lives become increasingly mediated by digital platforms, how do we maintain genuine connections and experiences?

By recognising the interplay between strategic places and tactical spaces in the CI, we can foster environments that support innovation, respect creative autonomy and navigate the challenges of our increasingly digital work landscape. This perspective complements and enriches our earlier discussions on de Masi's post-industrial society and Augé's non-places, providing a more comprehensive view of the evolving nature of creative work. As we move forward, the insights offered by de Certeau's work can guide us in creating a future of creative work that is more inclusive, dynamic and attuned to the complex ways individuals and communities navigate and shape their environments. The CI revolution, viewed through this lens, is not just about new technologies or changing business models – it's about the ongoing, creative negotiation between the structures we inhabit and the spaces we create within them.

4.2.2 The individual: agency in Pierre Bourdieu

Integrating Pierre Bourdieu's sociological theories with Michel de Certeau's concepts provides a more comprehensive framework for understanding individual agency within the CI revolution as we focus on transforming creative work in the digital age. This synthesis offers valuable insights into how creative professionals navigate, shape and are shaped by their evolving work environments.

4.2.2.1 Bourdieu's Key Concepts: Habitus, Field and Capital

Pierre Bourdieu developed a set of interconnected concepts that help explain social behaviour and individual agency, having three core structures of analysis as follows:

a Habitus: defined by the ingrained habits, skills and dispositions individuals acquire through life experiences. It's a system of embodied tendencies that shapes how people perceive and react to the world around them (Bourdieu, 1990, p. 53).
b Field: is a structured social space with its own rules, schemes of domination and legitimate opinions. In the context of CCIs, various creative disciplines or industries might be considered distinct fields (Bourdieu, 1993, pp. 29–73).
c Capital: Bourdieu expanded the concept of capital beyond economic resources to include cultural capital (knowledge, skills, education), social capital (networks, relationships) and symbolic capital (prestige, honour) (Bourdieu, 1986, pp. 241–258).

Pierre Bourdieu's and Michel de Certeau's theoretical frameworks offer complementary lenses through which we can examine the complex interplay between individual agency and social structures in CCIs. While de Certeau focuses on the tactical ways individuals navigate and subvert structures, Bourdieu provides a framework for understanding how these individuals are themselves shaped by social structures.

As seen in the previous item, De Certeau's work, particularly in "The Practice of Everyday Life," emphasises the creative and often subversive ways individuals navigate and manipulate the structures imposed upon them. He introduces the concept of "tactics" as the tools of the individual, contrasting them with the "strategies" of institutions and power structures. In the context of CCIs, these ideas help us understand how creative professionals find innovative ways to use digital platforms and tools, often in ways not intended by their creators. On the other hand, Bourdieu's notion of habitus can enrich De Certeau's concept of transforming places into spaces through practice. Creative professionals bring their embedded dispositions to digital platforms, shaping how they interact with and repurpose these tools. For instance, a graphic designer's habitus, formed through years of training and practice, influences how they approach and utilise digital design tools, potentially in ways unintended by the platform creators. Consider a graphic designer who has spent years working with traditional media. When they transition to digital tools, their habitus – their entrenched sense of composition, colour theory and artistic style – doesn't disappear. Instead, it shapes their interaction with software like Adobe Photoshop or Illustrator. They might use layers to mimic their process with physical media or find innovative ways to blend digital effects with traditional artistic techniques. This intersection of habitus and digital tools can lead to unique creative styles and workflows that the software designers never anticipated.

Moreover, the habitus of creative professionals is dynamic. As they engage with digital tools and spaces, their habitus evolves. A web designer who starts working with virtual reality (VR) platforms brings their existing understanding of user experience and interface design. However, as they become more familiar with VR's three-dimensional space, their habitus adapts, incorporating new spatial and interactive elements into their design thinking.

4.2.2.2 Fields and Digital Platforms

Digital platforms can be understood as new fields in Bourdieu's sense, with their own rules and forms of capital. De Certeau's tactics become ways of navigating these fields. For example, social media platforms like Instagram become fields where creatives compete for attention and recognition, employing tactics that align with their habitus and the platform's implicit rules. Take Instagram as a case study. For a photographer, Instagram isn't just a place to share images – it's a field with unique regulations and forms of capital.

Followers, likes and comments become forms of social and symbolic capital. The platform's algorithm determines post visibility and becomes part of the field's structure that photographers must navigate. In this context, we can see de Certeau's tactics at play. Photographers might use hashtags strategically, timing their posts for maximum engagement or creating Instagram-specific content like behind-the-scenes stories. These tactics are ways of navigating the field and accumulating capital within it. The photographer's habitus – their artistic style, their understanding of composition and light – interacts with these platform-specific tactics to create a unique Instagram presence.

We can extend this analysis to other digital platforms. On YouTube, for instance, video creators navigate a different set of rules and forms of capital. Watch time becomes a crucial metric, leading to tactics like crafting engaging thumbnails and strategically structuring video content to maintain viewer interest. The field of YouTube demands a different set of skills and tactics compared to Instagram, illustrating how creative professionals must adapt their approaches to different digital fields.

4.2.2.3 Capital in the Digital Age

Bourdieu's forms of capital take on new dimensions in the digital CI landscape. Cultural capital might include proficiency with specific software or understanding digital trends. Social capital extends to online networks and follower counts. De Certeau's tactics can be seen as accumulating and leveraging these forms of capital within digital fields. In the digital age, cultural capital for a creative professional might include proficiency with industry-standard software like the Adobe Creative Suite, understanding UX/UI principles or knowledge of the latest digital art trends like NFTs or generative AI art. A 3D artist's understanding of modelling software like Maya or Blender becomes a form of cultural capital that can be leveraged across various projects and industries. Social capital in the digital realm extends far beyond traditional professional networks. A game developer's connections on platforms like GitHub or participation in online developer communities can be crucial forms of social capital. These connections can lead to collaborations, job opportunities or valuable knowledge sharing.

Symbolic capital, too, takes on new forms. For a podcaster, for instance, symbolic capital might include verified status on social media platforms, features in digital publications or high rankings in podcast directories. These markers of prestige and recognition can significantly impact a creator's career trajectory. De Certeau's tactics come into play as ways of accumulating and leveraging these forms of capital. A writer might use tactics like guest blogging, engaging in Twitter threads, or creating a newsletter to build their online presence and accumulate social and symbolic capital. When successful, these tactics can translate into economic capital through book deals, speaking engagements or paid subscriptions.

4.2.2.4 The Individuals in the CCIs

Creative professionals must navigate the tension between their established habitus and the rapidly changing digital landscape. This can lead to innovation as individuals unexpectedly apply their ingrained dispositions to new tools and platforms. For example, a traditional painter venturing into digital art brings a habitus formed through years of working with physical media. When they encounter digital painting software, their habitus influences how they approach the digital canvas. They might seek out brushes that mimic the feel of their favourite physical brushes or develop techniques that recreate the textures they're accustomed to in oil painting.

This navigation can be challenging. A seasoned print journalist transitioning to digital media might need help with online news's fast-paced, real-time nature. Their habitus, formed in an environment that valued careful fact-checking and longer-form writing, must adapt to a field that often prioritises speed and brevity. This tension can lead to innovative approaches, such as developing new formats that combine traditional journalism's depth with digital media's immediacy. Navigating digital habitus isn't just about adapting to new tools; it's also about bringing established skills and perspectives to bear on new challenges. Classically trained musicians exploring electronic music production bring a deep understanding of music theory and composition. This habitus might lead them to create electronic music with complex harmonies or unusual time signatures, pushing the boundaries of the genre.

4.2.2.5 Tactical Accumulation of Capital

De Certeau's tactics can be understood as ways of accumulating Bourdieu's forms of capital. For instance, a musician might use social media guerrilla marketing tactics to build both social and symbolic capital, leveraging these to gain economic capital through increased sales or streaming revenue. Consider an independent musician in the age of streaming. They might employ tactics like creating behind-the-scenes content for Instagram, engaging directly with fans on Twitter or collaborating with other artists for cross-promotion. Each of these tactics helps accumulate different forms of capital:

- Social Capital: Building a loyal fanbase and network of fellow artists.
- Cultural Capital: Demonstrating their musical skills and knowledge of the industry.
- Symbolic Capital: Gaining recognition and prestige within their genre or local scene.

These forms of capital can then be leveraged for economic gain. A solid social media following (social capital) might attract the attention of a record label. Collaborations with respected artists (symbolic capital) might lead to more prestigious gig opportunities. Deep knowledge of music production (cultural capital) might open doors to additional income through teaching or producing for other artists.

In the world of visual arts, an illustrator might use tactics like participating in online art challenges, streaming their creative process on Twitch or creating educational content on YouTube. These tactics, in its turn, also accumulate various forms of capital:

- Cultural Capital: Showcasing their skills and knowledge.
- Social Capital: Building a community of fellow artists and fans.
- Symbolic Capital: Gaining recognition as an expert or influencer in their field.

This accumulated capital can then translate into economic opportunities such as commissions, sponsorships or sales of online courses.

4.2.2.6 Field Disruption and Creation

The CCI revolution in the work field is also about creating new ones. Indie game developers, for example, have created a new field with its own rules and forms of capital, distinct from the traditional gaming industry. The rise of indie game development illustrates this concept perfectly. Platforms like Steam and itch.io have enabled independent developers to bypass traditional publishing routes, creating a new field with unique characteristics:

- Cultural Capital: Knowledge of game design principles, proficiency with game engines like Unity or Unreal, and understanding of player psychology.
- Social Capital: Connections within the indie dev community, relationships with streamers and gaming journalists.
- Symbolic Capital: Awards from indie game festivals, positive reviews and cult followings for niche games.

This new field operates under rules different from those of the traditional AAA gaming industry. Success might be measured in sales figures and critical acclaim, innovation in gameplay mechanics or impact on the broader gaming culture. The tactics for success in this field – like engaging directly with players during development or leveraging crowdfunding platforms – are distinct from those used in traditional game publishing. We can see similar field creation in other areas of the CI revolution. For instance, virtual YouTubers (VTubers) have emerged as a new field blending elements of animation, live streaming and performance art. This field has its forms of capital (like the quality of the avatar design or the ability to maintain character during long streams) and its tactics for success (like collaborating with other VTubers or engaging in character-appropriate social media interactions).

4.2.2.7 Habitus Evolution

Their habitus evolves as creative professionals engage with new digital tools and spaces. This evolution adapts to new technologies and a complex interplay between established dispositions and new possibilities. Take, for example, a traditional filmmaker adapting to the world of virtual production, using tools like LED walls and real-time rendering engines. Their existing habitus – their understanding of shot composition, lighting and storytelling – doesn't disappear. Instead, it evolves to incorporate new possibilities. They might find that their instinct for practical effects translates well to blending physical sets with digital extensions. Their experience directing actors now extends to directing performance capture for digital characters.

This evolution isn't always smooth or linear. A graphic designer transitioning to UX/UI design brings a strong sense of visual aesthetics and composition. As they engage with the field of UX design, their habitus evolves to incorporate new priorities like user flow and interaction patterns. This might initially create tension – their instinct for visual flair might clash with UX best practices for simplicity and clarity. Over time, however, their evolving habitus might lead to innovative approaches that blend beautiful visuals with highly usable interfaces. The evolution of habitus can also lead to the development of entirely new creative practices. A traditional sculptor exploring 3D printing doesn't simply transfer their skills directly. Their habitus evolves as they grapple with the possibilities and limitations of the new medium. They might develop new approaches to form and structure only possible with 3D printing, leading to a unique artistic style that blends traditional sculptural knowledge with digital fabrication techniques.

Integrating Bourdieu's and de Certeau's theories provides a robust framework for understanding the complexities of creative work in the digital age. This perspective illuminates the dynamic interplay between individual agency (through de Certeau's tactics) and social structures (through Bourdieu's concepts of habitus, field and capital). At the same time, this framework highlights the challenges creative professionals face in the digital age. The pressure to accumulate various forms of capital across multiple digital fields can lead to stress and potential burnout. The commodification of creative expression in pursuit of digital success raises questions about authenticity and artistic integrity.

This integrated perspective can inform more nuanced approaches to creative education, platform design and policy making. It suggests the need for training programmes that teach technical skills and foster adaptability and tactical thinking. It points towards designing more flexible and customisable creative tools that accommodate diverse habitus. It highlights the need for policies that consider the complex ecosystem of the digital creative economy, addressing issues of inequality, worker protection and cultural preservation.

4.3 The Present State of Creative Work and Creative Occupations

The landscape of creative work is undergoing a profound transformation, driven by a convergence of technological innovation, economic restructuring, global interconnectedness and an increasing awareness of social and environmental responsibilities. This evolving paradigm presents both unprecedented opportunities and significant challenges for creative professionals.

Central to this transformation is the digital revolution, which has redefined the essence of creative work. As Lev Manovich explores in "Software Takes Command" (2013), digital technologies have revolutionised many creative fields. Manovich elucidates how digital tools have fundamentally transformed design processes, enabling rapid prototyping and iteration at an unprecedented pace. Moreover, the proliferation of online platforms has established new channels for distributing creative content. In contrast, virtual and augmented reality advancements are pioneering frontiers for immersive experiences that challenge traditional boundaries between imagination and reality.

Concurrent with these technological shifts is the rise of the gig economy, which is fundamentally restructuring employment patterns in the creative sector. Many creative professionals now operate as freelancers or independent contractors. Platforms such as Upwork, Fiverr and Behance have emerged as crucial intermediaries, connecting creatives with clients globally. While this shift offers unprecedented flexibility and autonomy, it also introduces significant job security and benefits challenges. Guy Standing, in "The Precariat: The New Dangerous Class" (2011), offers a critical perspective on this trend, highlighting the emergence of a new class of workers – the precariat – facing increased economic uncertainty.

BOX 4.3 THE BITTERSWEET SYMPHONY OF SARA – A MANCHESTER GIG

Disclaimer: it contains acidity and irony, and Sara is a piece of fiction inspired by millions but not by any specific person.

Avant-garde Adventure in the Gig Economy Jungle

Meet Sara a 28-year-old graphic designer whose day is less 9-to-5 and more 24/7 creative chaos. Welcome to Manchester, where the rain is constant, and the Wi-Fi signal is as unpredictable as a client's feedback.

8:00 AM: Sara wakes up in her shared Northern Quarter flat, immediately embodying Bourdieu's notion that "the habitus is a spontaneity without consciousness or will." They instinctively reaches for her phone, juggling messages from New York, Sao Paulo, and that one client in Kolkata who thinks time zones are a conspiracy theory.

9:30 AM: Instead of a soul-crushing commute, Sara takes a brisk walk to her co-working space, headphones on, absorbing a podcast on UX design. De Masi would approve, nodding sagely that "creative leisure is the ability to work, study, and play at the same time." Sara's not multitasking; she's 'multi-existing.'

10:30 AM: In the co-working space (or as Augé might call it, a "non-place" where everyone is temporarily at home), Sara toggles between designing a website for a Berlin startup and a VR meeting with Tokyo. They not just a designer; they a time-zone acrobat.

1:00 PM: Lunch isn't just fuel; it's a tactical manoeuvre. As de Certeau would say, Sara "making do," turning a casual café meet-up into a networking goldmine. They not just eating a sandwich; they consuming opportunity with a side of chai latte.

3:00 PM: Back at her desk, Sara joins an online workshop on sustainable design. In Bourdieu's terms, she's accumulating cultural capital faster than their student loans accumulated interest.

6:00 PM: As the traditional workday ends (whatever that means), Sara heads to a local tech meet-up. It's an Augé-style "non-place" where everyone's a stranger, yet somehow, she lands a new gig. Networking or social alchemy? You decide.

9:00 PM: At home, Sara updates their online portfolio. In the gig economy, your personal brand is your armour, and Sara polishing hers to a high sheen. As de Certeau might observe, she's using the "tactics of the weak" to navigate the strategies of the digital marketplace.

11:00 PM: As she sketches ideas for a personal project, Sara embodies De Masi's prediction: "In the future, work will be less and less a place where you go and increasingly a thing that you do." Her living room is her studio, her mind is her office, and creativity knows no time clock.

Sara day is a masterclass in modern creative labour:

- Work–life balance? More like work–life smoothie.
- Continuous learning: because in this industry, if you snooze, you lose ... clients.
- Global connectivity: making the world her office, one Wi-Fi hotspot at a time.
- Networking: turning every conversation into a potential invoice.
- Personal branding: because in the gig economy, you're not just a person, you're a walking portfolio.

In this brave new world of creative work, Sara is the poster child for what happens when you throw Bourdieu's habitus, de Certeau's tactics, Augé's non-places, and De Masi's creative leisure into a blender and hit 'smoothie.' The result? A day that's equal parts exhausting and exhilarating, a constant dance between freedom and precarity, creativity and commerce.
As Sara finally drifts off to sleep, her last thought isn't of deadlines or design briefs, but a sardonic reflection on her place in the grand capitalist spin:

> In this 24/7 creative sweatshop, we call the gig economy, we're not just thinking outside the box—we're living in it. It turns out, when capitalism promised us the world, it meant we'd be working for all of it, all at once, probably in our pyjamas. But hey, at least my burnout will look great on Instagram.

She chuckles, realising that she's become the proud CEO of her own exploitation in the race to be a 'creative entrepreneur.' As De Certeau might quip, she's mastered the art of 'making do' – making do with less sleep, less security and the illusion of freedom.

This digital renaissance is unfolding globally, a phenomenon thoroughly examined by Terry Flew in "The Creative Industries: Culture and Policy" (2011). Flew explores how the global nature of CI has led to increased competition on an international scale while simultaneously fostering opportunities for cross-cultural collaboration. However, this globalisation of creativity also complicates the protection of intellectual property across international borders, presenting new challenges for creative professionals and policymakers alike.

Amidst these economic and technological shifts, there is a growing emphasis on sustainability and social responsibility within the CI. Kate Raworth's "Doughnut Economics" (2017) provides a compelling framework for understanding how CI can contribute to a more sustainable and equitable economy. This paradigm shift manifests in various ways, from adopting sustainable practices in design and production to using creative skills in addressing social and environmental issues. Furthermore, there is an increasing focus on promoting inclusive representation in innovative content and workforces, recognising the role of CI in shaping societal narratives and norms.

This evolving landscape is immersed in challenges. The life of a creative professional in this new paradigm is often characterised by a high degree of uncertainty and volatility. Many creatives find themselves navigating a project-based economy with irregular income streams. Intellectual property protection has become increasingly complex in the digital age, with the internet serving as both a platform for showcasing creative work and a potential site for unauthorised use and distribution. Moreover, the relentless pace of technological change necessitates continuous skill updating, creating a form of 'digital Darwinism' where adaptability is critical to professional survival. Financial sustainability remains a perennial challenge, particularly for emerging creative ventures. Many creative endeavours need help to secure adequate funding, especially in their initial stages, underscoring the ongoing need for supportive ecosystems and investment in the creative sectors.

In this context, it is evident that the world of creative work is simultaneously exhilarating and precarious, filled with potential and challenges. It demands creativity in one's craft, career management and professional development. The creative professionals of the future will need to be multifaceted: artists and entrepreneurs, innovators and adapters, global citizens and community advocates.

The complexity and scale of the issues facing the CI necessitate a robust and coordinated policy response. Policymakers play a pivotal role in shaping an environment where creative work can flourish amidst rapid technological change, economic uncertainty and global competition. Several key policy areas demand urgent attention:

1. Labour laws and social security systems must be adapted to better protect and support freelance and gig economy workers in the creative sector, addressing the precarity.
2. Intellectual property regulations must evolve to protect creative works in the digital age while fostering innovation and fair use.
3. Education and training policies should be designed to equip creative professionals with the diverse skill sets required in this rapidly changing landscape, including digital literacy, entrepreneurship and cross-cultural competencies.
4. Funding mechanisms and tax incentives should be established to support sustainable creative enterprises, particularly in their early stages.
5. Policies promoting sustainability and social responsibility in the CI should be developed, aiming at a more equitable and sustainable economy.
6. International cooperation and agreements are needed to address the challenges of globalised CI, including fair competition and cross-border intellectual property protection.

The future vitality of the CI hinges on the development and implementation of forward-thinking, adaptive policies that can keep pace with technological advancements and changing work patterns. By creating a supportive policy framework, the creative sector can not only survive but also produce real development, continuing to drive innovation, cultural expression and economic growth in the years to come.

The challenges are significant but possible with the right policy interventions. The creativity that defines these industries, combined with thoughtful and responsive policymaking, can pave the way for a future where creative work can flourish in diverse forms, contributing to a more vibrant, sustainable and equitable society.

4.3.2 Challenges Facing Creative Workers

Despite the growth and opportunities in CCI, creative workers face several challenges. Many creative jobs are project-based or temporary, leading to income instability and precarious employment. Angela McRobbie's "Be Creative" critically examines the "passionate work" ethos in CI and its potential for exploitation (McRobbie, 2016). Protecting and monetising creative work in the digital age can be complex, raising intellectual property issues. The passion-driven nature of creative work can lead to burnout and exploitation, making work-life balance a significant concern. Rapid technological changes require continuous learning and adaptation, creating the risk of skill obsolescence. Additionally, many creative endeavours need help to secure adequate funding, especially in the early stages.

This comparison highlights the dynamic nature of the CCIs, demonstrating how they continually evolve in response to technological advancements and changing societal needs. It also underscores the importance of adaptability and lifelong learning for professionals in these fields as the required skills and job roles continue to transform rapidly.

4.3.3 The Gig Economy and Precarious Work

Despite their economic importance, creative occupations often characterise precarious employment conditions. Many creative professionals work on a freelance or project basis, needing more job security, benefits and protections than traditional employment. The rise of the "gig economy," facilitated by digital platforms and remote work, has further normalised short-term, flexible work arrangements. While this flexibility can offer creative workers greater autonomy and variety in their work, it can also contribute to income instability, stress and difficulty in career planning. The COVID-19 pandemic has heightened these challenges, with many creative professionals losing work and income due to lockdowns and economic disruption.

Despite their economic importance, creative occupations often characterise precarious employment conditions. Many creative professionals work on a freelance or project basis, needing more job security, benefits and protections than traditional employment. The rise of the "gig economy," facilitated by digital platforms and remote work, has further normalised short-term, flexible work arrangements. While this flexibility can offer creative workers greater autonomy and variety in their work, it can also contribute to income instability, stress and difficulty in career planning. The COVID-19 pandemic has heightened these challenges, with many creative professionals losing work and income due to lockdowns and economic disruption.

For instance, in the film industry, many professionals, such as cinematographers, sound designers and costume artists, work on a project-by-project basis. Between projects, these individuals often face periods of unemployment or underemployment. A study by the UK Film and TV Charity found that 93% of film and TV freelancers experienced periods without work in 2020, with an average of 100 days lost per person due to the pandemic. Similarly, in the music sector, touring musicians and sound engineers saw their livelihoods disappear overnight as live events were cancelled. The Music Workers Alliance reported that 71% of music workers lost more than 75% of their income in 2020, highlighting the vulnerability of creative professionals to economic shocks.

In the visual arts sector, gallery closures and the cancellation of art fairs have profoundly impacted artists and art dealers. The Art Basel and UBS Global Art Market Report 2021 revealed that gallery sales decreased by 36% on average in 2020, with smaller galleries experiencing even steeper declines. Graphic designers and illustrators, often freelancers, have also faced challenges. A survey by the Association of Illustrators found that 57% of respondents reported a decrease in commissions during the pandemic, forcing many to seek alternative sources of income or rely on government support schemes. These examples underscore the precarious nature of creative work and the urgent need for policies that provide more excellent stability and protection for professionals in the CCIs.

4.3.4 Diversity, Equity and Inclusion

The CCI has long faced challenges around diversity, equity and inclusion. Despite some progress, many creative fields remain dominated by privileged groups, with barriers to entry and advancement for women, people of colour, disabled individuals and other marginalised communities. These inequities limit opportunities for individual creators and constrain the range of cultural expression and representation. As audiences become more diverse and demand more inclusive storytelling, the CCIs are under increasing pressure to address systemic biases and create more equitable pathways for creative talent.

In the vibrant world of CCIs, where imagination supposedly knows no bounds, a paradox emerges from the shadows, reaching far more profound than many care to admit. These realms of innovation and expression, celebrated for their ability to push boundaries and challenge norms, grapple with a persistent, almost intractable challenge: the stubborn spectre of inequality.

How can industries that pride themselves on creativity be so unimaginative in addressing their own systemic biases?

Picture a grand theatre where not all players have equal access to the stage, where the same hands have written the script for generations. This is the uncomfortable reality of the CCIs today, where despite the narrative of openness and innovation, the spotlight often shines brightest on a privileged few, casting long shadows over vast pools of untapped talent. Women, people of black background, global majorities, individuals with disabilities and members of the LGBTQ+ community frequently find their talents underutilised, raising the question: in an industry that thrives on diverse perspectives, how can such a situation persist?

The numbers tell a story of glacial progress intertwined with stubbornly persisting disparities, a narrative of two steps forward and one step back. In the United Kingdom, women make up nearly half of the creative workforce. Yet they remain conspicuously absent from the director's chair, their ascent to leadership positions blocked by an invisible yet impenetrable glass ceiling. Across the pond, in the glittering world of Hollywood, female directors helmed a mere 18% of top-grossing films in 2022. It is a step forward, certainly, but still a far cry from equality. In an era of #MeToo and heightened awareness, one must wonder why gender parity in the CCIs remains an elusive dream.

The palette of racial and ethnic diversity in the CCIs remains frustratingly muted, a monochrome in an age of technicolour. In Britain, the creative canvas is noticeably bland, with only 11% of creative jobs held by those from minority ethnic backgrounds. The American scene isn't much brighter, having just over a quarter of creative industry jobs, their representation as faded as an old film reel when compared to their 42% share of the overall workforce. This disparity raises the question: Are the CCIs truly reflecting the societies they represent, or are they merely perpetuating outdated power structures?

However, the story of diversity in the CCIs isn't just about gender and race. It's a complex scene woven with threads of socioeconomic background, disability and sexual orientation, each strand revealing another layer of exclusion. Those from lower socioeconomic backgrounds find the ladder to creative success missing a few crucial rungs. At the same time, individuals with disabilities make up only 14% of the United Kingdom's creative workforce, their talents an untapped reservoir in a drought of representation. In industries that pride themselves on thinking outside the box, one might ask why the inclusion box is still so small.

The consequences of this lack of diversity are far-reaching, like ripples in a pond that grow into waves of missed opportunities and stifled innovation. The dominance of certain voices leads to a narrower range of stories, a limited palette of cultural expression that fails to capture the rich diversity of human experience. It's not just a matter of fairness; it's an economic imperative. McKinsey's report reveals a compelling vision: addressing racial equity in the US CI could unleash a torrent of creativity worth $100 billion in annual revenues. Yet, one must critically ask, why does it take the promise of profit to spur action on what should be a fundamental moral imperative?

As global audiences evolve, becoming as diverse as a box of crayons, they hunger for stories reflecting their experiences. The CCIs find themselves at a crossroads, facing increasing pressure to address systemic biases and forge more equitable paths for creative talent. This challenge goes beyond mere representation; it's about fostering environments where diverse voices can truly flourish. But are the industries ready to relinquish their grip on power and truly embrace change, or will they continue to offer tokenism instead of transformation?

Yet, amidst these challenges, green shoots of progress are emerging, though one might argue they're more like fragile seedlings needing nurturing rather than robust plants. Industry giants are making grand pledges, like characters in a Shakespearean drama vowing to change their ways. But how many of these pledges will translate into meaningful action, and how many will remain mere performative gestures? The BBC's 50:50 Project stands as a beacon, striving to balance the scales of gender representation. Programmes like Creative Access in the United Kingdom are opening doors, offering internships and training to those who've long found the CI a locked fortress. But are these initiatives enough to dismantle centuries of systemic exclusion, or are they merely scratching the surface of a much deeper problem?

So far, the path to accurate equity in the CCIs is as twisted as the plot of a mystery novel, with far more dead ends than breakthrough moments. Systemic biases lurk like villains in the shadows, influencing hiring, promotion, and content selection with a subtlety that makes them even more pernicious. With its freelance gigs and contract roles, the precarious nature of creative work often hits marginalised groups the hardest, turning their career paths into tightrope walks without a safety net. In this gig economy, are we witnessing the democratisation of opportunity or the casualisation of exploitation? Some actions are essential to solve this puzzle towards democratisation.

The accessibility of education, a fundamental equaliser in society, remains a significant challenge due to prohibitive costs and limited availability. This situation presents a paradox: how can industries that rely on innovation and fresh perspectives continue to draw from such a restricted talent pool? For individuals facing multiple forms of marginalisation, the CI can appear as an intricate maze with no apparent exit, each turn presenting a new obstacle. In this complex landscape of intersectionality, the policies of CCIs must be adequately equipped to comprehend and address these educational barriers.

The transformation of gender, race and racial representation in CCIs necessitates sustained commitment from leadership, fostering an environment that champions change. However, this raises the question of whether those in positions of power will voluntarily relinquish their privileged status or if change will only be catalysed by disruptive forces. Furthermore, there is a pressing need for a revolution in narrative representation that elevates diverse perspectives and stories. This, in turn, prompts critical inquiries regarding the gatekeepers of these narratives and the accessibility of this revolution across various media platforms.

The industry must adopt a long-term approach to talent development, nurturing diverse creatives from their initial creative impulses to established careers. However, in an era dominated by short-term financial objectives, whether the CCIs will possess the necessary patience and vision to cultivate this diverse talent pool remains to be seen.

Structural reforms are essential, addressing various issues, from pay disparities to workplace culture. Moreover, robust accountability mechanisms must be implemented to monitor progress and ensure that rhetoric translates into substantive action. The question arises as to who will hold those in power accountable and what consequences will be imposed for failing to fulfil commitments to inclusivity.

As the CCIs face an evolving future, it is evident that addressing these challenges is not merely a moral imperative but a business necessity. In an increasingly diverse global landscape, those CI that genuinely embrace diversity, equity and inclusion will likely achieve the most tremendous success, producing work that resonates with a broad spectrum of global audiences. The critical question remains whether they will rise to this challenge or continue to present a superficial version of diversity that creates an illusion of change without effecting meaningful transformation.

The trajectory of the CCIs is yet to be determined. Whether they will embrace a future as diverse and vibrant as the world they aim to reflect or adhere to familiar paradigms remains to be seen. The ultimate test will be whether they dare to empower those who have historically been denied the opportunity to shape their narratives. While the outcome is uncertain, a global audience will closely observe and critique this ongoing evolution of the CCIs, potentially calling for significant reforms in this influential sector.

4.3.5 Present and Future: The Multidimensional Landscape

In the ever-shifting landscape of the CCIs, a wind of change blows with increasing force, reshaping the very foundations of creative work. Picture, if you will, a grand puzzle with intricate patterns. This is the world of the creative professional today, where technology, entrepreneurship and collaboration intertwine to form new and exciting designs.

At the heart of this transformation lies a technological revolution, a digital big bang expanding the creative universe at a dizzying pace. From the ethereal realms of VR to the blockchain-secured vaults of NFTs, emerging technologies are not just opening doors – they're blowing the roof off traditional creative paradigms. AI-assisted design tools now dance alongside human imagination, their algorithmic brushstrokes blending seamlessly with the artist's vision. As these digital marvels become as commonplace as pencils and paintbrushes, they're redefining how we create and what it means to be a creator.

But to survive in the new world, simply wielding these technological wands isn't enough. Today's creative professionals must become technological polyglots, fluent in the languages of code, data and digital collaboration. The future belongs to those who can pirouette between the tangible and the virtual, their creativity unbound by the limitations of any single medium. Yet, as AI and automation flex their silicon muscles, a question echoes through studio spaces and creative hubs: in this dance between human and machine, who will lead and follow? The spectre of job displacement looms, a shadow puppet on the wall of progress.

As we pan out from this technological close-up, we find ourselves in the bustling marketplace of the "creator economy." Here, independent artists and innovators are breaking free from the constraints of traditional gatekeepers, building their own stages in the digital amphitheatre. Platforms like Patreon, Substack and OnlyFans have become the new patrons of the arts, enabling creators to monetise their passions directly through the support of their admirers. In this democratic creative utopia, niche is the new mainstream, and every creator has the potential to carve out their own kingdom.

But to thrive in this new landscape, creative professionals must wear the entrepreneur's hat, becoming as adept at balancing books as they are at balancing compositions. The successful creator of tomorrow is part artist, part marketer, part CEO – a Renaissance individual for the digital age. They must navigate the choppy waters of personal branding, financial management and networking with the skills they apply to their craft. As the lines between art and commerce blur, educational institutions find themselves racing to keep pace, their curricula evolving to nurture creative talent and business acumen.

Yet, the future of creative work is more than a solitary journey. The need for collaborative, interdisciplinary approaches has never been greater in a world grappling with challenges as vast and varied as climate change and social inequality. Imagine a symphony where scientists, engineers, policymakers and artists play their parts in harmony, their diverse expertise combining to compose solutions to our most pressing global issues. The creative professionals leading this orchestra can traverse disciplinary boundaries as easily as a melody flows between instruments.

In this rapidly evolving landscape, adaptability isn't just an asset – it's a survival skill. The creative professional of the future is a chameleon, continuously shedding old skills and adopting new ones to match the ever-changing environment. Lifelong learning becomes not just a noble aspiration, but a professional necessity. The boundaries between creative disciplines, once as rigid as canvas stretchers, now flex and bend, giving rise to hybrid roles that defy traditional categorisation. To navigate this fluid terrain, creatives must cultivate not just technical prowess, but the cognitive and interpersonal skills to thrive amidst complexity and change.

As the CCIs continue to grow in importance, nurturing this sector becomes not just an economic imperative but a cultural and social one. By investing in the skills, infrastructure and support systems needed for creative work to flourish, we're not just fostering economic growth – we're cultivating the very soul of our society. In the end, the future of work in the CCIs is a canvas awaiting our collective brushstrokes. By empowering and valuing the creative professionals at the heart of these industries, we have the opportunity to paint a future that is not only economically vibrant but culturally rich, inclusive and deeply fulfilling. As we step into this future, let us do so with the bold strokes of innovation, the vibrant colours of diversity and the intricate details of human creativity – for in this masterpiece of tomorrow, every creative voice has the

References

Association of Illustrators. (2020). *COVID-19 survey results*. Association of Illustrators.

Augé, M. (1995). *Non-places: Introduction to an anthropology of supermodernity*. Verso.

Bourdieu, P. (1986). The forms of capital. In J. Richardson (Ed.), *Handbook of theory and research for the sociology of education* (pp. 241–258). Greenwood.

Bourdieu, P. (1990). *The logic of practice*. Stanford University Press.

Bourdieu, P. (1993). *The field of cultural production: Essays on art and literature*. Columbia University Press.

Bourdieu, P. (2003). *Firing back: Against the tyranny of the* market 2. Verso.

CISAC. (2018). *Global collections report 2018*. International Confederation of Societies of Authors and Composers.

De Certeau, M. (1984). *The practice of everyday life*. University of California Press.

De Masi, D. (2000). *O ócio criativo*. Sextante.

Flew, T. (2011). *The creative industries: Culture and policy*. Sage Publications.

Manovich, L. (2013). *Software takes command*. Bloomsbury Academic.

McKinsey & Company. (2021). *The economic state of Black America: What is and what could be*. McKinsey & Company

McRobbie, A. (2016). *Be creative: Making a living in the new culture industries*. Polity Press.

Music Workers Alliance. (2020). *Music workers' COVID-19 emergency relief survey results*. Music Workers Alliance.

Raworth, K. (2017). *Doughnut economics: Seven ways to think like a 21st-century economist*. Random House Business.

Standing, G. (2011). *The precariat: The new dangerous class*. Bloomsbury Academic.

UNESCO. (2018). *Re|shaping cultural policies: Advancing creativity for development*. UNESCO Publishing.

The Film and TV Charity. (2020). *The looking glass report: Mental health and well-being in the UK film and TV industry*. The Film and TV Charity.

5

CREATIVE AND CULTURAL INDUSTRIES AND INNOVATION

In the summer of 1857, Manchester stood as a testament to the transformative power of innovation. Known as "Cottonopolis," the city's factories produced textiles at an unprecedented rate, embodying the essence of the Industrial Revolution. Yet, amidst this industrial fervour, Manchester sought to prove its cultural credentials by hosting the Art Treasures Exhibition – the most significant art show ever assembled.

Held in a purpose-built iron and glass structure in Old Trafford, the exhibition showcased over 16,000 works of art, including paintings, sculptures and decorative pieces. For 142 days, it drew over 1.3 million visitors, a testament to the city's ambition and the public's appetite for art. This juxtaposition of industrial ethos and artistic aspiration set the stage for a profound critique that would resonate through the ages.

In this context, John Ruskin, the eminent art critic and social thinker, was invited to deliver a keynote lecture at the Manchester Athenaeum. On 10 and 13 July 1857, Ruskin presented his seminal work, "The Political Economy of Art." Manchester's industrial elite was gathered inside the venue, adorned in silks and jewels. Outside, in stark contrast, factory workers gathered in smoke-filled streets, their faces tired by long hours and poor conditions. Ruskin, known for his distaste for industrialisation, saw Manchester as the epicentre of much of the wrong with modern society. He used this platform to challenge the very foundations of the city's alleged prosperity. His lecture was a passionate argument against the commodification of art and the dehumanising effects of industrial capitalism. He proclaimed:

> We have warped the word "economy" in our English language into a meaning that it has no business to bear. In our use of it, it constantly

DOI: 10.4324/9781003434252-6

> signifies merely sparing or saving; economy of money means saving money—economy of time, sparing time, and so on. But that is a wholly barbarous use of the word—barbarous in a double sense, for it is not English, and it is bad Greek; barbarous in a treble sense, for it is not English, it is bad Greek, and it is worse sense. Economy no more means saving money than it means spending money. It means, the administration of a house; its stewardship; spending or saving, that is, whether money or time, or anything else, to the best possible advantage. In the simplest and clearest definition of it, economy, whether public or private, means the wise management of labour; and it means this mainly in three senses: namely, first, *applying* your labour rationally; secondly, *preserving* its produce carefully; lastly, *distributing* its produce seasonably.
>
> *—John Ruskin, "The Roots of Honour," from Unto This Last and Other Essays on Political Economy (1860/1862)*

Ruskin's critique extended beyond art to encompass the broader impacts of industrialisation. He argued that the pursuit of wealth at the expense of human well-being and the environment was fundamentally flawed:

> It is not, in reality, the labour that is divided; but the men: Divided into mere segments of men – broken into small fragments and crumbs of life; so that all the little piece of intelligence that is left in a man is not enough to make a pin, or a nail, but exhausts itself in making a point of a pin or the head of a nail.
>
> *(Ruskin, 1857)*

Ruskin's lectures in Manchester marked a turning point in his career and the broader discourse on art, industry and society. His ideas would be further developed in his seminal work "Unto This Last" (1860), which influenced social reformers (such as the founders of the Labour Party and Mahatma Gandhi).

As we explore creative and cultural industries (CCIs) and innovation in this chapter, Ruskin's words from over 160 years ago provide a powerful starting point. They remind us of the ongoing tension between economic progress and human well-being and the potential of creativity to bridge this divide. In our contemporary context, where technology and innovation are rapidly reshaping the landscape of cultural production and consumption, Ruskin's challenge remains relevant: How can we harness the power of innovation in CCIs to enrich the human experience rather than diminish it?

This chapter will trace the evolution of innovation through successive industrial revolutions, examining how each wave of technological change has transformed creative work. It will explore Schumpeter's influential theories on innovation, particularly his concept of "creative destruction," and apply these ideas to the dynamic world of CCIs. Through examples spanning digital media, fashion, music, and more, we will investigate how CCIs are at the forefront of innovation, constantly reshaping cultural production and consumption.

There will be a look around how the new technologies are blurring the lines between creator and consumer, how digital platforms democratise access to creative content while raising new questions about value and ownership, and how sustainable and ethical concerns drive innovation in creative industries. Throughout, we will consider the double-edged nature of innovation in CCIs – its potential to unleash creativity and connect people across the globe and its capacity to disrupt traditional ways of working and exacerbate inequalities. Readers are invited to consider Ruskin's critique as these topics are reached. In exploring the transformative power of innovation in creative sectors, we must continually ask ourselves: What is the value of our creations? How can we ensure that our pursuit of progress doesn't come at the cost of our humanity? How can we use innovation tools to create a more just, sustainable and beautiful world?

By raising these questions, we can better understand the dynamic nature of CCIs in the 21st century and their potential to drive positive change in our society. The contrast between the luxury of the Art Treasures Exhibition and the harsh realities of industrial life in 1857 Manchester embodied the very contradictions Ruskin sought to address. Today, as we navigate the opportunities and challenges of the digital age, we face similar contradictions and ethical dilemmas. By examining the past and present of innovation in CCIs, this chapter aims to provide insights that can help shape a more equitable and enriching creative future.

5.1 An Overview of the Industrial Revolutions

5.1.1 The First: Steam and Coal

In the late 18th century, a profound transformation swept across Britain, forever transforming the fabric of society and the nature of human productivity. This seismic shift, which we now call the First Industrial Revolution, was not merely a series of technological innovations but a complex interplay of economic, social and cultural forces that would reshape the world. At the heart of this revolution lay a paradox: unprecedented economic growth coupled with wrenching social upheaval. As steam engines roared to life and factories threw smoke into once-clear skies, a new world was born – one of immense productive capacity and human cost.

Consider the humble steam engine, perhaps the most iconic innovation of the era. James Watt's improvements to this technology in the 1760s and 1770s unleashed a cascade of changes that would ripple through every aspect of society (Nuvolari et al., 2011). Steam power drove pumps that drained mines, allowing for deeper excavation of coal – the lifeblood of this new industrial age. It powered the machines that spun cotton into thread and wove cloth at speeds unimaginable to earlier generations. And it would soon propel ships across oceans and locomotives across continents, shrinking distances and knitting the world ever closer together.

But the steam engine was more than just a machine; it symbolised a new economic order. As historian E.A. Wrigley (2010) argues, the shift from an organic economy, limited by the constraints of plant photosynthesis, to a mineral-based economy powered by seemingly limitless coal reserves unlocked sustained economic growth. This transition allowed for a level of productivity that would have been inconceivable in earlier ages. Yet, as the gears of industry turned ever faster, they ground against the established rhythms of rural life. Nowhere was this tension more evident than in textiles, where a series of innovations – from James Hargreaves' Spinning Jenny to Edmund Cartwright's Power Loom – revolutionised production (Allen, 2009). These machines, marvels of human ingenuity, could produce cloth at a fraction of the time and cost of traditional methods. But they also turned obsolete the skills of hand spinners and weavers, many of whom were displaced and desperate.

It was in this context of rapid change and social dislocation that the modern industrial city was born. And no city more than Manchester embodied the promise and peril of this new age more than Manchester. Once a modest market town, Manchester exploded into a metropolis, its population swelling from around 25,000 in 1772 to 367,000 by 1851 (Williamson, 1990). The city became a reference of the new industrial order, and its labyrinths of factories were a testament to the transformative power of this revolution. Manchester's cotton mills were marvels of productivity, their spindles and looms churning vast quantities of cloth that would clothe the world. But they were also sites of exploitation and suffering. Children as young as nine worked long hours in dangerous conditions (Humphries, 2010), and women, drawn into factory work in unprecedented numbers, faced harsh conditions and societal disapproval (Berg, 1993).

The contrast between the wealth generated by Manchester's industries and the squalor in which many of its workers lived was stark. Friedrich Engels, who would later collaborate with Karl Marx, was so struck by the conditions he observed in Manchester that he penned his seminal work, "The Condition of the Working Class in England" (Engels, 1845). His vivid descriptions of overcrowded slums, polluted air and widespread disease painted a damning picture of industrial capitalism's human cost. Yet, viewing the Industrial Revolution solely through the lens of exploitation and misery would be a mistake. For many, the new industrial cities offered opportunities unimaginable in the rigid hierarchies of rural life. A new middle class of industrialists, managers and professionals emerged, their success stories fuelling dreams of social mobility (Gunn, 2000). And even among the working class, new forms of solidarity and political consciousness began to take shape.

For all its harshness, the factory system brought workers together in unprecedented numbers, creating the conditions for collective action. Though initially outlawed, trade unions began to form, fighting for better wages and working conditions (Thompson, 1963). Political movements like Chartism gained strength, demanding democratic reforms and universal suffrage (Royle, 1996). The concentration of people and problems in cities like Manchester sparked new thinking about public health, urban planning and social reform.

Innovation, too, was not solely the province of lone inventors or wealthy industrialists. The historian Maxine Berg (1991) has argued persuasively for the importance of incremental innovations and adaptations workers make in driving productivity gains. The factory floor became a site of constant experimentation and improvement as workers and managers sought to refine processes and increase efficiency. This culture of innovation extended beyond the factory walls. Manchester became known not just for its industry but for its intellectual ferment. The Manchester Literary and Philosophical Society, founded in 1781, became a forum for exchanging ideas, where industrialists rubbed shoulders with scientists and social reformers (Thackray, 1974). In this venture of industry and intellect, John Dalton developed his atomic theory, a breakthrough that would revolutionise chemistry and lay the groundwork for future scientific advances (Smith, 1856).

Though not fully understood at the time, the environmental consequences of this great transformation were profound. The shift to a coal-based economy began humanity's large-scale impact on the global climate (McNeill, 2000). The polluted air and water of industrial cities like Manchester were a starting point of the broader environmental challenges that would come to the fore in later centuries. As we reflect on the First Industrial Revolution from our vantage point in the 21st century, we are struck by its tremendous achievements and painful costs. It was a period of unprecedented economic growth and technological innovation that laid the foundations for the modern world. But it was also a time of great social upheaval, exploitation and environmental degradation. The tensions and contradictions of this era – between economic progress and social justice, technological innovation and human welfare, urban growth and quality of life – continue to resonate today. As of today, the world is embracing a period of rapid technological change and economic transformation, and the lessons of the First Industrial Revolution remain profoundly relevant.

The First Industrial Revolution ushered in an era of unprecedented productivity growth, fundamentally altering society's economic landscape and social fabric. This transformation was not merely a matter of technological change but a complex interplay of economic forces, social shifts and cultural adaptations.

Some aspects of the First Industrial Revolution can be summarised as follows:

BOX 5.1 THE FIRST INDUSTRIAL REVOLUTION: A SYNTHESIS

Productivity Leap

- Dramatic increase in productivity across various sectors, especially textiles
- Introducing machines like spinning jenny and power loom led to exponential output growth
- Steam engines played a crucial role, allowing for mechanisation and geographic flexibility
- Incremental innovations on factory floors significantly contributed to efficiency improvements

Economic Transformations

- Marked the beginning of sustained economic growth (GDP per capita in Britain grew 1.5% annually between 1780 and 1830)
- Structural changes: agricultural workforce declined; industrial sector expanded
- Emergence of factory system as dominant mode of production
- Financial innovations: rise of joint-stock companies and stock exchanges
- Bank of England's role expanded, laying groundwork for modern central banking

Social Upheaval

- Mass migration from rural areas to cities led to rapid, often chaotic urbanisation
- New social classes emerged: industrial working class and expanded middle class
- Harsh working conditions in factories sparked social unrest and labour movements
- Trade unions and political movements like Chartism gained strength

Cultural and Intellectual Impact

- Transformed conceptions of work, time and society
- Spurred development of modern economics (Smith, Ricardo, Marx)
- Public health concerns led to urban infrastructure improvements
- New rhythms of industrial work reshaped social norms and values

5.1.2 The Second: Steel and Power

The Second Industrial Revolution, which lasted roughly from the 1870s to the eve of World War I, would be no mere sequel to its predecessor but a transformation that would reshape the world in more profound and far-reaching ways. If the First Industrial Revolution was characterised by iron, coal and steam, its successor was defined by steel, electricity and chemistry. These new forces of production would not only accelerate the pace of change but fundamentally alter the very fabric of society, laying the groundwork for the modern world we inhabit today.

At the heart of this transformation was the Bessemer process, a method for mass-producing steel invented by Henry Bessemer in 1856. This seemingly technical and obscure innovation would be the key to a new age of construction and engineering. Suddenly, steel – stronger, lighter and cheaper than ever– became the material of choice for everything from railroads to skyscrapers (Misa, 1995). The skylines of cities like Chicago and New York began to reach for the heavens, a tangible symbol of the ambition and possibility of the age. But it was the harnessing of electricity that genuinely set this revolution apart. The invention of the dynamo and the perfection of the electric motor opened entirely new vistas of productivity and possibility. No longer were factories bound to the rhythms of daylight or the proximity of water sources. Electric lighting allowed for round-the-clock production, while electric motors provided flexibility and precision of power that steam engines could never match (Hughes, 1983).

The impact on productivity was staggering. In the United States, for instance, manufacturing output grew at an average annual rate of 4.3% between 1880 and 1900, while the number of workers increased by only 2.4% annually (Gordon, 2016). This surge in productivity was not just a matter of working harder or longer but of fundamentally reimagining the nature of work itself. Enter Frederick Winslow Taylor, the controversial father of scientific management. While often criticised for their dehumanising aspects, Taylor's time-and-motion studies represented a new way of thinking about work as something that could be systematically analysed and optimised (Kanigel, 1997). This approach, combined with innovations like the assembly line pioneered by Ransom Olds and perfected by Henry Ford, would transform not just how goods were produced but the very nature of work itself.

Yet, as with the First Industrial Revolution, these gains in productivity and efficiency came at a human cost. The pace and intensity of work in these new factories often increased stress and physical strain on workers. The division of labour, while increasing efficiency, also led to the deskilling of many jobs, turning skilled craftsmen into interchangeable machine operators (Braverman, 1974). The tension between economic progress and human welfare, evident in the mills of Manchester, had not disappeared but had taken on new forms.

The Second Industrial Revolution also saw the rise of a new middle class, fuelled by the explosion of white-collar jobs in management, engineering and administration. The growth of large corporations created new career paths and opportunities for advancement that would have been unthinkable a generation earlier (Chandler, 1977). Moreover, the fruits of this new industrial order began to touch the lives of ordinary people in ways both large and small. The advent of mass production made a wide range of consumer goods – from bicycles to sewing machines – affordable to a broader swath of society. The development of canned foods and refrigeration transformed diets and food safety. And new forms of transportation and communication, from the automobile to the telephone, began to shrink distances and connect people in unprecedented ways (Smil, 2005). Yet the most profound impact of the Second Industrial Revolution was not in the realm of production at all but in the sphere of knowledge and innovation. The rise of industrial research laboratories, pioneered by companies like General Electric and DuPont, marked the beginning of the systematic application of science to industry (Reich, 1985). This marriage of scientific inquiry and industrial production would prove to be one of the most fruitful partnerships in human history, giving birth to a seemingly endless stream of new materials, processes and technologies. The chemical industry exemplified this new approach. The development of synthetic dyes, beginning with William Perkin's accidental discovery of mauveine in 1856, sparked a revolution in industry and science. German companies like BASF and Bayer, recognising the potential of this new field, invested heavily in research and development, creating a model of industrial innovation that would be emulated around the world (Murmann, 2003).

However, as the frontiers of knowledge expanded, so too did the scale and potential consequences of human activity. The same chemical processes that produced vibrant dyes and life-saving medicines also gave birth to explosives and poison gases. While transformative, the ability to generate and transmit electricity on a massive scale also began to reveal the environmental costs of unchecked industrial development. The seeds of the 20th century's triumphs and tragedies were sown in the laboratories and factories of this second industrial age. The global impact of these changes was profound and often wrenching. As the new industrial powers of Germany and the United States began to challenge Britain's economic supremacy, the balance of global economic power began to shift. The demand for raw materials to feed the voracious appetite of these new industries intensified colonial exploitation and reshaped global trade patterns. The world was becoming more interconnected, competitive and conflictual (Beckert, 2014).

Yet amidst this tumult, new ideas and movements were taking shape that would profoundly influence the 20th century. Building on the foundations of the First Industrial Revolution, the labour movement gained strength and sophistication. The introduction of scientific management techniques paradoxically gave workers new tools to analyse and argue for the value of their labour (Montgomery, 1979). While rooted in earlier struggles, the women's suffrage movement gained momentum as women entered the workforce in more significant numbers and new roles.

As we reflect on the Second Industrial Revolution from our vantage point in the 21st century, we are struck by its uncanny resonance with our time. The debates over automation and job displacement, the concerns about the pace of technological change and its impact on society, and the excitement and anxiety about the transformative potential of new technologies – all find their echoes in this earlier period of rapid change and dislocation. Indeed, many of the institutions and assumptions we take for granted today – from the modern corporation to the idea of continuous technological progress – have their roots in this transformative era. The Second Industrial Revolution was a period of economic and technological change and a starting point for the modern world.

In the present era of rapid technological change – from artificial intelligence (AI) to biotechnology – the lessons of the Second Industrial Revolution remain profoundly relevant. They remind us of innovation's transformative power and the need to guide technological progress towards humane and sustainable ends. They caution us about the potential for technology to exacerbate inequality and social dislocation while showing us examples of how society can adapt and create new institutions to meet these challenges.

5.1.3 The Third: The Digital Revolution and the Internet

As the 20th century ended, a new wave of technological innovation began to reshape the global economy and society. This transformation, often called the Third Industrial Revolution or the Digital Revolution, marked a shift from mechanical and analogue electronic technology to digital and information technology. Unlike its predecessors, this revolution was characterised not by a single breakthrough but by a convergence of technologies that would fundamentally alter how we communicate, work and live.

At the heart of the Third Industrial Revolution lay the development and widespread adoption of digital technologies. The invention of the transistor in 1947 by William Shockley, John Bardeen and Walter Brattain at Bell Labs laid the groundwork for this transformation (Riordan & Hoddeson, 1997). This tiny device would become the building block of modern electronics, enabling the creation of increasingly powerful and compact computers. The subsequent development of integrated circuits in the late 1950s and early 1960s further accelerated this trend. Gordon Moore, co-founder of Intel, observed in 1965 that the number of transistors on a microchip doubled about every two years while the cost halved – a trend known as Moore's Law

(Moore, 1965). This exponential growth in computing power, coupled with falling costs, would drive the proliferation of digital technologies across all sectors of the economy.

The introduction of the personal computer in the 1970s and its rapid adoption in the 1980s marked a pivotal moment in the Third Industrial Revolution. Companies like Apple, IBM and Microsoft brought computing power into homes and offices, democratising access to information technology (Isaacson, 2014). This shift had profound implications for productivity and creativity, enabling individuals and small businesses to perform tasks that once required large, expensive mainframe computers. However, the development and widespread adoption of the Internet truly defined the Third Industrial Revolution. The creation of the World Wide Web by Tim Berners-Lee in 1989 transformed the Internet from a tool used primarily by academics and government agencies into a global network accessible to anyone with a computer and a phone line (Berners-Lee, 1999). The Internet revolution fundamentally altered how information was shared, businesses operated, and individuals communicated.

The early 2010s marked a significant acceleration in the evolution of social media and mobile technology, building upon the foundations laid by the Internet revolution. While LinkedIn was founded in 2003, it gained significant traction as the premier professional networking platform. The introduction of the iPhone in 2007 revolutionised mobile computing, paving the way for the explosive growth of the app economy. Twitter, launched in 2006, became a global phenomenon for real-time news and commentary. Instagram, founded in 2010, quickly rose to prominence as a photo-sharing platform, capitalising on the improved smartphone cameras. The decade also saw the meteoric rise of TikTok, which launched in 2016 and transformed short-form video content and became especially popular among younger users. These platforms, along with others like Facebook (founded in 2004), collectively reshaped how people communicate, share information and consume media, further cementing the internet's central role in daily life and accelerating the pace of the Digital Revolution.

As we move further into the 21st century, the technologies and trends of the Third Industrial Revolution continue to evolve and shape our world. The lines of this revolution and what some call the Fourth Industrial Revolution – characterised by the convergence of digital, biological and physical innovations – are becoming increasingly blurred (Schwab, 2017). The COVID-19 pandemic has accelerated many trends associated with the Third Industrial Revolution, from remote work to e-commerce to digital health solutions (Organisation for Economic Co-operation and Development [OECD], 2020). As we grapple with global challenges like climate change and inequality, the technologies and systems developed during this period will likely play a crucial role in shaping our responses.

Some crucial aspects of the Third Industrial Revolution are:

BOX 5.2 THE THIRD INDUSTRIAL REVOLUTION: A SYNTHESIS

Economic Transformations

- The rise of e-commerce challenged traditional retail models
- Growth of the service sector, especially in finance, consulting and software development
- The emergence of the "knowledge economy" where information and innovation drive growth
- Acceleration of globalisation and the rise of global value chains

Social and Cultural Impact

- Social media platforms reshaped communication and community
- Remote work and the gig economy transformed traditional work structures
- Education systems adapted to prepare students for a digital job market
- The rise of online learning platforms challenged traditional higher education models

Environmental Considerations and Sustainable Energy

- Integration of digital technologies with renewable energy and smart transport systems
- Innovations in renewable energy technologies challenged fossil fuel dominance
- The emergence of the Internet of Things (IoT) and smart grids for efficient resource use

Challenges and Criticisms

- Labour market disruptions due to automation
- The digital divide between those with and without access to digital technologies
- Concerns about data privacy, surveillance and concentration of power in tech companies
- Environmental challenges from energy consumption of data centres and electronic waste

Like its predecessors, the Third Industrial Revolution has brought about profound changes in how we live, work and interact with the world around us. It has created new opportunities and challenges, reshaped industries and labour markets and altered the balance of global economic power. As we stand on the cusp of further technological revolutions, this era's lessons and unresolved questions will continue to shape our future.

5.1.4 The Fourth

The threads of the digital age spun during the Third Industrial Revolution, are now intertwining with strands of the physical and biological worlds, creating a fabric of innovation called the Fourth Industrial Revolution. This revolution, a concept introduced by Klaus Schwab of the World Economic Forum, is not merely a continuation of its predecessor but a quantum leap into a future where the boundaries between man and machine, between the tangible and the virtual, begin to blur and fade (Schwab, 2017).

Imagine, if you will, a world where your refrigerator not only keeps your food cold but also orders groceries when supplies run low, where your car navigates city streets without your hands on the wheel, and where doctors can print replacement organs tailored to your DNA. This is not the stuff of science fiction but the emerging reality of the Fourth Industrial Revolution. It is a symphony of technologies, each playing its part in a grander composition. AI sits at the heart of this technological orchestra, the maestro conducting an ensemble of intelligent machines. These AI systems, far removed from the clunky robots of the past, are learning, adapting and even creating. They're driving our cars, diagnosing our illnesses, and even composing music (Russell & Norvig, 2020). Alongside AI, the Internet of Things hums quietly in the background, and a vast network of sensors and devices collect data and talk to each other, making our world more intelligent and responsive (Atzori et al., 2010).

However, the Fourth Industrial Revolution is not content to remain digital. It reaches out into the physical world through advanced robotics and 3D printing. Once confined to factory floors, robots vent into our homes and hospitals, becoming caregivers and companions (Siciliano & Khatib, 2016). 3D printers, meanwhile, are rewriting the rules of manufacturing, allowing us to create complex objects layer by layer, customised to our exact specifications (Ngo et al., 2018). Perhaps most provocatively, this revolution dares to tinker with the very building blocks of life itself. Biotechnology and genetic engineering are opening new frontiers in healthcare and human enhancement. We are on the brink of being able to edit our genes, cure inherited diseases, and perhaps even enhance our physical and cognitive abilities (Church & Regis, 2012).

As these technologies converge and interact, they're reshaping our economic landscape. Traditional business models are being upended by the rise of platforms and sharing economies. Companies like Uber and Airbnb have shown how technology can turn our cars and spare rooms into valuable assets, blurring the lines between consumer and producer (Parker et al., 2016). In this new world, the nature of work itself is changing. As machines become more capable, many jobs that once seemed secure are now under threat. Yet, as some doors close, others open. The Fourth Industrial Revolution is creating new roles that prize creativity, emotional intelligence, and technological savvy – skills that remain uniquely human (Frey & Osborne, 2017).

But with great power comes great responsibility, and the Fourth Industrial Revolution brings a host of ethical and social challenges. As more of our lives become digitised, privacy and data security questions loom large (Zuboff, 2019). The potential for these technologies to exacerbate existing inequalities is a pressing concern (Piketty, 2014). As we gain the ability to enhance human capabilities, we must grapple with profound questions about the nature of humanity itself (Bostrom & Sandberg, 2009). The environmental implications of this revolution are equally complex. On the one hand, intelligent technologies offer hope for more efficient resource use and cleaner energy (Ramchurn et al., 2012). On the other hand, the growing energy demands of our digital infrastructure raise concerns about sustainability (Sedlmeir et al., 2020).

On the global stage, the Fourth Industrial Revolution is redrawing the map of power and influence. Nations compete for technological supremacy and economic and military advantage (Lee, 2018). At the same time, the interconnected nature of these technologies creates new vulnerabilities, making cybersecurity a paramount concern (Singer & Friedman, 2014). Education, too, must evolve to keep pace with this changing world. The rapid march of technology demands a workforce committed to lifelong learning, constantly updating their skills to remain relevant (World Economic Forum, 2020). STEM education is more crucial than ever, but so is the cultivation of creativity and emotional intelligence – the qualities that set us apart from machines (National Academies of Sciences, Engineering, and Medicine, 2018). In healthcare, the convergence of digital, physical and biological technologies promises a revolution in preventing, diagnosing and treating disease. Personalised medicine, tailored to our genetic makeup, could transform our approach to healthcare (Ginsburg & Phillips, 2018). Telemedicine, accelerated by recent global events, is breaking down geographical barriers to care (Dorsey & Topol, 2016).

Yet, for all its promise, the Fourth Industrial Revolution is not without its critics. Some worry about widespread job displacement (Acemoglu & Restrepo, 2018), while others argue that the transformative potential of these technologies needs to be increased (Fernandez-Carmona et al., 2019). There are also valid concerns about the concentration of power in the hands of a few tech giants (Moore & Tambini, 2018).

As we stand on the threshold of this new era, we are filled with excitement and trepidation. The Fourth Industrial Revolution offers immense opportunities to increase efficiency, improve quality of life and solve some of our most pressing global challenges. But realising these benefits while mitigating risks will require thoughtful governance, inclusive policies and a commitment to ensuring that technological progress serves humanity. The future, as always, remains unwritten. Even though some visionaries are still dealing with the implications of the Fourth Industrial Revolution, some are already speaking of the fifth and sixth revolutions to come (Skobelev & Borovik, 2017). Whatever the future holds, one thing is sure: the pace of change shows no signs of slowing. As we weave this new technological standard, we must ensure that the pattern we create is one of progress, sustainability and shared prosperity for all humanity.

BOX 5.3 KEY TECHNOLOGIES DRIVING THE FOURTH INDUSTRIAL REVOLUTION

1. AI and Machine Learning: AI systems are becoming increasingly sophisticated and capable of learning, problem-solving and creativity. From autonomous vehicles to virtual assistants, AI permeates various aspects of our lives (Russell & Norvig, 2020).
2. Internet of Things (IoT): The proliferation of connected devices is creating vast networks of data-gathering sensors, enabling real-time monitoring and smart decision-making in fields ranging from manufacturing to healthcare (Atzori et al., 2010).
3. Robotics: Advanced robots are becoming more adaptive and flexible, expanding their potential applications beyond traditional industrial uses to services and even caregiving (Siciliano & Khatib, 2016).
4. 3D Printing: Also known as additive manufacturing, this technology is revolutionising production processes, enabling customisation and reducing waste (Ngo et al., 2018).
5. Biotechnology: Advances in genetic engineering, synthetic biology and neurotechnology are pushing the boundaries of what's possible in healthcare and human enhancement (Church & Regis, 2012).
6. Quantum Computing: While still in its early stages, quantum computing promises to revolutionise fields like cryptography, material science and complex system modelling (National Academies of Sciences, Engineering, and Medicine, 2019).
7. Blockchain: This distributed ledger technology has potential applications far beyond cryptocurrencies, including supply chain management, voting systems and identity verification (Tapscott & Tapscott, 2016).

Some aspects of economic and social life have been fundamentally affected by this social and economic revolution, such as:

5.1.4.1 Economic and Business Implications

The Fourth Industrial Revolution is reshaping the global economy and business landscape in profound ways:

1. New Business Models: The rise of platform economies and the sharing economy (e.g., Uber, Airbnb) are challenging traditional business models and blurring industry boundaries (Parker et al., 2016).
2. Shift in Labour Markets: While automation threatens many existing jobs, new roles emerge. There's an increasing premium on creative, emotional and technological skills that machines can't easily replicate (Frey & Osborne, 2017).
3. Customisation and Personalisation: Technologies like AI and 3D printing are enabling mass customisation, allowing businesses to tailor products and services to individual preferences at scale (Xu & Chen, 2016).
4. Supply Chain Transformation: IoT, AI and blockchain are making supply chains more transparent, efficient and resilient (Treiblmaier, 2018).
5. Data as a Key Asset: The ability to collect, analyse and leverage vast amounts of data is becoming a critical source of competitive advantage (Mayer-Schönberger & Cukier, 2013).

5.1.4.2 Social and Ethical Considerations

The rapid pace of change brought about by the Fourth Industrial Revolution raises significant social and ethical questions:

1. Privacy and Data Security: As more of our lives become digitised, concerns about data privacy and security are intensifying (Zuboff, 2019).
2. Inequality: There's a risk that the benefits of the Fourth Industrial Revolution could be unevenly distributed, exacerbating existing inequalities (Piketty, 2014).
3. Human Enhancement: Advances in biotechnology and neurotechnology raise ethical questions about the limits of human enhancement (Bostrom & Sandberg, 2009).
4. AI Ethics: As AI systems become more autonomous and influential, ensuring they make decisions aligned with human values becomes crucial (Russell, 2019).
5. Digital Divide: Ensuring equal access to the technologies driving the Fourth Industrial Revolution is a significant challenge (Van Dijk, 2006).

5.1.4.3 Environmental Impact and Sustainability

The Fourth Industrial Revolution offers both challenges and opportunities for environmental sustainability:

1 Smart Cities: IoT and AI technologies are enabling the development of smart cities that can manage resources more efficiently (Albino et al., 2015).
2 Circular Economy: Advanced technologies are facilitating the transition to a more circular economy, where waste is minimised and resources are used more efficiently (Geissdoerfer et al., 2017).
3 Clean Energy: AI and IoT are optimising renewable energy systems, while advances in materials science are improving energy storage technologies (Ramchurn et al., 2012).
4 Environmental Monitoring: Sensor networks and satellite technologies are enhancing our ability to monitor and respond to environmental changes (Pettorelli et al., 2016).
5 Energy Consumption: However, the increasing use of data centres and blockchain technologies raises concerns about growing energy consumption (Sedlmeir et al., 2020).

5.1.4.4 Geopolitical Implications

The Fourth Industrial Revolution is reshaping global power dynamics:

1 Technological Leadership: Countries are vying for leadership in key technologies like AI and quantum computing, seeing them as crucial for economic and military advantage (Lee, 2018).
2 Cybersecurity: As more critical infrastructure becomes connected, cybersecurity becomes a major national security concern (Singer & Friedman, 2014).
3 Regulatory Challenges: Governments are grappling with how to regulate rapidly evolving technologies that often transcend national boundaries (Yeung, 2019).

5.1.4.5 Education and Skills

The Fourth Industrial Revolution is necessitating changes in education and skill development:

1 Lifelong Learning: The rapid pace of technological change is making continuous learning and skill upgrading essential (World Economic Forum, 2020).

2 STEM Education: There's an increased focus on science, technology, engineering and mathematics (STEM) education, as well as on developing creativity and emotional intelligence (National Academies of Sciences, Engineering, and Medicine, 2018).
3 Digital Literacy: Basic digital literacy is becoming as fundamental as reading and writing (Gilster, 1997).

5.1.4.6 Healthcare Transformation

The convergence of digital, physical and biological technologies is revolutionising healthcare:

1 Personalised Medicine: Genomics and AI advances enable more personalised diagnosis and treatment (Ginsburg & Phillips, 2018).
2 Telemedicine: Digital technologies are expanding access to healthcare services, a trend accelerated by the COVID-19 pandemic (Dorsey & Topol, 2016).
3 3D Bioprinting: This technology promises to create replacement organs and tissues (Murphy & Atala, 2014).

5.1.4.7 Challenges and Criticisms

Despite its potential benefits, the Fourth Industrial Revolution faces several challenges and criticisms:

1 Job Displacement: There are concerns about widespread job losses due to automation and AI (Acemoglu & Restrepo, 2018).
2 Technological Determinism: Critics argue that the narrative of the Fourth Industrial Revolution often oversimplifies complex social and economic processes (Pfeiffer, 2017).
3 Hype vs. Reality: Some argue that the transformative potential of certain technologies (like blockchain or quantum computing) is overstated (Fernandez-Carmona et al., 2019).
4 Concentration of Power: There are concerns about the concentration of power in the hands of a few tech giants (Moore & Tambini, 2018).

5.2 Innovation in the Economic Point of View: Schumpeter

5.2.1 Waves and Types of Innovation

Joseph Schumpeter was one of the most influential economists of the 20th century, known for his theories on innovation, entrepreneurship and the dynamism of capitalist economies. His work has profoundly impacted our

TABLE 5.1 A Comparison between Revolutions

First Industrial Revolution (1760s–1840s)	*Second Industrial Revolution (1870s–1914)*	*Third Industrial Revolution (1960s–2010s)*	*Fourth Industrial Revolution (2010s–Present)*
Steam Engine	Electricity	Personal Computers	Artificial Intelligence
Spinning Jenny	Assembly Line	Internet	Internet of Things (IoT)
Power Loom	Telephone	Mobile Phones	3D Printing
Iron Production	Internal Combustion Engine	Semiconductors	Gene Editing (CRISPR)
Mechanised Factory	Mass Production	Digital Electronics	Quantum Computing
Textile Industry	Steel Production	Renewable Energy	Blockchain
Coal as Fuel	Oil and Gas as Fuel	Nuclear Energy	Advanced Robotics
Canal Systems	Railways	Fibre Optics	Autonomous Vehicles
Mechanical Tools	Chemical Synthesis	Space Technology	Virtual and Augmented Reality
Water Power	Electrical Power Grid	Digital Networks	5G Networks

Note: The date ranges provided are approximate and represent the generally accepted periods of each industrial revolution. There can be some overlap between periods, and the exact start and end dates may vary depending on different historical interpretations and geographical regions.

understanding of how innovation drives economic growth and transformation. An essential aspect of Schumpeter's theory is that innovations tend to cluster together in long waves or cycles rather than evenly distribute over time. He identified several types of these innovation waves:

1 Kondratiev Waves (45–60 years): The most prolonged economic cycles were named after Russian economist Nikolai Kondratiev. Schumpeter associated each Kondratiev wave with a significant technological revolution fundamentally altering the economy's structure. Examples include the Industrial Revolution (1780s–1840s), the Age of Steam and Railways (1840s–1890s), the Age of Steel, Electricity and Heavy Engineering (1890s–1940s), the Age of Oil, Automobiles and Mass Production (1940s–1990s) and potentially the Age of Information and Telecommunications (1990s–present).
2 Kuznets Swings (15–25 years): Named after Simon Kuznets, these are intermediate economic cycles often associated with infrastructure investments and demographic changes.

3 Juglar Cycles (7–11 years): Clément Juglar identified these medium-term cycles related to firm investment behaviour.
4 Kitchin Cycles (3–5 years): Named after Joseph Kitchin, these are short business cycles associated with inventory fluctuations.

In addition to describing innovation cycles, Schumpeter also distinguished between different types of innovation:

1 New Products: Introducing a new good or quality of an existing good. Examples include the first automobiles and smartphones.
2 New Methods of Production: The introduction of a new way of making products, such as the assembly line in manufacturing or computer-aided design.
3 New Markets: The opening of new markets for an industry's products. This could involve geographic expansion or tapping into new demographic segments.
4 New Sources of Supply: Securing a new source of raw materials or semi-finished goods. An example would be new oil reserves or new synthetic materials.
5 New Forms of Organisation: Changes in how firms or industries are organised. An example is the rise of "Fordism" – standardised mass production combined with high wages – in the early 20th century.

Joseph Schumpeter's theory of innovation is not merely a description of technological change but a comprehensive framework for understanding the multi-faceted nature of innovation and its role in economic transformation. Central to this framework is Schumpeter's distinction between different types of innovation, each of which plays a unique role in economic development.

The author identifies the first type of innovation as introducing a new good or a new quality of a good (Schumpeter, 1939). This type of innovation is the most easily recognisable, as it directly introduces new products into the market. Historical examples abound, from the introduction of the automobile in the early 20th century to the advent of the smartphone in the early 21st. These product innovations often open new markets and create new consumer demands, fundamentally altering the economic landscape (Christensen, 2013).

The second type of innovation is the introduction of a new method of production. These process innovations involve new ways of making existing products, often more efficiently or with new materials. Henry Ford's pioneering of the assembly line in manufacturing in the early 20th century is a prime example. More recent examples include using 3D printing in manufacturing or applying machine learning algorithms to optimise production processes. These innovations can lead to significant productivity gains and cost reductions.

The third type of innovation is opening a new market (Schumpeter, 1942). This could involve expanding into new geographic regions or targeting new demographic segments. The globalisation of commerce in the late 20th century, facilitated by innovations in transportation and communication technology, opened up vast new business markets (Friedman, 2005). On a smaller scale, a company might innovate by identifying and serving a previously overlooked market segment.

The fourth type of innovation involves securing a new source of raw materials or semi-finished goods (Freeman & Soete, 1997). This could include discovering new natural resources, such as oil reserves, or developing new synthetic materials. For example, the development of plastics in the mid-20th century provided a new source of supply for many industries (Bijker et al., 1987). Innovations in recycling and circular economy practices in recent years also fall under this category.

The fifth and final type of innovation is carrying out a new organisation in any industry. This could involve the creation or breaking up of a monopoly position or, more broadly, changes in the structure of an industry. The rise of "Fordism" in the early 20th century, which combined mass production with high wages and led to a mass consumer market, is an example of this type of organisational innovation. More recently, the emergence of the "sharing economy," exemplified by companies like Airbnb and Uber, represents a significant organisational innovation in several industries.

It's important to note that these types of innovation are not mutually exclusive and often occur in combination (Fagerberg, 2003). The development of the personal computer, for example, involved product innovations (the microcomputer itself), process innovations (the use of microprocessors and new production techniques), the opening of new markets (personal computing for homes and small businesses), new sources of supply (the development of new electronic components) and new industry organisation (the emergence of new hardware and software companies). Moreover, innovation is not a one-time event but an ongoing process. Successful innovations often lead to further innovations, creating a self-reinforcing cycle of economic change. For example, the digital revolution of the late 20th century continues to spur innovations in fields like AI, robotics and the Internet of Things.

The author emphasised that innovation is not just about technology but can encompass changes in products, processes, markets, inputs and industry structures. He saw entrepreneurs as the key agents driving innovation by introducing these "new combinations." In this sense, innovation was the engine of economic growth and a force of "creative destruction." He challenged the neoclassical economics view of perfect competition, arguing that dynamic, innovation-driven competition was more important for development than the static price competition assumed in traditional models. Accordingly, to this view, successful innovators enjoy temporary monopoly profits, which incentivise them to invest in innovation. These profits are then eroded as imitators enter the market, spurring the next round of innovation. This dynamic process, while disruptive, leads to higher productivity and living standards in the long run.

In today's rapidly changing digital and knowledge-based economy, these insights on the role of innovation and entrepreneurship in driving economic transformation are as relevant as ever. Concepts like "disruptive innovation," "creative destruction," and "innovation ecosystems" can trace their intellectual roots back to Schumpeter's work.

While some aspects of his theories remain debated, and innovation patterns have emerged since his time, Schumpeter's core ideas provide an enduring framework for understanding the dynamics of innovation and growth in capitalist economies. Particularly with the opportunities and challenges posed by AI, biotechnology, renewable energy and other emerging technologies, the vision of innovation as the driving force of economic change continues to resonate.

5.2.2 The Industrial Revolutions in Schumpeter's Lens

Joseph Schumpeter's ground-breaking theory of innovation and his concept of "long waves" or "Kondratiev waves" can be elegantly applied to the four industrial revolutions that have transformed our economic landscape (Schwab, 2017). With steam-powered marvels and mechanised textile production, the First Industrial Revolution (1760–1840) aligns with Schumpeter's first Kondratiev wave (Allen, 2009; Schumpeter, 1939). The luminaries of this age, such as James Watt and Richard Arkwright, embody the spirit of entrepreneurial innovation that Schumpeter held so dear (Landes, 2003; Mokyr, 2012).

Walking into the Second Industrial Revolution (1870–1914), the changing tempo accelerates, propelled by the electric dynamo, the internal combustion engine and the marvels of mass production (Gordon, 2016; Landes, 1969). This era, corresponding to Schumpeter's second Kondratiev wave, gave birth to titanic industries like steel, chemicals and automobiles (Chandler, 1990). Visionary figures like Thomas Edison and Henry Ford stand as the quintessential Schumpeterian innovators, their names etched into the annals of economic history (McCraw, 2007).

The Third Industrial Revolution (1960s–2000s), straddling the boundary between Schumpeter's fourth and fifth Kondratiev waves, heralds the dawn of the digital age (Dosi, 1988). This period saw a quantum leap in innovation, from the humble transistor to the global embrace of the internet (Castells, 2010). The characteristic industries of this time – electronics, telecommunications, software and biotechnology – reshaped the very fabric of our society (Freeman & Louçã, 2001). The luminaries of this revolution, figures like Bill Gates and Steve Jobs, embody the Schumpeterian ideal of the entrepreneur as a force for creative destruction (Isaacson, 2014).

And now, as we stand on the cusp of the Fourth Industrial Revolution, Schumpeter's ideas resonate with renewed vigour. AI, robotics, the Internet of Things and the promise of clean energy technologies are the instruments of this new wave of change (Brynjolfsson & McAfee, 2014). Though Schumpeter himself could not have foreseen these specific developments, his intellectual legacy provides an indispensable framework for understanding the innovation-driven metamorphosis of our economy (Perez, 2010). As we navigate the uncharted waters of this new era, Schumpeter's insights into the vital role of entrepreneurship and the ceaseless gale of creative destruction remain our essential compass (Fagerberg, 2003).

5.2.3 Types of Innovation and the Creative Industries

Schumpeter categorising innovation types provides a robust framework for understanding economic changes in the scope of CCIs. By distinguishing between different kinds of innovation, Schumpeter highlights how entrepreneurs can introduce "new combinations" that disrupt existing economic structures and drive economic development. From the arts and media to design and digital content, creative sectors are nestling of innovation, constantly pushing the boundaries of what is possible and driving economic and cultural transformation (Caves, 2000).

Product innovation is the most visible type of innovation in creative industries. Creating new cultural goods, such as a ground-breaking film, a best-selling novel or a chart-topping album, can significantly impact the market and popular culture (Hesmondhalgh, 2018). In the digital age, product innovations in creative industries also increasingly take the form of new digital content and experiences, such as virtual reality games or interactive online narratives.

Process innovations are also critical in creative industries, although they often happen behind the scenes. Developing new technologies and techniques for creating, distributing and consuming cultural content has transformed many creative sectors (Landry, 2012). The rise of digital animation and special effects, for example, has revolutionised filmmaking, while digital publishing has transformed the book industry (Thompson, 2013). The increasing use of data analytics and AI in creative industries also represents a significant process innovation, enabling new forms of personalisation and optimisation (Srnicek, 2016).

Opening new markets is another crucial type of innovation in creative industries. The globalisation of culture and the rise of the internet have created vast new audiences for cultural content and new opportunities for creative professionals to reach niche markets. For example, the growth of the Chinese film market has opened new opportunities for Hollywood studios. At the same time, the rise of online streaming has created new markets for independent musicians and filmmakers (Curtin & Sanson, 2016).

Innovations in sourcing new inputs are also prevalent in creative industries. For instance, the use of new materials and technologies in fashion and design can create entirely new types of products (Brydges & Hracs, 2019). In the music industry, new instruments and sound technologies have often spurred new genres and styles (Pinch & Bijsterveld, 2004). The increasing incorporation of user-generated content and data into creative processes, enabled by digital technologies, also represents a new source of inputs (Manovich, 2009).

Finally, *organisational innovations* are transforming the structure and dynamics of many creative industries. The rise of flexible, project-based forms of organisation in sectors like film and television production represents a significant organisational innovation, enabling greater agility and adaptability (Grabher, 2002). The growth of creative clusters and networks, facilitated by digital technologies, also allows new collaboration and knowledge sharing (Florida, 2002). In the art world, the increasing use of online platforms and social media is changing how artists connect with audiences and patrons (Joselit, 2013).

It's important to note that innovation in creative industries often involves a unique blend of artistic creativity and economic entrepreneurship (Howkins, 2002). Creative professionals frequently innovate to create financial value, express new ideas, challenge conventions and push the boundaries of their art (Becker, 1982). This means that the drivers and impacts of innovation in creative industries are often complex and multidimensional, involving a mix of cultural, social and economic factors (Potts & Cunningham, 2008).

Nonetheless, this framework provides a valuable starting point for analysing how innovation drives change and growth in creative industries. By highlighting the diverse types of innovation at play – from new products and processes to new markets, inputs and organisational forms – Schumpeter's theory helps us better understand the dynamic and transformative nature of creativity in the economy.

5.2.4 Creative Destruction in the Creative Industries

Joseph Schumpeter's "creative destruction" concept is perhaps his most enduring and influential contribution to our understanding of innovation and economic change. The term refers to the incessant innovation process by which new products, methods and organisations replace outdated ones (Schumpeter, 1942). Schumpeter argued that this process is the fundamental impulse that sets and keeps the capitalist engine in motion (McCraw, 2007).

At the heart of the concept is the idea that innovation is not just about creating new things but also about destroying old ones. As Schumpeter put it, creative destruction "incessantly revolutionises the economic structure from within, incessantly destroying the old one, incessantly creating a new one" (Schumpeter, 1942b, p. 83). This means that innovation is inherently disruptive, constantly challenging established ways of doing things and upsetting the status quo (Christensen, 2013). The automobile industry provides a classic example of creative destruction in action. The rise of the car in the early 20th century didn't just create a new industry; it also destroyed or transformed many others, from horse-drawn carriages and blacksmiths to railroads and urban design. More recently, the rise of digital photography destroyed the film photography industry, while streaming services have fundamentally disrupted the business models of traditional media companies (Gans, 2016).

Schumpeter saw this process of creative destruction as an essential fact of capitalism. In his view, it is not price competition that counts but competition from new commodities, technologies, sources of supply and types of organisations. This competition strikes not at the margins of existing firms but their foundations and lives.

The concept of creative destruction highlights the dynamic, evolutionary nature of the capitalist economy. It suggests that economic growth and development are not smooth, gradual processes but are characterised by constant upheaval and discontinuous change (Freeman & Louçã, 2001). It also emphasises the central role of the entrepreneur as an agent of innovation and change, constantly introducing new combinations that challenge the existing order.

However, the concept also highlights innovation's inherently conflictual and disruptive nature. The process of creative destruction necessarily involves winners and losers as new industries and firms rise and old ones decline (Perez, 2003). This can lead to significant social and economic dislocation, as workers lose their jobs and communities are disrupted. Moreover, the benefits of creative destruction are only sometimes evenly distributed. Schumpeter acknowledged that creative destruction could lead to the concentration of economic power as successful innovators gain market dominance. This has led some critics to argue that Schumpeter's vision celebrates the role of monopoly power in driving innovation (Dolfsma, 2004).

Despite these criticisms, creative destruction remains central to our understanding of innovation and economic change. It highlights the constant interplay of innovation and destruction that characterises dynamic economies and the central role of entrepreneurship in driving this process (Metcalfe, 1998). The concept also has important policy implications. It suggests that policies promoting innovation and growth should focus on supporting the creation of new industries and technologies and facilitating the smooth reallocation of resources from declining to rising sectors. It also highlights the importance of policies that support workers and communities affected by the disruptive impacts of innovation.

The concept of creative destruction is highly relevant to the dynamics of creative industries. These industries, including media, entertainment, design and the arts, are characterised by a constant drive for novelty and originality (Caves, 2000). In this context, innovation often takes the form of new creative products, styles and forms of expression that challenge and disrupt established norms and conventions.

For example, the rise of digital filmmaking and special effects in the 1990s and 2000s transformed how movies are made and experienced. The fashion industry is another creative sector where creative destruction is a constant force. The cyclical nature of fashion trends means that new styles and designs are constantly emerging, often in reaction to and at the expense of older ones. The rise of "fast fashion" in recent years, enabled by new technologies and globalised supply chains, has significantly disrupted the traditional fashion industry, challenged established players and created new opportunities for innovation.

In all these cases, creative destruction is driven by the inherent need for novelty and differentiation in creative industries. There is constant pressure to innovate and challenge the status quo in a market where the primary value is derived from originality and uniqueness (Caves, 2000). This means creative industries are inherently dynamic and unstable, with new ideas and forms constantly emerging and displacing older ones (Potts & Cunningham, 2008).

However, creative destruction in creative industries also has unique challenges and complexities. Unlike in other sectors, where innovation is often driven by technological change or efficiency gains, innovation in creative industries is usually more subjective and unpredictable (Caves, 2000). The success of a new innovative product or style depends not just on its objective qualities but also on its ability to capture the zeitgeist and resonate with audiences' changing tastes and preferences (Hirsch, 1972). Moreover, the disruptive impact of new ideas and forms in creative industries is only sometimes immediately apparent. Unlike in industries where innovation leads to clear and measurable efficiency gains, the value of new creative products and styles often emerges over time as they gain cultural significance and influence. This means that creative destruction in creative industries is usually more gradual and iterative, with new ideas and forms co-existing with older ones for extended periods before eventually displacing them (Potts & Cunningham, 2008).

Despite these complexities, the concept of creative destruction remains a powerful tool for understanding the dynamics of change and innovation in creative industries. It highlights the constant tension between tradition and innovation, between established and emerging forms, that characterises these sectors. It also emphasises the central role of creative entrepreneurs and innovators in driving this process, constantly introducing new ideas and challenging the status quo.

For policymakers and industry leaders, understanding the process of creative destruction in creative industries is crucial for fostering a dynamic and innovative creative economy. This means creating an environment that supports risk-taking and experimentation, values originality and uniqueness, and can adapt and evolve in response to changing tastes and technologies (Pratt & Jeffcutt, 2009). It also means supporting the creative entrepreneurs and innovators who drive the process of creative destruction, providing them with the resources, skills and opportunities they need to bring their ideas to life (Florida, 2002).

Ultimately, creative destruction reminds the world that change and disruption are inherent to the nature of creative industries. In an era where the only constant is change, the ability to innovate and adapt is not just a competitive advantage but a necessity for survival. By embracing the process of creative destruction and fostering an environment that supports and encourages innovation, we can ensure our creative industries' continued vitality and relevance in the face of a progressively changing world.

5.2.5 Schumpeterian Innovations in Creative and Industries: Examples

The CCIs, encompassing sectors such as media, entertainment, design and the arts, serve as a vibrant arena for innovation in the Schumpeterian tradition. You can find some examples below:

5.2.5.1 Introduction of a New Good

The creative industries are prolific in introducing new products that capture the public's imagination and reshape cultural landscapes. These innovations often blend technological advancements with artistic vision, creating entirely new categories of cultural goods, such as:

Digital Revolution in Art Consumption: The iPad's introduction in 2010 transformed digital content interaction, creating new possibilities in digital publishing, interactive storytelling and mobile gaming. Art galleries and museums developed apps for virtual tours and artwork exploration, increasing fine art accessibility. Digital art platforms like DeviantArt and ArtStation democratised art creation and distribution, leading to new forms of artistic expression such as generative art and interactive installations.

Streaming Services and Content Creation: Netflix's streaming service launch in 2007 and subsequent original content production introduced a new model of content creation and consumption. This innovation changed viewing habits, disrupted traditional TV networks, led to "binge-watching," and altered storytelling formats. It affected the entire entertainment ecosystem, changing success metrics, production budgets, acting careers and facilitating international content exchange.

Virtual (VR) and Augmented Reality (AR) in Entertainment: Consumer-grade VR headsets and AR applications created new forms of immersive entertainment, expanding beyond gaming into virtual art exhibitions, immersive journalism and AR-enhanced live performances. The potential of VR and AR in creative industries is still being explored, with applications in virtual concerts, immersive storytelling in film and AR-based virtual art installations.

Innovative Musical Instruments and Production Tools: Introducing new instruments and production tools, such as synthesisers and digital audio workstations (DAWs), has led to new genres and democratised music production. Cloud-based DAWs enable global collaboration, AI-powered tools offer automated services, and blockchain technology is being explored for managing music rights and royalties.

E-Books and Digital Publishing: E-readers like the Amazon Kindle created a new market for digital books, affecting pricing models, enabling self-publishing, and leading to interactive and multimedia books. This has impacted reading habits, spawned new literary forms like the "Kindle Single," and democratised the publishing industry by allowing new voices to reach readers without traditional gatekeepers.

5.2.5.2 Introduction of a New Method of Production

Innovations in production methods have transformed how creative content is made and distributed, often leading to entirely new aesthetic possibilities and business models. Relevant examples are:

Digital Animation and Computer-Generated Images (CGI): Digital animation techniques, pioneered by Pixar, have revolutionised the film industry. *Toy Story* (1995) was the first fully computer-animated feature film, setting a new industry standard. The technology has evolved to create photorealistic effects, blurring the line between animation and live-action. CGI's impact extends beyond animated films, transforming visual effects in live-action movies and finding applications in architectural visualisation, product design and medical imaging. It has raised questions about film performance and authorship.

3D Printing in Fashion and Design: 3D printing has introduced new production methods in fashion and industrial design. Designers like Iris van Herpen use it to create intricate pieces impossible with traditional methods. It enables rapid prototyping and small-batch production of custom designs. 3D printing allows for customisation, on-demand production and sustainable design. It could potentially democratise design and manufacturing.

AI in Creative Processes: AI is introducing new production methods across creative fields. Tools like AIVA and Amper Music can compose original scores, while GAN technology creates AI-generated artworks. This raises questions about creativity and authorship. AI is also used in recommendation algorithms and predictive tools for creative projects.

Virtual Production in Film and Television: LED walls and real-time rendering engines, as used in *The Mandalorian* (2019), represent a shift in visual effects integration. This method allows real-time compositing of digital backgrounds, reducing post-production time and costs. Virtual production could decentralise the film industry and open new creative possibilities.

Algorithmic Composition and Generative Art: Algorithms generate new music and visual artworks. Generative music creates ever-changing compositions, while artists like Refik Anadol use machine learning for data-driven artworks. This approach raises questions about authorship and creativity and opens possibilities for interactive and personalised art experiences.

5.2.5.3 Opening of a New Market

Creative industries have been adept at opening new markets, often by tapping into previously underserved demographics or creating entirely new categories of cultural consumption. Some relevant examples are:

Streaming and the Global TV Market: Netflix's global expansion strategy, focusing on local-language content in markets like India, Brazil and South Korea, has opened new markets for high-quality, streaming-first television content. Shows like *Money Heist* and *Squid Game* have found global audiences, challenging English-language content dominance. This strategy has increased investment in local production industries, fostered cultural exchange, challenged the Hollywood-centric content distribution model and created opportunities for non-English-speaking creators to reach global audiences.

Gaming and New Demographics: Nintendo's Wii and mobile games like "Candy Crush Saga" opened up new markets for casual gamers, attracting previously uninterested demographics. Games like "Fortnite" have expanded beyond gaming to become social platforms and virtual concert venues. This expansion has led to the gamification of non-gaming activities, the rise of esports and mobile gaming becoming a significant industry.

Podcasting and Audio Entertainment: Podcasting has created a new audio entertainment and education market. Shows like "Serial" demonstrated the potential for long-form investigative journalism in audio format. Companies like Gimlet Media have established a professional podcast production industry. Podcasting has revitalised audio storytelling, created new opportunities for creators and advertisers and built engaged communities around specific topics or personalities.

STEM Toys and Edutainment: Companies like LittleBits and Kano have created a market at the intersection of toys and education, teaching coding and electronics through play. This "edutainment" market expands the toy industry into STEM education, reflecting societal shifts towards valuing STEM skills and gamification of learning. These products also address the gender gap in STEM fields by making coding and electronics more accessible to all children.

Virtual Influencers and Digital Celebrities: Creating virtual influencers like Lil Miquela has opened a new market in the influencer economy. These AI-powered, computer-generated characters engage with followers, endorse products and even release music. This phenomenon raises questions about celebrity and authenticity in the digital age, creates new brand opportunities and could be used to create persistent digital avatars for real celebrities.

5.2.5.4 Conquest of a New Source of Supply

Innovations in sourcing new inputs have led to novel creative outputs and reshaped industry supply chain, such as:

User-Generated Content Platforms: Platforms like YouTube, TikTok and Instagram have provided new sources of talent and content for the entertainment industry. Many social media stars have transitioned to mainstream media, reshaping the talent pipeline. This democratisation of content creation has altered the media landscape, challenging traditional gatekeepers, creating new paths to stardom and allowing diverse voices to find audiences. It has also led to new business models like influencer marketing and new forms of content.

Sustainable and Recycled Materials in Fashion: The fashion industry has seen a significant trend towards sustainable and recycled materials. Companies like Adidas have created shoes from ocean plastic, while Stella McCartney pioneers' sustainable materials in high fashion. This includes innovative materials like Piñatex and mushroom leather. This shift challenges the traditional fast fashion model, creating new supply chains, potentially reducing environmental impact and responding to changing consumer preferences.

Crowdsourcing in Design: Platforms like 99designs have created a new supply source for graphic design services, allowing businesses to crowdsource design work globally. This has disrupted traditional design agency models and opened opportunities for freelance designers worldwide. While it has democratised access to design services, it has also raised concerns about the devaluation of design work and the ethics of speculative work.

Big Data as Creative Input: Big data has become a new source of input for creative decisions. Companies like Netflix and Spotify use viewer and listener data to inform content creation and curation. This data-driven approach is changing decision-making in creative industries, allowing for more personalised experiences. However, it raises questions about the role of human intuition and the potential for reinforcing biases or creative homogenisation.

AI-Generated Content: AI is becoming a new source of creative content, with applications in automated journalism, chatbots and conceptual art. Tools like GPT-3 and DALL-E can generate human-like text and images. This raises profound questions about creativity, authorship and the value of human labour in creative industries. The legal and ethical implications of AI-generated content, particularly around copyright and authenticity, are still being debated.

5.2.5.5 New Organisation of an Industry

The creative industries have seen numerous innovations in organising themselves as an industry (shaping a whole system of productive chain). Representative examples are:

Gig Economy in Creative Services: Platforms like Fiverr and Upwork have created new marketplaces for freelance creative services, transforming how creative professionals work. This offers more flexibility and diverse opportunities but also brings challenges like job insecurity. It provides businesses with access to a global talent pool but raises questions about labour rights and fair compensation.

Blockchain in Music Rights Management: Blockchain technology is reshaping music rights and royalties tracking and distribution. Platforms like Musicoin and Ujo Music are experimenting with blockchain-based systems that could disintermediate traditional industry players. This could create more transparent and efficient systems but faces adoption challenges and environmental concerns.

Direct-to-Consumer Models in Publishing: Authors like Andy Weir have found success self-publishing online, bypassing traditional gatekeepers. Platforms like Amazon's Kindle Direct Publishing have facilitated this shift. This has democratised publishing but created challenges in discoverability and quality control.

Virtual Production Studios: The COVID-19 pandemic accelerated remote work adoption in film and TV production. Companies like Ziva Dynamics and Unity are creating virtual production tools for collaborative filmmaking in virtual environments. This could decentralise the industry but requires significant upfront investment.

Subscription Models in Creative Software: Adobe's shift to a subscription-based model for its Creative Suite in 2013 marked a change in creative software distribution and monetisation. This provides more regular revenue for companies and potentially lowers upfront costs for users, but it has been criticised for potentially increasing long-term costs.

Collaborative Consumption in Fashion: Clothing rental services like Rent the Runway and peer-to-peer fashion resale platforms like Depop represent a shift towards collaborative consumption in fashion. These models could reduce waste and provide broader access to clothing but face logistical challenges and need to change consumer attitudes towards clothing ownership.

The creative industries stand at the forefront of Schumpeterian innovation, embodying the "creative destruction" process that drives economic progress. From the introduction of new goods like virtual reality experiences and AI-generated art to new methods of production like virtual film sets and 3D-printed fashion, to the opening of new markets through global streaming platforms and mobile gaming, to the conquest of new sources of supply through user-generated content and sustainable materials, to new ways of organising industries through blockchain and the gig economy – the creative sectors are constantly reinventing themselves and, in the process, reshaping our cultural and economic landscape. These innovations are not merely technological; they represent fundamental shifts in creating, distributing and consuming culture. They challenge traditional notions of authorship, ownership and value in the creative economy. Also, these industries blur the lines between creator and consumer, between professional and amateur, and between different creative disciplines.

The pace and scale of these changes present both opportunities and challenges. On one hand, they offer unprecedented opportunities for creativity, accessibility and diversity in cultural production. They allow for more personalised and immersive cultural experiences, and they open new avenues for creative expression and entrepreneurship. On the other hand, they raise important questions about the future of creative work, the ethics of AI and data-driven creativity, the sustainability of new business models and the potential for technological disruption to exacerbate existing inequalities in the creative industries.

For policymakers, the challenge will be to create regulatory frameworks that encourage innovation while protecting the rights of creators and the interests of consumers. For creative professionals, ongoing learning and adaptation will be crucial to navigate this rapidly changing landscape. For businesses, anticipating and quickly responding to technological and cultural shifts will be essential for survival and success.

Ultimately, CCIs remind us that innovation is not just about technology but about reimagining how we express ourselves, tell our stories and make sense of the world around us. As these industries continue to evolve, they will undoubtedly play a crucial role in shaping our economy, culture and society.

References

Acemoglu, D., & Restrepo, P. (2018). The race between man and machine: Implications of technology for growth, factor shares, and employment. *American Economic Review*, 108(6), 1488–1542.

Albino, V., Berardi, U., & Dangelico, R. M. (2015). Smart cities: Definitions, dimensions, performance, and initiatives. *Journal of Urban Technology*, 22(1), 3–21.

Allen, R. C. (2009). *The British industrial revolution in global perspective*. Cambridge University Press.

Atzori, L., Iera, A., & Morabito, G. (2010). The internet of things: A survey. *Computer Networks*, 54(15), 2787–2805.

Beckert, S. (2014). *Empire of cotton: A global history*. Knopf.

Becker, H. S. (1982). *Art worlds*. University of California Press.

Berg, M. (1991). On the origins of capitalist hierarchy. In B. Gustafsson (Ed.), *Power and economic institutions*. Edward Elgar.

Berg, M. (1993). What difference did women's work make to the industrial revolution? *History Workshop Journal*, 35(1), 22–44.

Bijker, W. E., Hughes, T. P., & Pinch, T. J. (1987). *The social construction of technological systems: New directions in the sociology and history of technology*. MIT Press.

Berners-Lee, T. (1999). *Weaving the web: The original design and ultimate destiny of the World Wide Web by its inventor*. Harper San Francisco.

Bostrom, N., & Sandberg, A. (2009). Cognitive enhancement: Methods, ethics, regulatory challenges. *Science and Engineering Ethics*, 15(3), 311–341.

Braverman, H. (1974). *Labor and monopoly capital: The degradation of work in the twentieth century*. Monthly Review Press.

Brydges, T., & Hracs, B. J. (2019). What are the fashion risks? The challenges of the slow fashion movement for independent fashion designers. *International Journal of Consumer Studies*, 43(6), 547–557.

Brynjolfsson, E., & McAfee, A. (2014). *The second machine age: Work, progress, and prosperity in a time of brilliant technologies*. W.W. Norton & Company.

Castells, M. (2010). *The rise of the network society*. Wiley-Blackwell.

Caves, R. E. (2000). *Creative industries: Contracts between art and commerce*. Harvard University Press.

Chandler, A. D. (1977). *The visible hand: The managerial revolution in American business*. Harvard University Press.

Chandler, A. D. (1990). Scale and scope: *The dynamics of industrial capitalism*. Harvard University Press.
Curtin, M., & Sanson, K. (2016). *Precarious creativity: global media, local labor*. University of California Press.
Christensen, C. M. (2013). *The innovator's dilemma: When new technologies cause great firms to fail*. Harvard Business Review Press.
Church, G. M., & Regis, E. (2012). *Regenesis: How synthetic biology will reinvent nature and ourselves*. Basic Books.
Dolfsma, W. (2004). The logic of collective consuming: Consumers as subcontractors on electronic markets. *Business Ethics: A European Review*, 13(1), 42–49.
Dorsey, E. R., & Topol, E. J. (2016). State of telehealth. *New England Journal of Medicine*, 375(2), 154–161.
Dosi, G. (1988). Sources, procedures, and microeconomic effects of innovation. *Journal of Economic Literature*, 26(3), 1120–1171.
Engels, F. (1845). *The condition of the working class in England*. Otto Wigand.
Fagerberg, J. (2003). Schumpeter and the revival of evolutionary economics: An appraisal of the literature. *Journal of Evolutionary Economics*, 13(2), 125–159.
Fernandez-Carmona, M., Bellotto, N., & Coşar, S. (2019). Social service robots in shopping malls: Current trends and future research directions. *International Journal of Social Robotics*, 11(1), 1–18.
Florida, R. (2002). *The rise of the creative class*. Basic Books.
Freeman, C., & Louçã, F. (2001). *As time goes by: From the industrial revolutions to the information revolution*. Oxford University Press.
Geissdoerfer, M., Savaget, P., Bocken, N. M., & Hultink, E. J. (2017). The circular economy–A new sustainability paradigm? *Journal of Cleaner Production*.
Gilster, P. (1997). *Digital literacy*. Wiley.
Ginsburg, G. S., & Phillips, K. A. (2018). Precision medicine: From science to value. *Health Affairs*, 37(5), 694–701.
Gordon, R. J. (2016). *The rise and fall of American growth: The U.S. standard of living since the Civil War*. Princeton University Press.
Grabher, G. (2002). The project ecology of advertising: Tasks, talents and teams. *Regional Studies*, 36(3), 245–262.
Gunn, S. (2000). *The public culture of the Victorian middle class: Ritual and authority and the English industrial city, 1840–1914*. Manchester University Press.
Hesmondhalgh, D. (2018). *The cultural industries*. SAGE Publications Limited.
Hirsch, P. M. (1972). Processing fads and fashions: An organization-set analysis of cultural industry systems. *American Journal of Sociology*, 77(4), 639–659.
Howkins, J. (2002). *The creative economy: How people make money from ideas*. Penguin UK.
Hughes, T. P. (1983). *Networks of power: Electrification in Western society, 1880–1930*. Johns Hopkins University Press.
Humphries, J. (2010). *Childhood and child labour in the British Industrial Revolution*. Cambridge University Press.
Isaacson, W. (2014). *The innovators: How a group of hackers, geniuses, and geeks created the digital revolution*. Simon & Schuster.
Joselit, D. (2013). *After art*. Princeton University Press.
Kanigel, R. (1997). *The one best way: Frederick Winslow Taylor and the enigma of efficiency*. Viking.

Landes, D. S. (1969). *The unbound Prometheus: Technological change and industrial development in Western Europe from 1750 to the present*. Cambridge University Press.

Landry, C. (2012). *The creative city: A toolkit for urban innovators*. Earthscan.

Lee, K. F. (2018). *AI superpowers: China, Silicon Valley, and the new world order*. Houghton Mifflin Harcourt.

Manovich, L. (2009). The practice of everyday (media) life: From mass consumption to mass cultural production? *Critical Inquiry*, 35(2), 319–331.

Mayer-Schönberger, V., & Cukier, K. (2013). *Big data: A revolution that will transform how we live, work, and think*. Houghton Mifflin Harcourt.

Metcalfe, J. S. (1998). *Evolutionary economics and creative destruction*. Psychology Press.

Montgomery, D. (1979). *Workers' control in America: Studies in the history of work, technology, and labor struggles*. Cambridge University Press.

Moore, M., & Tambini, D. (2018). *Digital dominance: The power of Google, Amazon, Facebook, and Apple*. Oxford University Press.

Murphy, S. V., & Atala, A. (2014). 3D bioprinting of tissues and organs. *Nature Biotechnology*, 32(8), 773–785.

McCraw, T. K. (2007). *Prophet of innovation: Joseph Schumpeter and creative destruction*. Harvard University Press.

McNeill, J. R. (2000). *Something new under the sun: An environmental history of the twentieth-century world*. W.W. Norton & Company.

Misa, T. J. (1995). *A nation of steel: The making of modern America, 1865–1925*. Johns Hopkins University Press.

Mokyr, J. (2012). *The enlightened economy: An economic history of Britain 1700–1850*. Yale University Press.

Moore, G. E. (1965). Cramming more components onto integrated circuits. *Electronics*, 38(8), 114–117.

Murmann, J. P. (2003). *Knowledge and competitive advantage: The coevolution of firms, technology, and national institutions*. Cambridge University Press.

National Academies of Sciences, Engineering, and Medicine. (2018). *How people learn II: Learners, contexts, and cultures*. The National Academies Press.

National Academies of Sciences, Engineering, and Medicine. (2019). *Quantum computing: Progress and prospects*. The National Academies Press.

Ngo, T. D., Kashani, A., Imbalzano, G., Nguyen, K. T., & Hui, D. (2018). Additive manufacturing (3D printing): A review of materials, methods, applications and challenges. *Composites Part B: Engineering*, 143, 172–196.

Nuvolari, A., Verspagen, B., & von Tunzelmann, N. (2011). The early diffusion of the steam engine in Britain, 1700–1800: A reappraisal. *Cliometrica*, 5(3), 291–321.

OECD. (2020). *Digital economy outlook 2020*. OECD Publishing.

Perez, C. (2003). *Technological revolutions and financial capital: The dynamics of bubbles and golden ages*. Edward Elgar Publishing.

Piketty, T. (2014). *Capital in the twenty-first century*. Harvard University Press.

Perez, C. (2010). Technological revolutions and techno-economic paradigms. *Cambridge Journal of Economics*, 34(1), 185–202.

Pettorelli, N., Owen, H. J., & Duncan, C. (2016). How do we want satellite remote sensing to support biodiversity conservation globally? *Methods in Ecology and Evolution*, 7(6), 656–665.

Pfeiffer, S. (2017). The vision of "Industrie 4.0" in the making—a case of future told, tamed, and traded. *NanoEthics*, 11(1), 107–121.
Pinch, T., & Bijsterveld, K. (2004). Sound studies: New technologies and music. *Social Studies of Science*, 34(5), 635–648.
Potts, J., & Cunningham, S. (2008). Four models of the creative industries. *International Journal of Cultural Policy*, 14(3), 233–247.
Pratt, A. C., & Jeffcutt, P. (2009). *Creativity, innovation and the cultural economy*. Routledge.
Ramchurn, S. D., Vytelingum, P., Rogers, A., & Jennings, N. R. (2012). Putting the 'smarts' into the smart grid: A grand challenge for artificial intelligence. *Communications of the ACM*, 55(4), 86–97.
Reich, L. S. (1985). *The making of American industrial research: Science and business at GE and Bell, 1876–1926*. Cambridge University Press.
Riordan, M., & Hoddeson, L. (1997). *Crystal fire: The invention of the transistor and the birth of the information age*. W.W. Norton & Company.
Royle, E. (1996). *Chartism*. Routledge.
Ruskin, J. (1857). *The political economy of art*. George Routledge and Sons. https://archive.org/details/in.ernet.dli.2015.202545/page/n3/mode/2up. Accessed on 10 September 2024.
Ruskin, J. (1862). *Unto this last and other essay on political economy*. Project Gutenberg.
Russell, S., & Norvig, P. (2020). *Artificial intelligence: A modern approach* (4th ed.). Pearson.
Singer, P. W., & Friedman, A. (2014). *Cybersecurity and cyberwar: What everyone needs to know*. Oxford University Press.
Schumpeter, J. A. (1939). *Business cycles: A theoretical, historical and statistical analysis of the capitalist process*. McGraw-Hill.
Schumpeter, J. A. (1942). *Capitalism, socialism and democracy*. Harper & Brothers.
Schwab, K. (2017). *The fourth industrial revolution*. Currency.
Sedlmeir, J., Buhl, H. U., Fridgen, G., & Keller, R. (2020). The energy consumption of blockchain technology: Beyond myth. *Business & Information Systems Engineering*, 62, 599–608.
Skobelev, P. O., & Borovik, S. Y. (2017). On the way from Industry 4.0 to Industry 5.0: From digital manufacturing to digital society. *Industry 4.0*, 2(6), 307–311.
Siciliano, B., & Khatib, O. (Eds.). (2016). Springer *handbook of robotics*. Springer.
Smil, V. (2005). *Creating the twentieth century: Technical innovations of 1867–1914 and their lasting impact*. Oxford University Press.
Smith, J. L. (1856). *Memoir of John Dalton and history of the atomic theory up to his time*. H. Baillière.
Thackray, A. (1974). Natural knowledge in cultural context: The Manchester model. *The American Historical Review*, 79(3), 672–709.
Tapscott, D., & Tapscott, A. (2016). Blockchain revolution: How the technology behind Bitcoin is changing money, business, and the world. *Portfolio*.
Thompson, J. B. (2013). *Books in the digital age: The transformation of academic and higher education publishing in Britain and the United States*. Polity Press.
Thompson, E. P. (1963). *The making of the English working class*. Victor Gollancz Ltd.
Treiblmaier, H. (2018). The impact of the blockchain on the supply chain: A theory-based research framework and a call for action. *Supply Chain Management: An International Journal*, 23(6), 545–559.

Williamson, J. G. (1990). *Coping with city growth during the British Industrial Revolution*. Cambridge University Press.

Wrigley, E. A. (2010). *Energy and the English industrial revolution*. Cambridge University Press.

World Economic Forum. (2020). *The future of jobs report 2020*. World Economic Forum.

Van Dijk, J. A. G. M. (2006). Digital divide research, achievements and shortcomings. *Poetics*, 34(4–5), 221–235.

Xu, X., & Chen, X. (2016). Customer value co-creation in social media: Conceptualization and scale development. *International Journal of Information Systems in the Service Sector*, 8(4), 1–20.

Yeung, K. (2019). Regulation by blockchain: The emerging battle for supremacy between the code of law and code as law. *The Modern Law Review*, 82(2), 207–239.

Zuboff, S. (2019). *The age of surveillance capitalism: The fight for a human future at the new frontier of power*. Public Affairs.

6

CREATIVE AND CULTURAL INDUSTRIES AND PUBLIC POLICY

6.1 Perspectives on Creative and Cultural Industries Policies: Rationales

Cultural and creative industries (CCIs) can be robust drivers of growth, social cohesion and national identity engines in today's interconnected world. Governments worldwide have recognised this potential, crafting diverse policy frameworks to nurture and harness the power of these industries. This chapter invites readers to explore the policy models to support CCIs, examine the underlying rationales and assess the impact on creative sectors and broader socio-economic landscapes.

The rationale for public policies in CCIs is rooted in several economic and social considerations. While market mechanisms can drive innovation and efficiency in many sectors, they often need to catch up in fully capturing the value and addressing the unique challenges of CCIs. This necessitates state intervention through well-crafted public policies.

One primary justification for government involvement is the presence of market failures in the creative sector. These failures occur when the free market fails to allocate resources efficiently or fails to produce socially optimal outcomes (Towse, 2019). In CCIs, market failures can manifest in several ways:

1 Information asymmetry: Consumers often need more complete information about the quality of cultural goods before consumption, leading to the undervaluation of creative products.

DOI: 10.4324/9781003434252-7

2 Public goods characteristics: Many cultural products, once created, can be consumed by additional users at little or no extra cost, making it difficult for creators to capture the total value of their work.
3 Natural monopolies: In some areas of cultural production, high fixed costs and low marginal costs can lead to natural monopolies, potentially stifling diversity and innovation.

Another crucial aspect is the presence of positive externalities in CCIs. Externalities are the effects of an economic activity on unrelated third parties. In the case of CCIs, these are often positive, meaning they benefit society beyond the immediate consumers or producers. Examples include:

1 Educational externalities: Exposure to arts and culture can enhance critical thinking and creativity, benefiting society beyond the cultural sector (Crossick & Kaszynska, 2016).
2 Innovation spillovers: Creative industries often drive innovation that spills over into other sectors of the economy (Bakhshi & McVittie, 2009).
3 Social cohesion: Cultural activities can foster social bonds and community identity, contributing to social stability and cohesion (Belfiore & Bennett, 2007).

State intervention through public policies can help internalise these positive externalities, ensuring that the total social value of creative activities is recognised and supported.

Furthermore, public policies in CCIs aim to ensure that the economic potential of these industries translates into tangible social benefits. These benefits can include:

1 Job creation: CCIs are often labour-intensive and can create significant employment opportunities, particularly for young people (UNESCO, 2022).
2 Urban regeneration: Cultural initiatives can be crucial in revitalising urban areas, attracting investment and improving quality of life (Grodach & Loukaitou-Sideris, 2007).
3 Cultural diversity: Public support can help maintain and promote diverse cultural expressions that might not be commercially viable but are socially valuable (Throsby, 2010).
4 Soft power: A thriving cultural sector can enhance a country's international reputation and influence (Nye, 2004).

Policies can also create an environment where CCIs thrive economically and contribute significantly to societal well-being by addressing market failures, internalising positive externalities and promoting tangible social benefits. This balanced approach recognises culture and creativity's unique value as economic drivers and essential components of social progress.

However, it's important to note that designing effective policies for CCIs is complex and context-dependent. Policymakers must carefully consider the specific characteristics of their cultural ecosystems, balancing economic objectives with cultural and social goals. Different countries have developed varied strategies to support their CCIs in the last decades, reflecting their unique circumstances, priorities and challenges.

Policies can be defined as systematic courses of action governments produce to address specific issues or achieve desired societal outcomes. They represent the government's intentions and are implemented through various instruments such as laws, regulations, executive orders and funding priorities (Birkland, 2015). In the context of CCIs, public policies encompass various interventions designed to support, regulate and promote creative sectors, from tax incentives for film production to copyright laws protecting artistic works. These policies are formulated through complex processes involving multiple stakeholders, including policymakers, industry representatives, cultural institutions and civil society organisations.

The relevance of public policies and state participation in guiding market forces towards social progress must be considered, particularly in CCIs. While market mechanisms can drive innovation and efficiency, they may only sometimes align with broader societal goals such as cultural preservation, equitable access to creative content or nurturing diverse artistic expressions (Throsby, 2018). State intervention through well-crafted public policies can help correct market failures, internalise positive externalities generated by creative activities, and ensure that the economic potential of CCIs translates into tangible social benefits. By setting strategic frameworks and providing targeted support, governments can foster an environment where creative industries thrive economically and contribute to social cohesion, cultural diversity and sustainable development (UNESCO, 2022). This balanced approach recognises the unique value of culture and creativity as economic drivers and essential components of societal well-being.

BOX 6.1 POLICIES: WHAT, WHY AND HOW?

What: CCI policies are comprehensive strategic frameworks designed to nurture, support and develop cultural and creative sectors.
Why: These policies are essential for:

1. Directing economic growth towards a holistic development strategy
2. Leveraging the unique value of CCIs for societal and cultural benefit
3. Fostering innovation and creativity across various sectors
4. Preserving and promoting cultural heritage while encouraging new forms of expression

How: CCI policies are implemented through a multifaceted approach, including:

1. Financial incentives (e.g., grants, tax breaks, subsidies)
2. Regulatory frameworks (e.g., intellectual property protection, fair competition laws)
3. Educational initiatives (e.g., arts education, creative skills training)
4. Infrastructure development (e.g., cultural spaces, digital platforms)
5. International promotion and cultural diplomacy
6. Public-private partnerships
7. Support for research and development in creative technologies

Each nation tailors these elements to its specific context, cultural strengths and long-term goals.

As we stand at the threshold of a new era in global cultural and economic dynamics, it is imperative to critically examine the policies that have shaped different approaches in CCIs over the past few decades. The turn of the millennium ushered in a period of unprecedented globalisation, technological integration and homogenised consumption trends. While these forces undeniably fostered economic growth and cultural exchange, they also gave rise to unforeseen challenges and deepening disparities.

The first cycle of global CCI policies, emerging in the late 1990s, was a product of its time. It embraced the promise of an interconnected world, where borders seemed to fade in the face of digital innovation and global markets. However, in our pursuit of growth and integration, we often overlooked the importance of diversity and the persistence of inequalities. The result was a widening chasm of social and economic disparities, felt acutely in both the Global North and South.

The year 2020 marked a pivotal moment in this trajectory. The global pandemic disrupted our way of life and catalysed reassessment and change. It accelerated the integration of artificial intelligence and information and communication technologies into our markets, reshaping the landscape of production and consumption. Moreover, it challenged our assumptions about globalisation and highlighted the need for more resilient, equitable systems. As the world navigates this new phase of the 21st century, the approach of policies for CCIs must evolve. We can only afford to pursue innovation and GDP growth with careful consideration of their broader impacts. The potential for CCIs to exacerbate wage gaps, media monopolies and various forms of social divide – be it gender, race or digital – demands our attention and action.

As we stand at this crossroads in 2024, the creative industries offer a vision of how we might come together, reimagining our shared future through the lens of human ingenuity and cultural expression. The path forward must be clarified and easy, but the creative industries have repeatedly shown their capacity for adaptation and innovation (UNESCO, 2022). As they navigate the challenges of this new landscape – from digital disruption to cultural wars – they continue to play a crucial role in shaping our understanding of ourselves and our world. In doing so, they reflect our society and help shape its future, offering new ways of seeing, thinking and being in an increasingly complex world.

The following pages will offer a panoramic flight around a few models of policies for CCIs and will highlight an overview of commonalities and differences among these policies.

6.2 A Global View of Policies for CCIs

In this overview of CCI policies across 13 diverse countries, readers will gain insight into three crucial cultural policy and management aspects. The exploration begins with examining funding models and sector prioritisation, revealing how nations balance public and private investment and which cultural sectors are receiving global attention. The discussion then lands on policy stability and efforts to address inequalities, highlighting the interplay between political environments, cultural policy consistency and various strategies to promote diversity and rectify historical imbalances. Finally, the analysis turns to the organisational structures countries employ to oversee their cultural policies, from centralised ministries to specialised agencies, demonstrating how governmental approaches shape the development of cultural sectors. Throughout this journey, readers will encounter resumed and comparative analyses of established cultural powerhouses and emerging players in the global creative economy, uncovering key trends, unique national strategies, and the challenges countries face in nurturing their CCIs in an increasingly digital and globalised world. The proposal is a panoramic view and not an in-depth analysis, so it can guide your future research to uncover specificities if you want more information about one of these countries.

6.2.1 Part 1: Model for Funding and Sectors Prioritised

The funding models and sector prioritisation in CCIs reflect each country's economic structure, cultural heritage and policy priorities. Developed economies tend to have more sophisticated hybrid models, balancing public and private investments, while emerging economies are still evolving their approaches. This diversity in funding strategies highlights the complex nature of supporting cultural production in a globalised digital age. For instance,

France's model of solid-state support and public-private partnerships exemplifies the European tradition of viewing culture as a public good. This approach has allowed France to maintain a robust film industry and protect its cultural heritage. In contrast, the United States' primarily private sector-driven model reflects its market-oriented economy, resulting in globally dominant entertainment industries but potentially underserving less commercially viable cultural sectors.

Interestingly, despite varied economic and cultural backgrounds, there's a noticeable convergence in the prioritised sectors across countries. This trend suggests a global recognition of specific industries – particularly film, digital media and music – as critical drivers of cultural expression and economic growth in the 21st century.

South Korea's focus on K-pop, film, gaming and animation showcases a strategic approach to leveraging cultural soft power for economic gain. The global success of Korean popular culture demonstrates how targeted support for specific sectors can yield significant returns. Similarly, India's emphasis on its film industry (Bollywood) capitalises on a long-standing cultural strength while adapting to new digital platforms (Table 6.1).

TABLE 6.1 Global Models for CCIs Funding

Country	*Model for Funding*	*Sectors Prioritised*
United Kingdom	Hybrid, significant public funding and tax incentives	Film, TV, digital media, music, performing arts
France	Strong state support, tax incentives, public-private partnerships	Film, audiovisual, literature, visual arts, heritage
Australia	Hybrid, with public funding and tax incentives	Film, TV, digital games, design, visual arts
United States	Primarily private sector-driven, limited public funding	Film, TV, digital media, music
Brazil	Hybrid, significant public funding (e.g., Lei Rouanet)	Audiovisual, music, literature, traditional expressions
South Korea	Hybrid, strong government support, growing private involvement	K-pop, film, gaming, animation
China	Predominantly state-driven, increasing market approaches	Film, digital media, cultural tourism, traditional crafts
Colombia	Hybrid, emphasis on tax incentives (Orange Economy)	Audiovisual, music, digital content, cultural tourism

(*Continued*)

TABLE 6.1 (Continued)

Country	*Model for Funding*	*Sectors Prioritised*
Canada	Hybrid, significant public funding and tax incentives	Film, TV, digital media, music, literature, video games
Italy	Hybrid, public funding, tax incentives, growing private sector	Film, fashion, design, literature, cultural heritage
Argentina	Hybrid, public funding and tax incentives	Film, TV, music, literature
India	Primarily private sector-driven with some government support	Film (Bollywood), music, animation, digital media
Spain	Hybrid, significant public funding and tax incentives	Film, TV, music, literature, cultural tourism

The comparison reveals that while most countries employ a hybrid funding model, the balance between public and private involvement varies significantly. Countries like France and South Korea demonstrate strong state support, while the United States and India lean more towards private sector-driven models. This spectrum reflects differing philosophies on the role of government in cultural production and preservation. Colombia's emphasis on the "Orange Economy" represents an innovative approach to conceptualising and supporting CCIs, particularly in a developing economy context. The Latin American country aims to attract investment and foster digital content and cultural tourism growth by framing creative industries as a critical economic sector.

6.2.2 Part 2: Policy Stability and Actions to Address Inequalities

Policy stability in the CCI sector is closely tied to each country's broader political and economic stability. Nations with longer-standing democratic traditions or centralised governance tend to exhibit more consistent cultural policies. However, this stability only sometimes correlates with the effectiveness or progressiveness of these policies. The challenge lies in maintaining policy continuity while adapting to rapidly changing technological and social landscapes that impact cultural production and consumption.

China's stable policy environment, aligned with its Five-Year Plans, allows for long-term strategic development of cultural industries. This approach has enabled significant growth in digital media and cultural tourism. However, it also raises questions about the balance between state control and artistic freedom. In contrast, Brazil's fluctuating policies reflect its complex political landscape. The Lei Rouanet (Rouanet Law), a significant cultural funding mechanism, has undergone multiple changes with different administrations, creating uncertainty in the sector. Despite these challenges, Brazil's commitment to programmes like Cultura Viva demonstrates an ongoing effort to democratise culture amid political changes.

Addressing inequalities within the cultural sector is common across most countries, reflecting a growing awareness of the importance of diverse representation in artistic expression. However, the approaches vary widely, from quota systems to targeted funding programmes, demonstrating that there is no one-size-fits-all solution to this complex issue.

Canada's strong focus on supporting Indigenous arts and regional development stands out as a comprehensive approach to addressing historical inequalities and promoting cultural diversity. This policy direction supports underrepresented voices and enriches the country's overall cultural landscape (Table 6.2).

TABLE 6.2 Global Policy Stability and Inequalities Approach in CCIs

Country	*Policy Stability*	*Actions to Address Inequalities*
United Kingdom	Relatively stable across governments	Regional development, diversity quotas in public funding
France	Stable, with long-term cultural policy traditions	Cultural democratisation efforts, support for regional cultures
Australia	Fluctuating, with changes in government priorities	Indigenous arts support, regional development initiatives
United States	Fluctuating, limited federal-level consistency	Limited federal initiatives, some local programmes
Brazil	Fluctuating, significant changes with political shifts	Programmes like Cultura Viva for democratising culture
South Korea	Stable, long-term strategic planning	Efforts to spread industries beyond Seoul
China	Stable, aligned with Five-Year Plans	Developing cultural industries in less developed regions
Colombia	Fluctuating, changes in government priorities	Support for diverse expressions, including marginalised communities
Canada	Relatively stable across governments	Strong focus on supporting Indigenous arts and regional development
Italy	Fluctuating with changes in government, some long-term traditions	Efforts to support southern regions and preserve local cultural traditions

(*Continued*)

TABLE 6.2 (Continued)

Country	*Policy Stability*	*Actions to Address Inequalities*
Argentina	Fluctuating with significant changes in political shifts	Programmes to support regional cultural development and indigenous expressions
India	Relatively stable with growing focus on creative industries	Efforts to promote diverse linguistic and regional cultural expressions
Spain	Relatively stable with some fluctuations due to regional autonomy	Support for regional cultures and languages due to autonomous community structure

The data shows a clear divide between countries with stable cultural policies (like South Korea and Canada) and those experiencing frequent fluctuations (such as Brazil and Argentina). This instability can challenge long-term planning and development in the CCI sector. However, it's noteworthy that even in countries with fluctuating policies, there are consistent efforts to address cultural inequalities, suggesting a global recognition of this issue's importance.

Spain's approach to supporting regional cultures and languages within its autonomous communities' structure offers an exciting model for countries with diverse internal cultural landscapes. This decentralised approach allows for the preservation and promotion of local cultural identities within a national framework.

6.2.3 Part 3: Leading Policy Organisms and Dedicated CCI Institutions

The organisational structure of cultural policy administration provides insight into how different countries prioritise and manage their CCIs. A dedicated ministry or department for culture is almost universal, indicating the recognised importance of this sector. However, the scope and influence of these bodies vary considerably, reflecting differences in governmental structures and the perceived role of culture in national development.

The United Kingdom's Department for Digital, Culture, Media & Sport (DCMS) exemplifies a comprehensive approach, integrating traditional cultural sectors with digital media and sports. This structure reflects the United Kingdom's recognition of the interconnected nature of these fields in the modern economy and their collective contribution to the country's soft power and creative industries. In contrast, the United States stands out because it lacks a centralised federal body for cultural policy. The limited roles of the National Endowment for the Arts (NEA) and National Endowment for the

Humanities (NEH) reflect a more decentralised approach, with significant responsibility falling to state-level initiatives and the private sector. This model has led to a diverse and dynamic cultural landscape but can also result in uneven support across regions and disciplines.

Establishing dedicated CCI institutions represents a more focused approach to nurturing specific sectors within the broader cultural landscape. These institutions often reflect national priorities and strengths, such as film agencies in countries with solid cinematic traditions.

France's Centre National du Cinéma et de l'Image Animée (CNC) is a prime example of a specialised institution that has played a crucial role in maintaining the country's influential position in global cinema. The CNC's comprehensive support for film production, distribution and preservation has been instrumental in sustaining France's unique cinematic culture. Similarly, South Korea's Korea Creative Content Agency (KOCCA) has been pivotal in the global success of Korean popular culture. KOCCA has helped position South Korea as a major exporter of cultural content by providing targeted support for sectors like K-pop, animation and gaming (Table 6.3).

TABLE 6.3 Global Leading Policy Organisms for CCIs

Country	*Leading Policy Organism*	*Dedicated CCI Institutions*
United Kingdom	Department for Digital, Culture, Media & Sport (DCMS)	Creative Industries Council
France	Ministry of Culture	Centre National du Cinéma et de l'Image Animée (CNC)
Australia	Department of Infrastructure, Transport, Regional Development and Communications	Australia Council for the Arts, Screen Australia
United States	No centralised federal body; NEA and NEH play limited roles	No dedicated federal-level institution
Brazil	Ministry of Culture (subject to political changes)	ANCINE (National Film Agency), Cultura Viva programme
South Korea	Ministry of Culture, Sports and Tourism	Korea Creative Content Agency (KOCCA)
China	Ministry of Culture and Tourism	China Animation Comic Game Industry Association
Colombia	Ministry of Culture (reinstated in 2023)	Orange Economy Council

(Continued)

TABLE 6.3 (Continued)

Country	*Leading Policy Organism*	*Dedicated CCI Institutions*
Canada	Department of Canadian Heritage	Canada Council for the Arts, Telefilm Canada
Italy	Ministry of Culture	Istituto Luce Cinecittà (for film industry)
Argentina	Ministry of Culture	National Institute of Cinema and Audiovisual Arts (INCAA)
India	Ministry of Culture and Ministry of Information and Broadcasting	National Film Development Corporation (NFDC)
Spain	Ministry of Culture and Sport	Institute of Cinematography and Audiovisual Arts (ICAA)

This comparison highlights the diversity in approaches to cultural policy administration. While most countries have centralised cultural ministries, their effectiveness and reach vary. The United States stands out with its decentralised approach, relying more on private initiatives and state-level programmes. The presence of dedicated CCI institutions in most countries underscores a trend towards specialised support for high-potential cultural sectors, particularly in audiovisual industries.

India's dual ministry approach, with separate ministries for Culture, Information, and Broadcasting, reflects the country's vast and diverse cultural landscape. This structure allows for focused attention on traditional artistic forms and the rapidly growing media and entertainment sectors. The National Film Development Corporation (NFDC) supports India's influential film industry, balancing commercial success with artistic and cultural objectives.

In conclusion, examining CCI policies across various countries reveals a complex global landscape characterised by diverse approaches, shared challenges and evolving strategies. From the market-oriented models of the United Kingdom and the United States to the more state-centric approaches of France and China and the hybrid systems seen in countries like Brazil, South Korea and Canada, it's clear that there is no one-size-fits-all solution to fostering vibrant and sustainable creative economies. Each nation grapples with balancing economic imperatives with cultural preservation, addressing regional disparities and adapting to rapid technological changes. The varying degrees of policy stability and efforts to address inequalities further underscore the intricate nature of developing effective CCI policies.

As we look to the future, it is evident that CCIs will continue to play a crucial role in shaping national identities, driving economic growth and fostering social cohesion. The global trends identified in this chapter – including the push for more inclusive and equitable policies, the need for adaptability in the face of digital transformation, and the growing recognition of CCIs' contribution to sustainable development – point towards a future where CCI policies must become more holistic, flexible and responsive to both local needs and global dynamics. Policymakers, industry leaders and cultural practitioners worldwide must collaborate to create frameworks that drive innovation and economic prosperity, preserve cultural diversity, promote social equity and contribute to the overall well-being of societies. As CCIs continue to evolve, so must the policies supporting them, ensuring that creativity remains a powerful force for positive change in our increasingly interconnected world.

References

Bakhshi, H., & McVittie, E. (2009). Creative supply-chain linkages and innovation: Do the creative industries stimulate business innovation in the wider economy? Innovation: Management. *Policy & Practice*, 11(2), 169–189.

Belfiore, E., & Bennett, O. (2007). Rethinking the social impacts of the arts. *International Journal of Cultural Policy*, 13(2), 135–151.

Birkland, T. A. (2015). *An introduction to the policy process: Theories, concepts, and models of public policy making*. Routledge.

Crossick, G., & Kaszynska, P. (2016). *Understanding the value of arts & culture: The AHRC Cultural Value Project*. Arts and Humanities Research Council.

DCMS (Department for Digital, Culture, Media & Sport). (2023b). *DCMS sectors economic estimates 2022: Employment*. https://www.gov.uk/government/statistics/economic-estimates-earnings-2023-and-employment-october-2022-to-september-2023-for-the-dcms-sectors-and-digital-sector

Grodach, C., & Loukaitou-Sideris, A. (2007). Cultural development strategies and urban revitalization: A survey of US cities. *International Journal of Cultural Policy*, 13(4), 349–370.

Nye, J. S. (2004). *Soft power: The means to success in world politics*. Public Affairs.

Throsby, D. (2010). *The economics of cultural policy*. Cambridge University Press.

Throsby, D. (2018). *Art, politics, money: Revisiting Australia's cultural policy*. Currency House.

Towse, R. (2019). *A textbook of cultural economics*. Cambridge University Press.

UNESCO. (2022). *Re|shaping policies for creativity – Addressing culture as a global public good*. UNESCO. https://en.unesco.org/creativity/publications/reshaping-policies-creativity-addressing-culture-global

7

THE CHALLENGES AND OPPORTUNITIES IN THE MEASUREMENT OF CREATIVE AND CULTURAL INDUSTRIES AND ECONOMIC DEVELOPMENT

In an increasingly interconnected global economy, the role of creative and cultural industries (CCIs) in driving economic development has raised significant attention from policymakers, economists and cultural practitioners alike. As nations strive to diversify their economic bases and tap into the potential of the knowledge economy, CCIs have emerged as a promising sector capable of generating both monetary value and social impact (Throsby, 2008; UNESCO, 2018). However, quantifying the precise contribution of CCIs to economic development presents a complex challenge. Traditional economic indicators, such as Gross Domestic Product (GDP), often fail to capture the total value created by creative and cultural activities (Bakhshi et al., 2015; Cunningham & Potts, 2015). This chapter approaches the intricate relationship between CCIs and economic development, examining available data and analytical approaches.

Our exploration begins with a critical assessment of conventional economic metrics, highlighting their limitations in measuring the multifaceted impact of CCIs. The need for more GDP as a sole measure of economic well-being has been widely recognised (Stiglitz et al., 2009), and this shortcoming is particularly acute when it comes to capturing the value of cultural and creative activities. The chapter examines alternative approaches and complementary indicators that provide a more comprehensive picture of CCIs' economic and social contributions. Also, it brings attention to the diverse data sources on CCIs worldwide and gives a global overview of the sector's financial footprint. This comprehensive approach allows us to paint a more accurate picture of CCIs' contribution to national and regional economies, drawing on data from international organisations such as UNESCO and UNCTAD, national statistical offices (NSOs) and industry reports (UNCTAD, 2021; UNESCO, 2022).

DOI: 10.4324/9781003434252-8

This chapter also presents two examples of research aimed at developing innovations in measuring CCIs to illustrate the practical aspects of knowledge exchange between research and policy. These examples, conducted by the author of this book, ground our analysis in real-world contexts. The first case study examines the interplay between GDP and creative occupations in Brazil. The second explores the Relative Values Project, an innovative research initiative representing a significant step towards developing a more nuanced understanding of CCIs' socio-economic impacts. The Relative Values Project, through a co-creative partnership with arts organisations in Britain and Brazil, aimed to construct a new narrative about the transformational change generated by cultural activities. By building multidimensional indicators in collaboration with arts organisations, the project offers a fresh perspective on measuring CCIs' impact beyond traditional economic metrics.

This chapter aims to go beyond mere statistical analysis, delving into the qualitative aspects of CCIs' impact on economic development. Doing so seeks to provide a more holistic understanding of the sector's role in shaping modern economies and societies. This approach aligns with recent scholarship emphasising the need for a more nuanced understanding of cultural value and its relationship to economic outcomes (Throsby & Zednik, 2014). Navigating this complex landscape, we will also identify gaps in current data and methodologies, highlighting areas where further research and more refined measurement tools are needed. This critical approach will contribute to more accurately assessing CCIs' economic impact and inform future policy decisions and research directions in this vital field.

The chapter concludes by discussing the policy implications of our findings and proposing directions for future research. By comprehensively analysing the available data on CCIs and economic development, the aim is to equip policymakers, researchers and industry practitioners with the insights needed to foster a thriving creative economy in diverse global contexts.

7.1 Limitations of GDP and Quantitative Metrics

The Evolution and Strengths of GDP (Gross Domestic Product)

GDP is the total monetary value of all finished goods and services produced within a country's borders in a specific time, typically a year or quarter. It can be calculated using three main approaches: the production approach, the income approach and the expenditure approach (Landefeld et al., 2008). The development of GDP represented a significant advancement in economic measurement, providing a standardised, comprehensive and simple tool for comparing economic growth across countries and guiding economic policy.

The strengths of GDP as an economic indicator are numerous. It offers a uniform measure for comparisons across countries and periods, attempts to capture all economic activity within a nation's borders and distils complex financial data into a single, easily understood figure. Governments and international organisations use GDP as a critical indicator for economic policymaking, including monetary and fiscal policy decisions. At the same time, businesses rely on GDP forecasts for strategic planning and investment decisions (Coyle, 2014).

7.1.1 Early Critiques and Adaptations

Even as GDP gained prominence, economists recognised its limitations. Simon Kuznets warned against using GDP as a measure of welfare, noting that "the welfare of a nation can scarcely be inferred from a measure of national income" (Kuznets, 1934). In the 1970s, Nordhaus and Tobin proposed adjustments to GDP for leisure time, unpaid work and environmental damage, introducing their Measure of Economic Welfare (MEW) (Nordhaus & Tobin, 1972). Around the same time, Richard Easterlin's research highlighted the disconnect between rising GDP and stagnant happiness levels in developed countries, sparking debates about the relationship between economic growth and well-being (Easterlin, 1974).

7.1.1.1 Limitations of GDP in Capturing Cultural and Creative Value

As the importance of CCIs has grown, the shortcomings of GDP in reflecting their actual value have become more pronounced. These limitations can be categorised into several key areas:

1 Exclusion of Non-Market Activities

GDP primarily focuses on market transactions, overlooking many cultural activities that don't involve direct monetary exchange. This omission is particularly problematic for CCIs, where significant value is often created outside traditional market structures. Amateur arts and crafts, community festivals, volunteer work in cultural organisations, open-source creative projects and peer-to-peer sharing of cultural content contribute to cultural richness. Still, they are largely invisible in GDP calculations.

Throsby (2001) argues that these non-market activities often form the foundation of a society's cultural capital. He proposes the concept of "cultural capital" as a complement to traditional economic measures, encompassing both tangible assets (like heritage buildings) and intangible ones (like conventional knowledge and practices). Klamer (2017) goes further, suggesting that the most valuable aspects of culture often lie outside the market sphere. He introduces the concept of the "value-based economy," where cultural and social values are given equal weight to economic ones in assessing societal progress.

2 Inability to Measure Quality

GDP is inherently quantity-focused, failing to differentiate between high- and low-quality cultural products. This quantitative bias can lead to significant distortions in valuing cultural and creative outputs. For example, mass-produced art might contribute more to GDP than a single, highly influential original artwork, and blockbuster films with significant box office returns would be valued more in GDP terms than lower-budget, critically acclaimed films that may have more significant cultural impact (Klamer, 2017). Bakhshi et al. (2015) highlight the need for new metrics to capture the qualitative aspects of cultural production. They propose approaches like expert evaluations, audience impact assessments and longitudinal studies of cultural influence to complement traditional economic measures.

3 Disregard for Long-Term Value

The long-term cultural and social impacts of creative works often fail to be reflected in GDP calculations, which typically focus on annual or quarterly economic activity. This short-term focus fails to capture the enduring value of many cultural and creative outputs, such as cultural heritage's educational value, art's inspirational effects on future generations and the long-term influence of innovative designs (Bakhshi et al., 2015). Throsby (2010) introduces the concept of "cultural sustainability," arguing that the preservation and development of cultural capital should be considered alongside economic and environmental sustainability in policymaking.

4 Neglect of Digital Value

The digital revolution has dramatically changed how cultural content is created, distributed and consumed. GDP struggles to account for many aspects of the digital creative economy, significantly undervaluing digital cultural production. Free digital content, user-generated content, value created through data collection and analysis and new digital cultural experiences all present challenges for traditional economic measurement (OECD, 2018).

Bakhshi and Throsby (2012) explore the concept of "cultural value in the digital age," arguing for new frameworks that can capture the unique ways digital technologies enable cultural creation, distribution and consumption.

5 Failure to Capture Externalities

CCIs often generate positive externalities that benefit society but are not reflected in market transactions. These spillover effects, such as enhanced social cohesion, improved mental health and well-being, increased tourism, innovation spillovers, urban regeneration and educational benefits, remain largely invisible in GDP calculations (Throsby, 2010).

Sacco et al. (2013) developed the concept of "culture 3.0," emphasising the role of culture as a platform for social and economic development.

They argue that traditional financial measures fail to capture the transformative potential of culture in areas like social innovation, lifelong learning and sustainable development.

6 Inability to Reflect Cultural Diversity

GDP treats all economic activity equally, failing to account for the importance of cultural diversity. This can lead to policies prioritising economic growth at the expense of cultural richness and diversity. The undervaluation of minority cultural expressions, traditional cultural practices and diverse local cultural productions in GDP calculations poses significant challenges to maintaining and promoting cultural diversity (UNESCO, 2009).

Yúdice (2003) argues for a broader understanding of culture as a resource for social and economic development, emphasising the need to value diverse cultural expressions and practices in an increasingly globalised world.

7.2 The Need for Qualitative and Alternative Metrics

Recognising the limitations of Gross Domestic Product (GDP) in capturing the full value of CCIs, researchers and policymakers have developed various alternative metrics. These approaches aim to provide a more comprehensive and nuanced understanding of the cultural and creative sectors' contributions to society and the economy (Throsby, 2008). This paper synthesises five critical categories of alternative metrics: cultural participation indicators, cultural vitality indices, creative economy frameworks, well-being indicators and innovation metrics.

7.2.1 Cultural Participation Indicators

Cultural participation indicators measure engagement with cultural activities, offering insight into the reach and impact of CCIs. UNESCO's Framework for Cultural Statistics (2009) provides guidelines for collecting and analysing these indicators, emphasising both active and passive forms of cultural participation. Key metrics include attendance rates at cultural events, time spent on creative pursuits, digital engagement with cultural content, cultural education participation and media consumption patterns.

These indicators provide a more direct measure of how artistic and creative outputs are consumed and valued by society, addressing some of the limitations of GDP in capturing non-market cultural activities (Crossick & Kaszynska, 2016).

7.2.2 Cultural Vitality Indices

Cultural vitality indices are composite measures that assess the overall health of a community's cultural ecosystem. Jackson et al. (2006) developed a comprehensive framework for measuring cultural vitality in communities, emphasising three main dimensions: opportunities for cultural participation, cultural participation itself and support for cultural activities.

Components often included in cultural vitality indices are:

Presence of cultural institutions
Availability of cultural education
Support for local artists and creators
Cultural diversity measures
Community engagement in culture

Markusen and Gadwa (2010) build on this work, proposing the concept of "creative placemaking" to understand and measure how cultural activities contribute to community development and quality of life.

7.2.3 Creative Economy Frameworks

Creative economy frameworks offer holistic approaches that consider the broader economic impacts of creativity, including direct, indirect and induced effects across various economic sectors. The UNCTAD Creative Economy Report series (2008, 2010, 2013) has been instrumental in developing and promoting these broader frameworks, emphasising the interconnectedness of culture, economy and technology in driving creative sector growth.

Critical components of creative economy frameworks include:

Direct economic contributions of CCIs
Indirect effects on other sectors
Induced effects through increased spending
Creative intensity of occupations
Innovation metrics related to creative activities

These frameworks attempt to capture the total economic impact of CCIs, addressing GDP's limitation in measuring spillover effects and intersectoral influences (Potts & Cunningham, 2008).

7.2.3.1 Well-being Indicators

Well-being indicators attempt to capture the contribution of culture and creativity to the overall quality of life, recognising that the value of cultural activities extends beyond economic measures to include social, psychological and community benefits. The New Zealand Treasury's Living Standards Framework (2018), for example, incorporates cultural identity as one of its crucial well-being domains, including indicators such as a sense of belonging, the ability to express identity and engagement with artistic practices.

Fujiwara et al. (2014) researched the well-being value of culture in the United Kingdom, using large-scale survey data to monetise the benefits of cultural participation. Their findings suggest that the well-being value of cultural engagement often far exceeds the market value captured by traditional economic measures.

The OECD's Better Life Index includes measures of civic engagement and social connections, which are often influenced by cultural participation. This provides a more holistic view of societal progress beyond GDP (OECD, 2020).

7.2.3.2 Innovation Metrics

Innovation metrics measure the role of CCIs in driving innovation across the economy, recognising that creative activities often spark new ideas, processes and technologies that benefit multiple sectors. Bakhshi et al. (2008) demonstrate how creative industries support innovation on the broader economy, emphasising the need for metrics that capture these spillover effects.

Key innovation metrics related to CCIs include:

Patents and trademarks in creative fields
Cross-sector collaboration rates
Adoption of creative technologies
Creative problem-solving methodologies
Cultural and creative education in STEM fields (STEAM approach)

The European Commission's Cultural and Creative Cities Monitor (2019) includes innovation metrics in its assessment of cultural and creative city performance, recognising the crucial role of CCIs in driving urban innovation and economic development. Cunningham and Potts (2015) propose a four-model framework for understanding the relationship between creative industries and innovation. They argue that the innovation model is increasingly dominant, necessitating new metrics to capture these complex relationships.

Developing these alternative metrics represents a significant advancement in our ability to measure and understand the total value of CCIs. By addressing many of GDP's limitations, these new approaches provide a more comprehensive picture of the cultural, social and economic impacts of CCIs. However, challenges still need to be solved in data collection, standardisation and integration of these metrics into policy-making processes.

Future research should focus on refining these metrics, improving data collection methodologies and developing frameworks to integrate these diverse measures into cohesive assessments of CCI value. Additionally, policymakers and industry stakeholders should increase the adoption of these alternative metrics to ensure that the total value of CCIs is recognised and supported in economic and cultural policy decisions.

7.3 Challenges in Measuring Intangible Assets and Spillover Effects

The CCIs have gained increasing recognition for their economic and social contributions. However, accurately measuring their value remains a significant challenge due to the unique characteristics of cultural and creative production. Below, you will find the four critical difficulties in quantifying intangible assets and externalities in CCIs, focusing on four main areas: intangible assets, knowledge spillovers, network effects and cultural externalities.

7.3.1 Intangible Assets

CCIs rely heavily on intangible assets, which are notoriously difficult to quantify using traditional economic measures. This reliance systematically undervalues creative sectors in national accounts and financial statements (Haskel & Westlake, 2018). The challenges in measuring intangible assets in CCIs span several categories, including intellectual property (IP) valuation, brand value and reputation, human capital and organisational culture.

IP valuation in CCIs is particularly complex due to the difficulty in predicting future earnings from copyrights, trademarks and design rights. The variability in the lifespan and impact of creative works further complicates this process. Similarly, brand value and reputation in creative industries are highly intangible and subject to rapid fluctuations, making them challenging to measure accurately.

Human capital in CCIs, comprising skills, creativity and know-how, presents its own measurement challenges. The implicit nature of much creative knowledge and the rapid evolution of skills in these sectors make it difficult to quantify this crucial asset. Additionally, the value of collaborative creativity, which is often central to CCIs, takes a lot of work to measure using traditional metrics.

Organisational culture and creative ecosystems also contribute significantly to the value of CCIs but are inherently intangible. The innovative potential of creative organisations and the value of creative networks and clusters are examples of assets crucial to CCIs but challenging to quantify.

Haskel and Westlake (2018) argue that traditional accounting and economic measures need to be equipped to capture the value of these intangible assets. They propose several approaches to address this issue, including developing new accounting standards for intangible assets, creating satellite accounts for intangibles in national economic statistics and using big data and AI to track the creation and use of intangible assets.

7.3.2 Knowledge Spillovers

Ideas and innovations from CCIs often diffuse into other sectors, creating value that is difficult to track and attribute. This diffusion process, usually informal and occurring through multiple channels, presents significant measurement challenges (Bakhshi et al., 2008). One of the primary difficulties in measuring knowledge spillovers from CCIs is attribution. Tracing the origin of creative ideas as they spread across sectors and quantifying the contribution of creative inputs to innovations in other fields is a complex task. This challenge is compounded by the often-lengthy time lag between introducing innovative ideas and their impact in different sectors, making it challenging to link current economic outcomes to past creative investments.

The informal nature of knowledge transfer in creative sectors adds another layer of complexity. Tacit knowledge exchange, often facilitated through social networks and creative clusters, is significant in CCIs but challenging to track through traditional economic metrics. Furthermore, the wide-ranging influence of innovative ideas across diverse industries makes it challenging to measure how creative methodologies (e.g., design thinking) impact other sectors.

To address these challenges, Bakhshi et al. (2008) propose several approaches, including developing more sophisticated input–output models to track creative inputs across the economy, using network analysis to map knowledge flows between creative and non-creative sectors, and conducting longitudinal studies to track the long-term impacts of creative innovations.

7.3.2.1 Network Effects

The value created through creative clusters and ecosystems often exceeds the sum of individual contributions, known as network effects. These synergistic effects are difficult to measure using traditional economic metrics, leading to the potential undervaluation of creative hubs and cultural districts (Pratt & Jeffcutt, 2009).

Measuring network effects in CCIs involves several challenges. Quantifying informal collaboration and knowledge exchange between co-located creative businesses is complex, as is assessing the collective drawing power of innovative clusters. While significant, the cumulative attraction of talent and investment to creative hubs is difficult to attribute directly to the presence of creative ecosystems.

Enhanced innovation through knowledge exchange within creative networks is another crucial aspect of network effects that poses measurement challenges. Tracking the flow of ideas within these networks and quantifying the innovation premium of creative cluster participation require new methodological approaches.

Pratt and Jeffcutt (2009) emphasise the complexity of these network effects and propose a "cultural ecosystem" approach that considers the interdependencies between various actors in creative clusters. Comunian (2011) suggests using social network analysis techniques to map and quantify the complex relationships within creative ecosystems, providing a more nuanced understanding of how value is created and distributed in these networks.

7.3.3 Cultural Externalities

The broader societal benefits of cultural activities, or cultural externalities, represent a significant portion of the value created by CCIs. However, these benefits are often intangible and challenging to quantify, remaining largely invisible in traditional economic measures (Throsby, 2010).

Cultural externalities include enhanced national or local identity, improved intercultural understanding, educational and cognitive benefits, and health and well-being impacts. Measuring these effects presents numerous challenges. For instance, quantifying the economic value of a stronger cultural identity or assessing the long-term benefits of cultural heritage preservation is complex and often subjective.

While widely recognised, cultural engagement's educational and cognitive benefits are difficult to measure in economic terms. This includes challenges in quantifying how cultural engagement contributes to lifelong learning and assessing the spillover effects of creative skills on other domains. Similarly, while cultural participation has been linked to health and well-being benefits, measuring healthcare cost savings or quantifying mental health improvements presents significant methodological challenges.

Throsby (2010) proposes several approaches to better capture these cultural externalities, including using contingent valuation methods to estimate willingness to pay for cultural benefits, developing cultural satellite accounts to track non-market cultural activities and employing multi-criteria analysis to assess the diverse impacts of cultural investments.

The challenges in measuring intangible assets and externalities in CCIs are multifaceted and complex. Traditional economic metrics and accounting practices often need to be revised to capture the full value created by these sectors. Addressing these challenges requires interdisciplinary approaches that combine economic analysis with insights from cultural studies, sociology, psychology and other relevant fields.

As the creative economy continues to grow in importance, refining our ability to measure and value these intangible assets and externalities becomes increasingly crucial. This will provide a more accurate picture of the economic contribution of CCIs and inform better policymaking and investment decisions in these vital sectors. Future research should focus on developing and refining new methodologies that can capture the unique value-creation processes in CCIs, ensuring that the full impact of these industries is recognised and supported.

The limitations of GDP and traditional quantitative metrics in capturing the total value of CCIs are significant and multifaceted. From excluding non-market activities to the inability to measure quality, long-term value and digital contributions, GDP falls short of providing a comprehensive picture of the cultural and creative economy. Developing and adopting alternative metrics for measuring the impact of CCIs is a challenging yet crucial endeavour. These new metrics are essential for several interconnected reasons. Firstly, they are vital in informing evidence-based policymaking by providing more accurate and comprehensive measures of CCIs' contributions, leading to better-targeted policies and support mechanisms for the sector. Secondly, they allow for a more precise assessment of CCIs' contribution to development. They offer a fuller understanding of how culture and creativity drive social and economic progress, which can inform broader development strategies.

Moreover, these alternative metrics are instrumental in justifying public and private investment in CCIs. By demonstrating the wide-ranging impacts of cultural and creative initiatives, they can help secure much-needed funding and support. Additionally, new metrics are crucial for recognising diverse forms of value creation and acknowledging and promoting the various ways CCIs contribute to society beyond mere economic output. Lastly, developing these metrics significantly aligns economic measures with societal goals. By capturing a broader range of cultural and social values, they can help ensure that monetary policies are more closely attuned to overall societal well-being. In essence, adopting alternative metrics for CCIs is not just about better measurement but about fostering a more holistic and nuanced understanding of the role of culture and creativity in our societies and economies.

As economies evolve, with intangible assets and creative capital playing increasingly central roles, the need for more sophisticated measurement approaches becomes more pressing. Future research and policy efforts should focus on:

- Developing robust, comprehensive frameworks that capture the full spectrum of value created by CCIs.
- Integrating qualitative and quantitative approaches to provide a more nuanced understanding of cultural and creative impacts.
- Leveraging new technologies, such as big data analytics and AI, to track and measure the complex interactions within creative ecosystems.
- Fostering interdisciplinary collaboration between economists, cultural theorists, data scientists and policymakers to develop innovative measurement methodologies.
- Promoting international standardisation of new metrics to enable meaningful comparisons and benchmarking across countries and regions.

By addressing these challenges and embracing new approaches to measuring the value of CCIs, societies can ensure that the vital contributions of culture and creativity to our societies and economies are fully recognised, supported and nurtured.

7.4 Sources of Data in CCIs Worldwide

Collecting and analysing data on CCIs is a complex and multifaceted endeavour involving various sources and methodologies. This section explores the primary data sources for CCIs worldwide, examining their strengths, limitations and challenges in collecting and harmonising data across different contexts. Below, you can find an overview of the primary sources of data for CCIs that can be useful for research and policymaking:

7.4.1 International Organisations

International organisations are crucial in collecting, analysing and disseminating data on CCIs worldwide. Their work often provides the foundation for cross-country comparisons and global analysis, shaping policy discussions and research agendas.

7.4.1.1 UNESCO (United Nations Educational, Scientific and Cultural Organisation)

UNESCO has been at the forefront of efforts to measure and analyse cultural activities globally, providing crucial frameworks and methodologies for understanding CCIs.

Key contributions:

- **Framework for Cultural Statistics (FCS)**: First developed in 1986 and revised in 2009, the FCS provides a conceptual foundation for defining and measuring cultural activities (UNESCO, 2009). The FCS defines six cultural domains (Cultural and Natural Heritage; Performance and Celebration; Visual Arts and Crafts; Books and Press; Audiovisual and Interactive Media; Design and Creative Services) and two related domains (Tourism, Sports and Recreation).
- **Culture for Development Indicators (CDIS)**: A suite of 22 indicators measuring the contribution of culture to sustainable development across seven dimensions: Economy, Education, Governance, Social Participation, Gender Equality, Communication, and Heritage (UNESCO, 2014). For example, the CDIS measures the contribution of cultural activities to GDP, cultural employment and household expenditure on culture.
- **Periodic Reports on the Convention on the Protection and Promotion of the Diversity of Cultural Expressions:** These quadrennial reports provide valuable data on policies and measures implemented by member states to support CCIs. They cover cultural policies, international cooperation, preferential treatment and integration of culture in sustainable development policies.

- **Institute for Statistics (UIS)**: UNESCO's statistical arm produces global databases on cultural employment, trade in cultural goods and services and cultural participation. For instance, the UIS data on feature films provides information on the number of national films produced, the market share of domestic films and cinema admissions across countries.

Strengths:

- Comprehensive coverage of cultural domains, providing a holistic view of CCIs
- Standardised definitions and methodologies, enabling cross-country comparisons
- Global scope and participation of member states, offering a truly international perspective
- Integration of culture into broader development frameworks, highlighting CCIs' wider societal impacts

Limitations:

- Reliance on national data sources of varying quality, potentially affecting data consistency
- Challenges in ensuring timely and regular data updates due to resource constraints and varying national capacities
- Limited granularity in some areas of CCIs, particularly emerging digital subsectors
- Difficulties in capturing informal cultural activities, which are significant in many developing countries

Furthermore, UNESCO's Culture|2030 Indicators UNESCO has recently developed the Culture|2030 Indicators framework to monitor the contribution of culture to the implementation of the UN 2030 Agenda for Sustainable Development. This framework includes 22 indicators across four thematic dimensions: Environment and Resilience, Prosperity and Livelihoods, Knowledge and Skills, and Inclusion and Participation. For example, under Prosperity and Livelihoods, the framework measures cultural employment, cultural businesses, household expenditure on culture, and trade in cultural goods and services. This initiative demonstrates UNESCO's ongoing efforts to integrate cultural data into broader development metrics and to provide policy-relevant information on CCIs' contributions to sustainable development.

7.4.1.2 UNCTAD (United Nations Conference on Trade and Development)

UNCTAD has been instrumental in highlighting the economic potential of CCIs, particularly in developing countries, through its focus on trade in creative goods and services.

Key contributions:

- **Creative Economy Reports:** Published in collaboration with UNDP, these reports provide a global analysis of trade in creative goods and services (UNCTAD, 2008, 2010, 2018). The reports classify creative industries into nine categories: Traditional Cultural Expressions, Performing Arts, Audiovisuals, New Media, Creative Services, Design, Publishing, Visual Arts, and Crafts.
- **Creative Economy Network:** An online platform for sharing data, best practices and analysis on the creative economy. It facilitates knowledge exchange among policymakers, researchers and creative professionals.
- **Creative Economy Outlook:** Regular publications update trends in the creative goods and services trade. For example, according to UNCTAD's Creative Economy Outlook 2022, the global market for creative goods has shown significant growth. The report indicates that the value of the international creative goods market reached $715 billion in 2020, despite the challenges posed by the COVID-19 pandemic. This represents a substantial increase from the $509 billion reported in 2015.
- **Global Database on Creative Economy:** UNCTAD maintains a comprehensive database on international trade in creative goods and services, covering over 200 countries and territories. Data on creative goods goes back to 2002 and on creative services to 2006.

Strengths:

- Focus on international trade in creative goods and services, providing crucial data on the global creative economy
- Emphasis on developing countries and emerging markets, highlighting the potential of CCIs for economic development
- Consistent time series data on creative exports and imports, enabling trend analysis
- Detailed product-level data, allowing for granular analysis of specific creative sectors

Limitations:

- Limited coverage of domestic cultural production and consumption, which are significant aspects of CCIs
- Challenges in capturing digital trade in creative services, an increasingly important component of the creative economy

- Difficulty in distinguishing between creative and non-creative components of goods, potentially leading to overestimation of creative trade
- Reliance on customs data, which may not fully capture intangible or digital creative products

Furthermore, UNCTAD's analysis of South-South trade in creative goods UNCTAD's research has highlighted the growing importance of South-South trade in creative goods. For example, their analysis showed that between 2002 and 2015, South-South trade in creative goods more than tripled, from $7.8 billion to $27.8 billion. This trend is particularly significant in sectors like design, where developing countries have become major exporters. For instance, China has emerged as the world's largest exporter of creative goods, with its exports growing from $32 billion in 2002 to $168 billion in 2015. This data has been crucial in highlighting the shifting dynamics of the global creative economy and the growing role of developing countries in CCIs.

7.4.1.3 WIPO (World Intellectual Property Organisation)

WIPO provides valuable data on IP rights, which is crucial for many CCIs. Its work offers insights into countries' and industries' innovation and creative outputs.

Key contributions:

- **WIPO IP Statistics Data Centre:** This centre provides data on patents, trademarks, industrial designs and other forms of IP across countries. For example, it offers time series data on trademark applications by sector, including those related to CCIs.
- **Studies on Copyright Industries:** Periodic reports on the economic contribution of copyright-based industries. These studies use a standardised methodology to measure the value added, employment and trade performance of industries that rely on copyright protection.
- **Global Innovation Index:** Annual rankings of countries' innovation capabilities, including creative outputs. The creative outputs pillar includes indicators such as trademark applications, industrial designs, ICTs and business model creation.
- **Creative Economy Notes:** A series of publications focusing on specific aspects of IP in the creative economy. For example, a recent note examined the role of IP rights in the global film industry.

Strengths:

- Comprehensive data on IP registrations and applications, providing a proxy for creative and innovative activity

- Standardised methodologies for measuring copyright industries, enabling cross-country comparisons
- Global coverage and long-time series, allowing for trend analysis and international benchmarking
- Detailed sector-specific data offering insights into different segments of the creative economy

Limitations:

- Focus on formal IP registrations may underrepresent informal creative activities, which are significant in many developing countries
- Challenges in linking IP data directly to economic outcomes in CCIs, as not all IP translates into market success
- Limited coverage of non-IP-intensive cultural activities, potentially undervaluing certain forms of traditional or community-based cultural expression
- Difficulty in capturing the total value of IP in the digital age, where enforcement and monetisation challenges are prevalent

As a highlight, WIPO's analysis of the economic contribution of copyright industries WIPO's studies on the economic contribution of copyright industries have provided valuable insights into the importance of CCIs in national economies. For example, a study in Canada found that copyright-based industries contributed 5.59% to GDP and 5.96% to employment in 2019. In China, these industries accounted for 7.35% of GDP and 8.46% of national employment in 2018. These studies have been conducted in over 50 countries, offering a rich dataset for understanding the economic impact of copyright-intensive creative sectors across different economic contexts.

7.4.2 National Statistical Offices

NSOs are primary sources of official statistics on CCIs within individual countries. Their approaches and coverage vary significantly, reflecting differences in national priorities, resources and conceptions of CCIs.

Key roles of NSOs in CCI data:

- Conducting cultural participation surveys to measure engagement with various cultural activities
- Compiling economic statistics on cultural and creative sectors, including GDP contribution, employment and business demographics
- Developing national satellite accounts for culture to provide a more comprehensive picture of the cultural economy
- Collecting data on cultural employment and occupations, including both cultural and non-cultural sectors

Examples of leading practices:

- **United Kingdom's Department for Digital, Culture, Media & Sport (DCMS):** Produces annual Creative Industries Economic Estimates, using a robust methodology for defining and measuring the creative economy (DCMS, 2021). The DCMS approach includes both creative industries and creative occupations outside these industries, providing a comprehensive view of the creative economy.
- **Statistics Canada:** Developed the Canadian Framework for Culture Statistics and produced regular reports on the cultural economy (Statistics Canada, 2011). Their approach includes culture and sport domains and provides detailed data on GDP, jobs and consumer spending related to culture.
- **Australian Bureau of Statistics:** The ABS conducts comprehensive surveys on cultural participation and produces detailed satellite accounts of cultural and creative activity (ABS, 2020). These satellite accounts provide insights into the direct and indirect economic contribution of cultural and creative activities.
- **Netherlands' Centraal Bureau voor de Statistiek (CBS):** Produces the Culture and Media Monitor, which provides detailed statistics on cultural participation, employment in the cultural sector and government expenditure on culture.
- **Brazil's Instituto Brasileiro de Geografia e Estatística (IBGE):** Developed the System of Information and Cultural Indicators (SIIC) in collaboration with the Ministry of Culture. IBGE produces regular reports on the cultural economy, including data on cultural employment, household expenditure on culture and the contribution of cultural activities to GDP.
- **Colombia's Department of National Statistics (DANE):** DANE has developed the Satellite Account of Culture and Orange Economy in partnership with the Ministry of Culture. This account provides detailed information on the economic contribution of cultural and creative activities, including their share of GDP, employment figures and export data. The initiative is part of Colombia's broader strategy to promote its "Orange Economy" (creative economy).
- **Korea's Ministry of Culture, Sports and Tourism:** Conducts an annual survey on the creative industries, providing detailed data on revenues, employment and exports across various creative sectors.

Strengths:

- Detailed national-level data, often with regional breakdowns
- Integration with broader economic and social statistics, allowing for contextual analysis
- Ability to conduct specialised surveys and data collection exercises tailored to national priorities
- Official status, providing credibility and often mandatory reporting from businesses

Limitations:

- Lack of international comparability due to varying definitions and methodologies
- Resource constraints, particularly in developing countries, leading to gaps in data collection
- Challenges in keeping pace with rapidly evolving digital and creative sectors
- Potential political influence on definitions and methodologies, particularly in countries where CCIs are seen as strategically important

7.4.3 Industry Associations and Trade Bodies

Industry associations and trade bodies often collect and publish data specific to their sectors, providing valuable insights into the dynamics of creative industries. These organisations directly access industry players and can often provide timelier and sector-specific data than official statistics.

Examples of crucial industry data sources:

- **International Federation of the Phonographic Industry (IFPI)**: Publishes annual Global Music Reports with data on recorded music revenues and consumption patterns. For example, their 2021 report revealed that global recorded music revenues grew by 7.4% in 2020, despite the COVID-19 pandemic, driven by streaming growth.
- **International Publishers Association (IPA)**: This organisation produces annual reports on global publishing statistics. Its data covers book publishing across various markets, including information on new titles published, market size and digital vs. print sales.
- **Motion Picture Association (MPA)**: Releases data on global box office revenues and film industry economics. Their THEME Report provides a comprehensive analysis of the global theatrical and home/mobile entertainment market.
- **Interactive Software Federation of Europe (ISFE)**: Provides data on the European video game market, including information on market size, player demographics and gaming platforms.
- **World Association of Newspapers and News Publishers (WAN-IFRA)**: WAN-IFRA publishes the World Press Trends report, which offers insights into newspaper circulation, advertising revenues and digital news consumption.
- **International Confederation of Societies of Authors and Composers (CISAC)**: Produces the Global Collections Report, providing data on royalties collected for creators across different repertoires (music, audiovisual, visual arts, drama, literature).

Strengths:

- Detailed industry-specific data, often providing granular insights not available from official sources
- Access to proprietary information from member companies, offering unique perspectives on industry dynamics
- Timely insights into market trends and developments, often more up-to-date than government statistics
- Global coverage for many industries, allowing for international comparisons
- Deep understanding of sector-specific issues and metrics

Limitations:

- Potential bias towards more prominent industry players, as smaller or informal actors may be underrepresented
- Inconsistent methodologies across different associations, making cross-sector comparisons challenging
- Limited coverage of informal or emerging subsectors that may not have established industry bodies
- Potential conflict of interest in data presentation, as associations may have advocacy agendas
- Varying levels of methodological transparency and data accessibility

7.5 Challenges in Data Collection and Harmonisation

The measurement and analysis of CCIs have gained significant attention in recent years due to their growing economic importance and cultural significance (UNESCO, 2009). However, despite the rich data sources, researchers and policymakers need help collecting and harmonising data on CCIs worldwide. These challenges stem from the creative economy's complex and rapidly evolving nature and methodological and practical issues in data collection (Bakhshi et al., 2013).

One of the primary challenges in CCI data collection is the need for a universally accepted definition of what constitutes the CCIs. Countries define CCIs differently based on cultural, economic and political contexts (OECD, 2018). For example, some nations include software development in their definition of creative industries, while others do not. This variability in definitions leads to significant difficulties in international comparisons and can result in under- or over-estimating the size and impact of CCIs depending on the definition used (Flew, 2012).

Moreover, there are ongoing debates over including specific sectors, such as gastronomy, sports or gambling, within the scope of CCIs. The challenge of distinguishing between creative and non-creative activities within industries further complicates this definitional issue (Throsby, 2008). As new forms of creative expression and business models continually emerge, static definitions of CCIs are increasingly challenged, making it difficult to develop consistent time series data.

To address these definitional challenges, various international organisations have proposed standardised frameworks. UNESCO's FCS and the OECD's work on developing guidelines for measuring cultural and creative sectors represent significant efforts in this direction (OECD, 2018; UNESCO, 2009). Additionally, academic proposals for more flexible and inclusive definitions of CCIs have emerged, such as the work by Bakhshi et al. (2013), which advocates for a more dynamic approach to defining creative industries.

The rapid digitalisation of many creative activities poses another set of significant challenges for traditional data collection methods. Capturing value creation in free digital services, measuring cross-border digital transactions and accounting for user-generated content and prosumption activities have become increasingly complex (OECD, 2020). The economics of streaming and on-demand content delivery, as well as the impact of social media platforms on creative industries, require new measurement approaches that are still in development. These digital challenges can lead to a potential underestimation of the economic contribution of digital CCIs in official statistics and create difficulties in measuring cultural participation in online environments. The OECD's work on measuring the digital economy, including efforts to develop new indicators for digital trade, represents a step towards addressing these issues (OECD, 2020). Researchers such as Hadley et al. (2021) have also tried to develop new metrics for digital cultural participation.

A third major challenge is measuring the informal sector and non-market activities within CCIs. Many cultural and creative activities occur outside formal economic structures, making them difficult to capture in official statistics. These include amateur and volunteer cultural activities, informal cultural employment and entrepreneurship, traditional cultural practices, and community-based cultural events (Throsby, 2010). The implications of this challenge are particularly pronounced in developing countries, where a significant portion of creative activities may occur in the informal sector. This can lead to underestimating the true scope and impact of CCIs and create difficulties in designing appropriate support policies for informal creative workers (UNESCO, 2018). To address this, some countries have begun developing cultural satellite accounts to capture non-market activities. The use of time-use surveys to measure participation in informal cultural activities and the adaptation of ILO methodologies for measuring informal employment in the cultural sector are other promising approaches (ILO, 2018).

Data gaps in developing countries present another significant challenge. Many developing nations need more financial resources, human capital and institutional capacity to collect comprehensive data on their cultural and creative sectors (UNESCO, 2018). This results in an incomplete global picture of CCIs, with significant blind spots in the Global South. It also creates difficulties in assessing the potential of CCIs for development in these countries and challenges in designing appropriate policies and support measures. International organisations have responded to this challenge with capacity-building initiatives, such as UNESCO's Culture|2030 Indicators programme. South-South cooperation in cultural statistics and using alternative data sources (e.g., big data, satellite imagery) to complement traditional surveys are other strategies being explored to address these data gaps (UNESCO, 2019).

Finally, even when data is available, ensuring its comparability across different sources, countries and periods remains a significant challenge. Inconsistent classifications and definitions, varying data collection methodologies and frequencies, and challenges reconciling data from various administrative systems contribute to this issue (OECD, 2018). The rapid evolution of industry structures and business models, mainly due to digitalisation, can make historical comparisons problematic. These harmonisation challenges make meaningful international comparisons of CCIs difficult to assess global trends and patterns in the creative economy. They also create obstacles to evidence-based policy-making at the international level. Efforts to address these challenges include international initiatives to standardise cultural statistics, the development of crosswalks between different classification systems, and promoting metadata sharing and methodological transparency (OECD, 2018; UNESCO, 2009).

In conclusion, while significant progress has been made in measuring CCIs, substantial challenges remain. Addressing these challenges requires collaboration between NSOs, international organisations, researchers and industry stakeholders. As the creative economy continues to evolve, so must our approaches to measuring and understanding its dynamics. Future research should focus on developing more robust methodologies for capturing digital and informal creative activities, improving data collection in developing countries and enhancing the comparability of CCI data across different contexts.

Developing new economic models is another important avenue. These models should be more sophisticated and capable of better capturing the value creation processes in CCIs, including non-market and spillover effects. Improving metadata standards is also crucial to developing more comprehensive standards for CCI statistics to enhance transparency and comparability. Fostering public-private partnerships is also a crucial strategy, encouraging collaboration between government statistical agencies, academic researchers and private sector data providers to create more comprehensive datasets on CCIs. Additionally, integrating cultural and creative indicators into broader development metrics is essential, as well as working to incorporate

CCI measures into broader frameworks for measuring social progress and sustainable development.

As the creative economy continues to evolve and grow, developing robust, comprehensive and nuanced data sources will be crucial for informed policymaking and a deeper understanding of the role of CCIs in social and economic development. By addressing current challenges and embracing innovative data collection and analysis approaches, we can work towards a more accurate and holistic understanding of the creative economy's impact and potential. This ongoing effort to improve CCI data collection and analysis reflects the growing recognition of the sector's importance in driving innovation, economic growth and cultural enrichment. As these initiatives progress, they will provide policymakers, researchers and industry stakeholders with increasingly valuable tools for understanding and nurturing the creative economy in diverse forms.

7.6 A Brief Representative (find the complete report in www.valiatileandro.com) Case I: Brazilian CCIs GDP Based on Creative Occupations

The measurement of GDP for the CCIs in Brazil, as presented by Valiati et al. (2023), represents an innovative approach to quantifying the economic contribution of these sectors using a creative occupations methodology. This work, commissioned by Itau Foundation, offers valuable insights into new ways of capturing the impact of the creative economy, particularly in developing country contexts. It provides a template for other nations seeking to understand better and leverage their creative sectors.

A key strength of the approach is its use of the creative intensity model to define the boundaries of the CCI sector. This model, initially developed by Bakhshi et al. (2013), identifies creative sectors based on the percentage of workers in creative occupations. This allows the definition to evolve with economic changes over time. The researchers applied five criteria to evaluate creative occupations in Brazil: ability to generate new processes, resistance to mechanisation, non-repetitive work, creative contribution to the value chain and work involving interpretation rather than mere transformation. This methodology resulted in the identification of 13 creative sectors, ranging from fashion and artisanal activities to software development and visual arts.

The GDP calculation takes an income-based approach, aiming to capture the nuances of the CCI sector better than traditional production or expenditure methods. The researchers combined data from multiple sources to estimate four key components: wage mass, profit mass, taxes and other remunerations like digital income. Importantly, this method allows for the inclusion of both formal and informal economic activity, addressing a significant gap in many previous studies of the creative economy in developing countries.

This approach to measuring CCIs offers several advantages over traditional methods. Focusing on creative occupations rather than industry classifications can better capture the dynamic nature of creative work that often spans multiple sectors. The income-based calculation also provides a more comprehensive picture of economic value creation in CCIs, including informal and digital activities that conventional GDP measurements may miss.

Methodology: The researchers employed an innovative income-based approach to calculate the GDP of CCIs, diverging from traditional production or expenditure methods. This approach was chosen to capture better the nuances and specificities of the creative sector, including informal economic activities and digital income streams.

The calculation of GDP for CCIs was based on four main components:

1 Wage Mass (WM): Calculated using data from the Continuous National Household Sample Survey (PNADc), which covers both formal and informal employment. This approach allowed for a more comprehensive capture of labour income in the sector, including second jobs and informal work.
2 Profit Mass (PM): Estimated using data from the Annual Service Survey (PAS) and the Annual Industrial Survey – Enterprise (PIA-Enterprise). The researchers applied a double-weighting method based on wage mass and business fabric composition to estimate revenues for specific CCI sectors.
3 Taxes: Calculated using data from the Tables of Resources and Uses (TRU) provided by the Brazilian Institute of Geography and Statistics (IBGE).
4 Other Remunerations: This category included income from digital sources, such as data from the Central Office for Collection and Distribution (ECAD) for music rights.

The researchers also incorporated data from the Rouanet Law accountability reports to capture information on intermittent or freelance work and rentals, which are significant in the CCI sector.

Sectors Considered: The study used a creative intensity model to define the boundaries of the CCI sector. This dynamic approach identifies creative sectors based on the percentage of workers in creative occupations. The researchers applied five criteria to evaluate creative occupations:

1 Ability to generate new processes
2 Resistance to mechanisation
3 Non-repetitive work
4 Creative contribution to the value chain
5 Work involving interpretation rather than mere transformation

Based on these criteria, 13 creative sectors were identified:

1 Fashion
2 Artisanal activities
3 Publishing
4 Cinema, radio and TV
5 Music
6 Development of software and digital games
7 Other information technology services
8 Architecture
9 Advertising and business services
10 Design
11 Performing arts
12 Visual arts
13 Museums and heritage

This comprehensive list encompasses various creative activities, from traditional cultural industries to more technology-driven sectors. The results indicate that the GDP contribution of CCIs in Brazil was between 2% and 3.5% in 2020, placing it among the top ten sectors of the economy. While this figure is broadly in line with global UNESCO estimates of around 3% GDP contribution for CCIs, the methodology reveals exciting insights into the composition of this economic activity in Brazil.

Key findings include:

1 Profit mass and taxes represent a significant portion of the CCI sector's GDP, reflecting the prevalence of micro-entrepreneurs and small businesses in the sector.
2 The wage mass of the CCI sector showed an increasing trend in recent years, but with some volatility. It averaged about 0.19% of the national GDP over the ten-year period covered by the PNADc data.
3. Second incomes, captured through the PNADc, represented, on average, 1.82% of the wage mass in the CCI sector.
4 The profit mass of the CCI sector represented about 2% of the national GDP in 2020.
5 While income from digital sources is growing, it still represents a relatively small portion of the CCI sector's total GDP. This is partly due to measurement challenges rather than necessarily reflecting the true economic impact of digital activities.
6 The study revealed significant regional variations in the contribution of CCIs to GDP, with São Paulo state being a clear outlier regarding its share of CCI economic activity.

The work also highlights several ongoing challenges in measuring the creative economy. The researchers note difficulties in fully capturing income from the digital sector, second jobs and rental activities, which likely leads to some underestimation of the sector's actual economic impact. There are also limitations in the available data, particularly around informal economic activity and disaggregated financial information for creative businesses. Despite these challenges, the Brazil methodology offers valuable lessons for measuring CCIs in other contexts, especially developing economies. The creative occupations approach allows for a more dynamic and context-specific definition of the creative economy compared to static industry classifications. The income-based GDP calculation method also provides a framework for capturing economic activity that may be missed by traditional national accounts, particularly informal and digital transactions.

The study's recommendations for improving data collection are also noteworthy. These include developing better microdata on revenues and profits in creative sectors, improving tracking of digital income streams and creating mechanisms to capture gig economy activity in CCIs. Implementing such measures could significantly enhance the accuracy and comprehensiveness of creative economy measurements globally.

As the global economy continues to evolve towards knowledge-based and creative activities, such innovative measurement techniques will be crucial for informing effective policy and investment decisions in the CCI sector. The work done in Brazil demonstrates the potential for more nuanced and comprehensive assessments of the creative economy's contribution to national GDP.

Moreover, this approach to measuring CCIs can have broader implications for economic policy and development strategies. A more accurate picture of the creative economy's size and composition can help policymakers better target support and investment in these sectors. This is particularly important in developing economies where CCIs can offer opportunities for inclusive growth and job creation.

The methodology also highlights the importance of considering formal and informal economic activities in assessing the true impact of CCIs. This is especially relevant in countries with large informal sectors, where traditional GDP measurements may significantly underestimate the contribution of creative work.

Furthermore, the focus on creative occupations rather than industry classifications aligns well with emerging trends in the labour market, such as the rise of the gig economy and increasing fluidity between sectors. This approach may prove more adaptable to future changes like work and the structure of creative industries.

In conclusion, the work done by Valiati et al. in measuring the GDP contribution of CCIs in Brazil represents a significant advancement in our understanding of the creative economy. While further refinement and adaptation may be needed for application in different national contexts, this methodology offers a promising template for more accurate and comprehensive assessments of the economic value of creative and cultural activities. As countries worldwide seek to diversify their economies and tap into the potential of the creative sectors, such innovative measurement techniques will be invaluable in guiding policy and investment decisions. The complete study is here: https://issuu.com/itaucultural/docs/obs34_eng

7.7 A Brief Representative Case II: Relative Values (find the complete report in www.culturalvalue.org)

The Relative Values project, funded by the UK Arts and Humanities Research Council (AHRC), was a ground-breaking initiative led by principal investigators Dr. Leandro Valiati and Professor Paul Heritage. The project aimed to develop a new methodology for evaluating arts organisations' socio-economic impact in fragile urban communities. This collaborative research effort brought together People's Palace Projects at Queen Mary University of London and the Federal University of Rio Grande do Sul's Centre of Studies in Creative Economy and Culture (NECCULT), focusing on four arts organisations in the United Kingdom and Brazil:

1. Contact Theatre (Manchester, United Kingdom)
2. Battersea Arts Centre (London, United Kingdom)
3. Maré Centre for the Arts (Rio de Janeiro, Brazil)
4. The Agency of Youth Networks (Rio de Janeiro, Brazil)

Co-created Methodology: A distinguishing feature of the Relative Values project was its deeply collaborative, co-created methodology. This approach was fundamental to developing a system that could effectively capture and articulate cultural activities' complex, nuanced impacts in vulnerable urban contexts. The co-creation process involved several key stages:

1. Initial consultations: The research team conducted in-depth discussions with each partner organisation to comprehensively understand their work, impact goals and the specific challenges they face in their respective communities.
2. Collaborative workshops: A series of workshops brought together researchers and representatives from the arts organisations to collectively define key areas of impact and brainstorm potential indicators. This ensured that the resulting framework would be both academically rigorous and practically relevant.
3. Iterative development: The questionnaires and survey methods were developed through an iterative process, with multiple rounds of feedback and refinement involving all stakeholders. This approach allowed for the incorporation of diverse perspectives and expertise.

4 Training of local agents: To ensure consistent and effective data collection, local agents from each organisation were trained to apply the questionnaires. This step was crucial in building capacity within the organisations and ensuring the sustainability of the evaluation process.
5 Joint analysis and interpretation: The research team worked closely with the partner organisations to analyse and interpret the results, ensuring that local context and insights were fully integrated into the findings.

This co-created approach resulted in a academically robust methodology deeply rooted in the practical realities and needs of the arts organisations and the communities they serve.

Methodology Structure: The research methodology combined quantitative and qualitative approaches, structured around three main axes:

1 Context: This axis involved gathering publicly available socio-economic data about each territory. It included indicators such as the Index of Multiple Deprivation (IMD), life expectancy, infant mortality rates and unemployment figures. This contextual information was crucial for understanding the baseline conditions in which each organisation operates.
2 Operations: Information about each arts organisation was collected via detailed questionnaires. This included data on organisational structure, funding sources, programming, audience demographics and economic results. The operational data provided insights into how each organisation functions within its context.
3 Impact: This core component involved surveying participants in the organisations' projects using a comprehensive questionnaire of approximately 40 questions. The survey was designed to capture various impacts, from individual-level changes to broader community effects.

System of Indicators: The project developed a sophisticated system of indicators covering three interconnected areas:

1 Context Indicators: These measured local development and social vulnerability, providing a clear picture of the challenges and opportunities in each territory.
   Example indicators:

   - IMD score
   - Life expectancy
   - Infant mortality rate
   - Unemployment rate
   - Access to public services (e.g., healthcare, education)

2 Operation Indicators: These reflected the organisations' self-image, focusing on the relationship between activities and territories, project implementation, audience profiles and economic results.
Example indicators:

- Number of projects delivered annually
- Percentage of participants from low-income backgrounds
- Diversity of creative teams (e.g., percentage of BAME artists)
- Annual budget and funding sources
- Number of partnerships with local organisations

3 Impact Indicators: The most innovative aspect of the methodology, these indicators focused on three key dimensions:
   a Individual capacity for agency: Measuring participants' ability to reflect, process social experiences, and develop everyday skills. Example indicators:
- Capacity for reflection
- Social mobilisation
- Increase in social capital
- Expansion of perspectives
   b Relationship to arts and creativity: Assessing changes in cultural engagement, understanding of the arts sector, and creative skills development. Example indicators:
- Cultural democracy
- Understanding of working in the arts sector
- Cultural engagement
- Perceived proximity to the arts sector
- Viability of working in the arts sector
- Creative skills development
   c Relationship to territory: Evaluating how participation affects individuals' connection to and understanding of their local area. Example indicators:
- Access to local spaces
- Lived space (changes in how participants move through and use their local area)
- Recognition of local creative networks
- Understanding of social reality
- Identification and belonging to the territory

Each indicator's performance was classified on a scale from Low (0.0–0.5) to Outstanding (0.9–1.0), providing a nuanced picture of impact across different dimensions.

Additionally, the methodology included indicators for direct territorial transformation:

Example indicators:

- New use for spaces
- Community engagement
- Better perception of the territory by residents
- New business creation
- Increased access to spaces within the territory
- Safety in public spaces
- Improved use of public spaces
- Creation of new social spaces
- More positive description of the territory
- Infrastructure improvements

Key Findings: The research yielded several significant findings:

1. Incubators of innovation: Small-scale arts organisations were found to create conditions for incubating creative economy initiatives in fragile urban communities, often acting as catalysts for local development.
2. Startup-like characteristics: These organisations' impact was characterised by qualities typically associated with rapid-growth startups, including innovation, entrepreneurship, resilience, networking, social capital development, sustainability and enhanced agency.
3. Breaking isolation: The methodology demonstrated the effectiveness of strategies these organisations develop to break their isolation from other makers/practitioners, fostering creative networks and knowledge exchange.
4. Alternative value creation: The research showed how peripheral, vulnerable urban communities use creativity as a positive value that offers an alternative to resource-intensive business models.
5. Territorial significance: The study highlighted the importance of understanding arts organisations' impact on their specific territories, revealing how their effectiveness is deeply tied to the local context.

Specific Results: The study produced detailed impact profiles for each participating organisation. For example:

Contact Theatre greatly impacted individual capacity for agency and outstanding performance in cultural democracy and proximity to the arts. However, it had only an intermediate impact on participants' understanding of social reality and sense of belonging.

Battersea Arts Centre demonstrated high impact on personal agency of participants and outstanding performance in cultural democracy and proximity to the arts. However, it showed lower impact on cultural engagement and territorial transformation.

Maré Centre for the Arts achieved a high impact on participants' personal agency, outstanding performance in cultural democracy and proximity to the arts, and a significant impact on participants' relationship to the territory.

The Agency of Youth Networks showed consistently high impact across all indicators of personal agency, outstanding performance in cultural democracy, and high impact on participants' understanding of social reality and sense of belonging.

Implications and Future Directions: The Relative Values methodology represents a significant advancement in measuring the impact of arts organisations in vulnerable communities. Combining economic and social indicators through a co-created process provides a more comprehensive and contextually relevant picture of value creation than traditional GDP-based approaches.

The project demonstrates the potential for arts organisations to act as key drivers of local development in areas facing multiple challenges. It also highlights the importance of context-specific measurement, recognising that the value created by these organisations is deeply tied to the territories in which they operate.

The Relative Values methodology shows promise for broader application and further refinement. The researchers have already adapted it into a toolkit for young artists and cultural producers developing new projects in fragile territories. Additionally, it will be used to evaluate 25 arts projects across Brazil between 2018 and 2024, providing an opportunity for longitudinal study and methodology refinement. This ongoing development and application will likely lead to more robust and generalisable indicators over time, while emphasising co-creation and local relevance. As such, the Relative Values project provides valuable insights into the current impact of arts organisations in vulnerable communities and lays the groundwork for more nuanced, context-sensitive impact evaluation in the cultural sector more broadly.

References

ABS (Australian Bureau of Statistics). (2020). Cultural and creative activity satellite accounts, Australia. https://www.abs.gov.au/statistics/people/people-and-communities/cultural-and-creative-activities/latest-release

Bakhshi, H., Freeman, A., & Higgs, P. (2013). A dynamic mapping of the UK's creative industries. Nesta. https://media.nesta.org.uk/documents/a_dynamic_mapping_of_the_creative_industries.pdf

Bakhshi, H., & Throsby, D. (2012). New technologies in cultural institutions: Theory, evidence and policy implications. International Journal of Cultural Policy, 18(2), 205–222.

Bakhshi, H., McVittie, E., & Simmie, J. (2008). Creating innovation: Do the creative industries support innovation in the wider economy? Nesta. https://media.nesta.org.uk/documents/creative-innovation.pdf

Bakhshi, H., Cunningham, S., & Higgs, P. (2015). Measuring the creative economy: A guide for policymakers. Nesta.

Coyle, D. (2014). GDP: A brief but affectionate history. Princeton University Press.
Crossick, G., & Kaszynska, P. (2016). Understanding the value of arts & culture: The AHRC cultural value project. Arts and Humanities Research Council.
Cunningham, S., & Potts, J. (2015). Creative industries and the wider economy. In C. Jones, M. Lorenzen, & J. Sapsed (Eds.), *The Oxford Handbook of Creative Industries* (pp. 387–404). Oxford University Press.
DCMS (Department for Digital, Culture, Media & Sport). (2021). DCMS sectors economic estimates 2019: Gross value added. https://www.gov.uk/government/statistics/dcms-economic-estimates-2019-gross-value-added/dcms-economic-estimates-2019-provisional-gross-value-added
Easterlin, R. A. (1974). Does economic growth improve the human lot? Some empirical evidence. In P. A. David & M. W. Reder (Eds.), Nations and Households in Economic Growth (pp. 89–125). Academic Press.
European Commission. (2019). The Cultural and Creative Cities Monitor: 2019 Edition. Publications Office of the European Union.
Flew, T. (2012). *The creative industries: Culture and policy*. Sage.
Fujiwara, D., Kudrna, L., & Dolan, P. (2014). Quantifying and valuing the wellbeing impacts of culture and sport. Department for Culture Media & Sport.
Hadley, S., Hogarth, S., & Butterick, M. (2021). Redefining cultural participation in a digital world. *Cultural Trends*, 30(4), 346–361.
To know more: www.culturalvalue.org or www.valiatileandro.com
International Labour Organization (ILO). (2018). *Women and men in the informal economy: A statistical picture.*
Klamer, A. (2017). *Doing the right thing: A value based economy*. Ubiquity Press.
Kuznets, S. (1934). National income, 1929–1932. 73rd US Congress, 2d session, Senate document no. 124.
Landefeld, J. S., Seskin, E. P., & Fraumeni, B. M. (2008). Taking the pulse of the economy: Measuring GDP. *Journal of Economic Perspectives*, 22(2), 193–216.
Markusen, A., & Gadwa, A. (2010). Creative placemaking. National Endowment for the Arts.
New Zealand Treasury. (2018). The treasury approach to the living standards framework. https://www.treasury.govt.nz/publications/tp/treasury-approach-living-standards-framework
Nordhaus, W. D., & Tobin, J. (1972). Is growth obsolete? In *Economic research: Retrospect and prospect, Volume 5, economic growth* (pp. 1–80). National Bureau of Economic Research.
OECD. (2018). Oslo manual 2018: Guidelines for collecting, reporting and using data on innovation, 4th edition. OECD Publishing. https://www.oecd.org/science/oslo-manual-2018-9789264304604-en.htm
OECD. (2020). *How's life? 2020: Measuring well-being*. OECD Publishing. https://www.oecd.org/statistics/how-s-life-23089679.htm
Potts, J., & Cunningham, S. (2008). Four models of the creative industries. International Journal of Cultural Policy, 14(3), 233–247.
Pratt, A. C., & Jeffcutt, P. (Eds.). (2009). *Creativity, innovation and the cultural economy*. Routledge.
Sacco, P. L., Ferilli, G., & Blessi, G. T. (2013). Understanding culture-led local development: A critique of alternative theoretical explanations. Urban Studies, 50(13), 2806–2821.
Statistics Canada. (2011). *Conceptual framework for culture statistics 2011*. https://www150.statcan.gc.ca/n1/pub/87–542-x/87–542-x2011001-eng.htm

Stiglitz, J. E., Sen, A., & Fitoussi, J. P. (2009). Report by the commission on the measurement of economic performance and social progress. https://ec.europa.eu/eurostat/documents/8131721/8131772/Stiglitz-Sen-Fitoussi-Commission-report.pdf
Throsby, D. (2001). *Economics and culture*. Cambridge University Press.
Throsby, D. (2008). The concentric circles model of the cultural industries. *Cultural Trends*, 17(3), 147–164.
Throsby, D. (2010). *The economics of cultural policy*. Cambridge University Press.
Throsby, D., & Zednik, A. (2014). The economic and cultural value of paintings: Some empirical evidence. In V. A. Ginsburgh & D. Throsby (Eds.), Handbook of the Economics of Art and Culture (Vol. 2, pp. 81–99). Elsevier.
UNCTAD. (2008). Creative economy report 2008. https://unctad.org/system/files/official-document/ditc20082cer_en.pdf
UNCTAD. (2010). Creative economy report 2010. https://unctad.org/system/files/official-document/ditctab20103_en.pdf
UNCTAD. (2018). Creative economy outlook: Trends in international trade in creative industries. https://unctad.org/system/files/official-document/ditcted2018d3_en.pdf
UNESCO. (2009). The 2009 UNESCO Framework for Cultural Statistics (FCS). UNESCO Institute for Statistics. https://uis.unesco.org/sites/default/files/documents/unesco-framework-for-cultural-statistics-2009-en_0.pdf
UNESCO. (2014). Culture for development indicators: Methodology manual. https://unesdoc.unesco.org/ark:/48223/pf0000229608
UNESCO. (2018). Re|Shaping cultural policies: Advancing creativity for development. https://unesdoc.unesco.org/ark:/48223/pf0000260678
UNESCO. (2019). Culture|2030 indicators. https://whc.unesco.org/en/culture2030indicators/
UNCTAD. (2022). Creative economy outlook: Trends in international trade in creative industries. United Nations Conference on Trade and Development. https://unctad.org/publication/creative-economy-outlook-2022
UNESCO. (2022). Re|Shaping cultural policies: Global report 2022. United Nations Educational, Scientific and Cultural Organization. https://www.unesco.org/reports/reshaping-creativity/2022/en
Valiati, L., Lang, F. D. S., Möller, G., & Saron, E. (2023). The gross domestic product of the economy of culture and the creative industries: An income approach. *Revista Observatório Itaú Cultural*, 34, 15–42.
Yúdice, G. (2003). *The expediency of culture: Uses of culture in the global era*. Duke University Press.

8

FUTURE DIRECTIONS

8.1 Creative and Cultural Industries: Economic Growth, Development and Future Prospects

As this book regularly states, while often used interchangeably, economic growth and development represent distinct economic theory and practice phenomena. This distinction is crucial for understanding the complexities of economic progress, particularly in the context of creative and cultural Industries (CCIs).

Economic growth typically refers to the increase in goods and services produced per capita over a specific period, usually measured by the growth rate of real gross domestic product (GDP) (Kuznets, 1973). However, as Amartya Sen (1999) and others have noted, growth alone is insufficient to measure a society's progress. Economic development encompasses broader qualitative changes in economic and social structures. Seers (1969) argued that development occurs when a country experiences poverty, unemployment and inequality reductions. Sen (1999) expanded this view, defining development as expanding fundamental freedoms people enjoy, including access to education, healthcare and political participation.

Studying the relationship between CCIs and economic development is paramount for several reasons:

a CCIs have become significant contributors to economic growth and employment worldwide. According to the United Nations Conference on Trade and Development (UNCTAD), the global creative goods and services market has experienced rapid expansion, with exports reaching $646 billion in 2020 (UNCTAD, 2021). CCIs have shown remarkable resilience

DOI: 10.4324/9781003434252-9

in economic downturns, often outperforming traditional sectors in growth and job creation. Understanding how CCIs drive economic growth and generate employment opportunities is crucial for policymakers seeking to promote sustainable and inclusive development.

b The study of CCIs and economic development sheds light on the role of creativity and innovation in fostering competitiveness and productivity. In an increasingly knowledge-based and globalised economy, the ability to generate new ideas, products and services has become a key determinant of success. CCIs, with their focus on creativity and intellectual property, are at the forefront of this innovation-driven economy. By examining how CCIs contribute to technological advancements, the development of new business models and the creation of high-value-added products and services, researchers can gain valuable insights into economic competitiveness and productivity drivers.

c Exploring the relationship between CCIs and economic development is essential for understanding the creative economy's broader social and cultural impact. As Amartya Sen (2004) reminds us, "Cultural matters are integral parts of our lives. If development can be seen as an enhancement of our living standards, then efforts geared to development can hardly ignore the world of culture." CCIs not only generate economic value but also contribute to the formation of cultural identities, the promotion of social cohesion and the enhancement of quality of life. By studying the interplay between CCIs and economic development, researchers can gain a more holistic understanding of the role of culture in shaping individual and societal well-being.

d The study of CCIs and economic development is critical for informing policy decisions and strategies to foster the creative economy's growth and sustainability. Governments worldwide increasingly recognise the potential of CCIs as drivers of economic and social development and are implementing policies to support their growth. However, the effectiveness of these policies depends on a deep understanding of the specific challenges and opportunities faced by CCIs, as well as the complex dynamics of the creative ecosystem. By providing evidence-based insights and recommendations, research on CCIs and economic development can guide policymakers in designing targeted interventions and creating an enabling environment for the creative economy to thrive.

e Finally, the study of CCIs and economic development is essential for addressing the challenges of the digital era and the changing nature of work. The rapid advancement of digital technologies has transformed the way cultural and creative goods and services are produced, distributed and consumed, creating new opportunities and disruptions in the creative economy. At the same time, the rise of automation and artificial intelligence is reshaping the future of work, with significant implications for employment and skills development in the CCIs. By examining the impact of these technological and societal shifts on CCIs and economic growth, researchers can contribute to developing strategies and policies that ensure the inclusivity and sustainability of the creative economy in the face of these challenges.

Studying the relationship between CCIs and economic development is vital for understanding the role of culture, creativity and innovation in driving economic growth, fostering social and cultural well-being and shaping the future of work. As the global economy continues to evolve and the creative economy expands, the insights generated by this field of research will be essential for informing policy decisions, business strategies and societal responses to the opportunities and challenges presented by contemporary. This complex interplay holds significant implications for global economies, cultural diversity and societal well-being. As we analyse this topic, it becomes clear that our understanding of CCIs' impact on economic development needs to evolve to keep pace with rapid technological advancements and shifting social paradigms.

As the field evolves, it has the potential to generate new theoretical insights and practical applications, contributing to both the academic discourse and the sustainable development of the creative economy. Future research could focus on the impact of digital technologies on CCIs, the role of CCIs in addressing global challenges like climate change, and the potential of CCIs to promote social inclusion and cultural diversity. Additionally, exploring the intersections between CCIs and other sectors, such as education, healthcare and urban planning, could yield valuable insights for policymakers and practitioners alike.

The interplay of CCIs and social economic development is a critical area of study that warrants increased attention from academia and policymakers. Looking ahead, some key areas demand focused attention from academia and policymakers:

1 Interdisciplinary research must be prioritised to develop more comprehensive frameworks for understanding CCIs' impact. The creative economy's complex nature requires insights from diverse fields, including economics, cultural studies, sociology and technology.
2 New metrics and methodologies are needed to measure the intangible value generated by CCIs accurately. Traditional economic indicators often need to catch up in capturing the full spectrum of value created by cultural and creative activities.
3 Education systems must evolve to better prepare individuals for the creative economy. This involves developing curricula that blend creative skills with digital literacy, entrepreneurship and cross-cultural competencies.
4 Policy innovation is crucial to keep pace with the rapidly evolving creative landscape. Flexible and adaptive policies that can respond to technological changes and shifting market dynamics are essential.

5 Sustainability principles should be integrated into CCI development strategies. This includes considering the environmental impact of creative industries and exploring ways to promote sustainable practices within the sector.
6 Efforts to bridge the global digital divide must intensify to ensure equitable participation in the international creative economy. This is crucial for leveraging CCIs' full potential for economic development across diverse regions.
7 The implications of artificial intelligence for creative processes, copyright and labour markets in CCIs require thorough investigation. As AI technologies advance, their impact on creative industries will likely be profound and multifaceted.
8 Frameworks to preserve and promote cultural diversity through CCIs need to be developed. This is essential for ensuring that economic growth in the creative sector doesn't come at the cost of cultural homogenisation.
9 The resilience of CCIs in global crises, such as the COVID-19 pandemic, warrants in-depth study. Understanding how creative industries adapt to and recover from such shocks can inform broader economic resilience strategies.
10 Models for effective collaboration between CCIs and other sectors, including technology, education and urban planning, should be explored. Such cross-sector partnerships could unlock new avenues for innovation and economic growth.

Researchers, educators and policymakers can contribute to a more comprehensive understanding of CCIs' role in economic development. This enhanced understanding will be crucial for shaping strategies that promote a more inclusive, sustainable and culturally vibrant future.

As we move forward, we must recognise the creative economy's dynamic nature and remain adaptable in our approaches to studying and fostering its growth. CCIs' potential to drive economic development is vast. However, realising this potential will require concerted efforts to bridge knowledge gaps, develop innovative policies and cultivate the skills needed for the future creative economy.

8.2 The Future of CCIs and Economic Development: A Roadmap for Policymakers and Academics

The relationship between CCIs and economic development presents challenges and opportunities as we look to the future. A coordinated effort from policymakers and academics is essential to fully harness CCIs' potential as economic growth and social progress drivers. This roadmap outlines key focus areas and suggests practical actions for both groups.

8.2.1 Interdisciplinary Research and Collaboration

8.2.1.1 For Policymakers

Establish dedicated funding streams for cross-disciplinary research projects.
Create interdisciplinary think tanks focused on CCIs and economic development.

8.2.1.2 For Academics

Develop joint degree programmes that combine arts, economics and technology.
Organise regular international conferences to facilitate dialogue between different disciplines.

8.2.2 Innovative Metrics and Methodologies

8.2.2.1 For Policymakers

Commission the development of new economic indicators that capture the intangible value of cultural and creative outputs.
Integrate these new metrics into national economic assessments and policy decision-making processes.

8.2.2.2 For Academics

Conduct longitudinal studies to track the long-term economic impact of CCIs, including spillover effects on other sectors.
Develop and refine methodologies for valuing intangible assets in the creative economy.

8.2.3 Education and Skill Development

8.2.3.1 For Policymakers

Revise national education policies to incorporate creative and digital skills across all levels of education.
Implement tax incentives for businesses that invest in creative skills training for their workforce.

8.2.3.2 For Academics

Design and pilot innovative curricula that blend artistic creativity with entrepreneurship and technology skills.

Research the changing skill requirements in CCIs to inform curriculum development.

8.2.4 *Policy Innovation and Adaptation*

8.2.4.1 *For Policymakers*

Establish 'regulatory sandboxes' for CCIs, allowing for controlled experimentation with new business models and technologies.
Create cross-departmental task forces to ensure coherent policy approaches to CCIs across different government sectors.

8.2.4.2 *For Academics*

Develop policy simulation models to predict the impact of different regulatory approaches on CCIs.
Conduct comparative studies of CCI policies across different countries to identify best practices.

8.2.5 *Sustainability and Global Equity*

8.2.5.1 *For Policymakers*

Introduce sustainability criteria in public funding and support programmes for CCIs.
Implement international cooperation programmes focused on developing CCI infrastructure in underserved regions.

8.2.5.2 *For Academics*

Research the environmental impact of different creative industries and develop sector-specific sustainability guidelines.
Conduct studies on barriers to participation in the global creative economy, focusing on developing countries.

8.2.6 *Emerging Technologies and AI*

8.2.6.1 *For Policymakers*

Establish ethical guidelines for AI use in creative processes, addressing issues of authorship and copyright.
Create retraining programmes for creative professionals whose roles may be impacted by technological advancements.

8.2.6.2 For Academics

Conduct interdisciplinary research on the implications of AI for creative labour markets and artistic expression.
Develop new pedagogical approaches that integrate emerging technologies into creative education.

8.2.7 Cultural Diversity and Resilience

8.2.7.1 For Policymakers

Implement quota systems in public funding for CCIs to ensure the representation of diverse cultural expressions.
Establish emergency support mechanisms for CCIs that can be rapidly deployed during crises.

8.2.7.2 For Academics

Research the economic value of cultural diversity in CCIs and its impact on innovation and market expansion.
Conduct case studies on how different CCIs adapted to and recovered from global crises like the COVID-19 pandemic.
Policymakers and academics can collaborate to create a more nuanced, adaptive and supportive environment for CCIs by focusing on these critical areas and implementing targeted actions. This collaborative approach recognises the creative economy's multifaceted nature and potential to drive sustainable, inclusive economic development. For the next decade, it will be crucial to maintain flexibility, continually refine our understanding of CCIs' role in shaping our economic and cultural landscapes and adapt our strategies accordingly. The future of CCIs and their impact on economic development holds great promise, but realising this potential will require ongoing commitment, innovation and cooperation between policymakers, academics and industry practitioners.

References

Adorno, T., & Horkheimer, M. (2002). *Dialectic of enlightenment*. Stanford University Press.

Americans for the Arts. (2017). https://www.americansforthearts.org/by-program/reports-and-data/research-studies-publications/arts-index.

Azoulay, P., Stuart, T., & Wang, Y. (2014). Matthew: Effect or fable? *Management Science*, 60(1), 92–109.

Banks, M. (2007). *The politics of cultural work*. Palgrave.

Banks, M., & O'Connor, J. (2009). After the creative industries. *International Journal of Cultural Policy*, 15(4), 365–373.

Baumol, W. J., & Bowen, W. G. (1966). *Performing arts: The economic dilemma*. Cambridge University Press.

Benjamin, W. (1936). The Work of Art in the Age of Mechanical Reproduction. In Illuminations (H. Zohn, Trans.). Schocken Books.

Bol, T., de Vaan, M., & van de Rijt, A. (2018). The Matthew effect in science funding. *Proceedings of the National Academy of Sciences*, 115(19), 4887–4890.

Cunningham, S. D. (2002). From cultural to creative industries: Theory, industry, and policy implications. *Media International Australia Incorporating Culture and Policy: Quarterly Journal of Media Research and Resources*, 1(102), 54–65.

De Masi, D. (2001). *O futuro do trabalho: fadiga e ócio na sociedade pós-industrial*. José Olympio.

Department for Culture, Media & Sport. (1998). *Creative industries mapping documents* 1998.

Department for Culture, Media & Sport. (2001). *Creative industries mapping documents* 2001.

Department for Culture, Media & Sport. (2016). *Creative industries economic estimates methodology*.

DiPrete, T. A., & Eirich, G. M. (2006). Cumulative advantage as a mechanism for inequality: A review of theoretical and empirical developments. *Annual Review of Sociology*, 32, 271–297.

European Commission. (2010). *Green paper: Unlocking the potential of cultural and creative industries*.

Flew, T. (2012). Origins of creative industries policy. In *The creative industries: Culture and policy*, Sage Publications Ltd.

Florida, R. (2002). *The rise of the creative class*. Basic Books.

Frey, B. (2000). *La economia del arte*. La Caixa.

Furtado, C. (1978). *Criatividade e dependência na civilização industrial* [Creativity and dependency in industrial civilization]. Paz e Terra.

Garnham, N. (2005). From cultural to creative industries: An analysis of the implications of the 'creative industries' approach to arts and media policy making in the United Kingdom. *International Journal of Cultural Policy*, 11(1), 15–29.

Ginsburgh, V., & Weyers, S. (2014). Nominees, winners, and losers. *Journal of Cultural Economics*, 38(4), 291–313.

Kaldor, N. (1966). *Causes of the slow rate of economic growth of the United Kingdom*. Cambridge University Press.

KEA European Affairs. (2006). The Economy of Culture in Europe: A Study Prepared for the European Commission." (https://ec.europa.eu/assets/eac/culture/library/studies/cultural-economy_en.pdf)

Kretschmer, M. (2005). Artists' earnings and copyright: A review of British and German music industry data in the context of digital technologies. *First Monday*, 10(1).

Kuznets, S. (1973). Modern economic growth: Findings and reflections. *The American Economic Review*, 63(3), 247–258.

Lacroix, J. G., & Trembley, G. (1997). The emergence of cultural industries into the foreground of industrialization and commodification: Elements of context. *Current Sociology*, 45(4), 11–37.

Lipietz, A. (1991). *Audácia: uma alternativa para o século 21*. Nobel.

Marcuse, H. (1955). *Eros and civilization*. Beacon.

Merton, R. K. (1968). The Matthew effect in science. *Science*, 159(3810), 56–63.

Musgrave, R. (1959). *The theory of public finance*. McGraw-Hill.

O'Connor, J. (2010). *The cultural and creative industries: A literature review*. Creativity, Culture and Education.

Oakley, K. (2004). Not so cool Britannia: The role of the creative industries in economic development. *International Journal of Cultural Studies*, 7(1), 67–77.

Potts, J., & Cunningham, S. (2008). Four models of the creative industries. *International Journal of Cultural Policy*, 14(3), 233–247.

Pratt, A. C. (2005). Cultural industries and public policy: An oxymoron? *International Journal of Cultural Policy*, 11(1), 31–44.

Rodrik, D. (2001). *The global governance of trade: As if development really mattered*. United Nations Development Programme.

Rowthorn, R., & Ramaswamy, R. (1997). *Deindustrialization: Causes and implications*. International Monetary Fund.

Ruskin, J. (1857). *The political economy of art*. Smith, Elder & Co.

Seers, D. (1969). The meaning of development. *International Development Review*, 11(4), 2–6.

Seltzer, K., & Bentley, T. (1999). *The creative age: Knowledge and skills for the new economy*. Demos.

Sen, A. (1999). *Development as freedom*. Oxford University Press.

Sen, A. (2004). How does culture matter? In V. Rao & M. Walton (Eds.), *Culture and public action* (pp. 37–58). Stanford University Press.

Thirlwall, A. (2005). *A natureza do crescimento econômico: um referencial teórico para compreender o desempenho das nações*. Ipea.

Throsby, D. (2001). *Economics and culture*. Cambridge University Press.

Throsby, D. (2008). The concentric circles model of the cultural industries. *Cultural Trends*, 17(3), 147–164.

United Nations Conference on Trade and Development. (2008). *Creative economy report 2008*.

United Nations Conference on Trade and Development. (2010). *Creative economic report* 2010. *Creative economy: A feasible development option*.

United Nations Conference on Trade and Development. (2021). *Creative economy outlook* 2021.

United Nations Educational, Scientific and Cultural Organization. (2009). *UNESCO framework for cultural statistics*. UNESCO Institute for Statistics.

United Nations Educational, Scientific and Cultural Organization. (2013). *Creative economy report 2013*.

United Nations Educational, Scientific and Cultural Organization. (2015). *Reshaping cultural policies: A decade promoting the diversity of cultural expressions for development*.

World Intellectual Property Organization. (2015). *Guide on surveying the economic contribution of the copyright industries: 2015 revised edition*.

INDEX

Note: **Bold** page numbers refer to tables; *italic* page numbers refer to figures and page numbers followed by "n" denote endnotes.

Kolibri 360 GmbH
Ferdinand-Jühlke-Straße 7
99095 Erfurt, Deutschland
produktsicherheit@kolibri360.de